MW00440455

# Jon McConal's Texas

# Jon McConal

## REPUBLIC OF TEXAS PRESS

*Lanham • Boulder • New York • Toronto • Oxford*

Published by Republic of Texas Press
An imprint of The Rowman & Littlefield Publishing Group, Inc.
4501 Forbes Boulevard, Suite 200
Lanham, MD 20706

Distributed by NATIONAL BOOK NETWORK

**Library of Congress Cataloging-in-Publication Data**

McConal, Jon, 1937–
    Jon McConal's Texas / Jon McConal.
        p. cm.
    Includes index.
    ISBN 1-55622-893-7
    1. Texas—Description and travel—Miscellanea. 2. Texas—History, Local—Miscellanea. 3. Texas—Biography. I. Title.

F391.2.M24      2002                                                    2001058925
976.4—dc21                                                                  CIP

Manufactured in the United States of America.

⊛™ The paper used in this publication meets the minimum requirements of American National Standard for Information Sciences—Permanence of Paper for Printed Library Materials, ANSI/NISO Z39.48-1992.

For Jane, a wonderful companion whose company has made watching those Texas sunsets even more awesome.

# Contents

# Contents

# Contents

# Foreword

I used to read Jon McConal's columns in the *Fort Worth Star-Telegram* when I was a little boy. He started writing them sometime during the mid-Crustacean period, I think it was. Nowadays, he's kind of crusty himself.

For all these years he has been a wanderer, visiting Texas outposts, wherever there was thunder or sunshine.

He retired recently and turned his thunder and sunshine over to a new generation of reporters. He was eager enough to rest all right because he is still a vigorous crustacean and knows it is "not too late to seek a newer world," lines once penned to describe another wanderer.

McConal loves real people. As a result, none of his people is seeking "closure" to the gate to the corral or anything else. No one whines about "wrong choices," or "having issues." Nobody has an "agenda" or "pushes the envelope." Not one ever "raises the bar" unless it's in a saloon or "takes his best shot" at anything, unless it's with a double-barrel shotgun.

Instead, the reader will be moved by his sometimes-poetic renderings of Texas people and their lives. To Jon, everything—rocks, trees, vegetation, rivers, the wind—is alive and breathing. These subjects evoke in him similes that are startling either in their beauty or their strangeness. They are often lyrical, sometimes funky, sometimes just plain weird. But they always get your attention. About an old church he writes, "the boards sounded as we walked over them like the rasping lungs of a heavy smoker." One particular smoker has a cough that sounds like "a flat tire running on the rim in gravel."

The Texas wilderness has "hunks of rain clouds," "ragged echoes," and "patches of midnight." A Texas tree is never just a tree. One is "a twisting oak with limbs that look like someone wringing his hands." Others "have edges of reds and yellows, just tipped by fall like colors made by a kid strumming through a giant coloring book and had just thrown colors at pieces of pictures." Thunder-clouds sometimes look "like giant purple-colored turkey eggs."

And Texas doesn't have just land. In one memorable case, it is "pasturelands of mesquite trees and fields of tall bluestem grass and milkweeds bonneted in white bursts of flowers."

This latter exaltation brings out the English teacher in me. I think that he and his fellow backroad mariners, John Tushim and Floyd "Doc" Keen, are not unlike a landlocked Ulysses and his mates ...the obscure, sometimes strange Texas towns and counties he visits not too very unlike those of the lotus eaters and the old Cyclops. The denizens abiding there *often* live unusual lives, and if they don't, they know someone who did.

He would roar past some sports or movie star, leaving "ragged echoes," as he might say, to get to some grizzled geezer sinking a sucker rod or a woman bartender in Texola with a Chihuahua named Chili Dog. Celebrity trivialities hold no interest for him.

The people he likes are the chosen people of poets, of Homer and of Wordsworth. Wordsworth wrote about them because, he said, they were "less under restraint and speak a plainer and more emphatic language" and are "incorporated with the beautiful and permanent forms of nature."

So, knowing that Jon thinks I'm saturated with some kind of incurable malady called *englishteacheritis*, I herewith make bold nevertheless to suggest that this book could be called a "Texas Odyssey" or "Lyrical Ballads for Texas." But *Jon McConal's Texas* is a fine title, and the book itself represents the Texas we should think of when we brag about this great state.

Tom Dodge
Midlothian, Texas
August 27, 2001

# Preface

I have a confession to make. For the past twenty years, I did have the best job in Texas.

I have had many people tell me that. They did not hesitate with their opinions.

"Hey, man, did you know you don't work? Ha. Ha. All you do is wander around the state looking for stories and people to talk to. Gosh, I wish I had your job. You got the greatest job in the world," they would gush. Then they would motion for me to lean over and they would whisper into my ear, their breath choked with deviled eggs, coffee, snuff, and assorted other True Texas breath enhancers. "You ever die, I want your job. Thank they might consider me? Hail, when I was in the third grade, the English teacher said I should become a writer because I made a B plus on a paper about my favorite dog. I never did, but I am certain I could if all I had to write about were the people like you write about."

I never agreed with them that I did indeed have the greatest job in Texas. I was afraid to make such a confession for one reason. I was afraid that if my bosses saw that I was having so much fun in my job they would think nobody could do a good job and have as much fun as I was having. Having made that decision, they would transfer or promote me to another position.

So I never confessed. But, today, after retiring on December 31, 2000, and having no fears of being promoted or transferred, I can confess. I did have the greatest job in Texas.

That job called on me to go out in the country, meet people, and write about them. And though I did spend a good portion of my time in territory where the *Fort Worth Star-Telegram* was sold and for whom I worked forty of my forty-three years in journalism, I frequently made treks to other areas like East Texas where the tragic story of Cynthia Ann Parker began and ended. My wife, Jane, who frequently went with me on my ramblings, and I discovered the grave of this woman of tragedy in early Texas history. We accidentally found the unmarked site in the long shadows of beautiful pine trees.

Other trips to East Texas carried me to Weeping Mary and to Crockett where a district court judge is using effectively a rather unusual punishment. He orders certain defendants to wear placards with bright lettering spelling out their crimes as they walk around the courthouse. I interviewed one of these defendants one day as he marched around the courthouse wearing a sign that read, "I have been convicted of selling marijuana." He assured me he would never commit that act again.

I also went many times to what I call West Texas where I was born and reared. On one of these journeys, a friend, Tom Dodge, and I stopped in the tiny town where Carl B. Bradley is buried. He was the original Marlboro cowboy. And what a cowboy he was. He drowned when his horse became trapped in a stock tank and Bradley could not free himself from the saddle. Also on that trip we met a woman in the tiny town of Matador who does all of her traveling on a riding lawn mower. She has even driven ten miles to a neighboring town to buy groceries. I asked her husband what he thought of this. He shrugged his shoulders and replied simply, "When a person reaches eighteen and they are bigger than you are, they can do any damn thang they want." He keeps her lawn mowers repaired.

I frequently had people who in one voice would say that I had the greatest job in the world and then ask, "But how in the world do you find enough people to write three of these in a week?" It is a good question. Before I wrote my final column, I figured I had traveled some 200,000 miles and interviewed more than 10,500 people in person. That equates to a town about the size of Mineral Wells, which is forty miles west of Fort Worth.

But I found my subjects by being a good listener. I contend that if you are a good listener, practically anyone you meet has a story worth telling. I found one in a man who lives in southern Johnson County. He had built his own casket, a beautiful piece of woodwork. He was in excellent health, so until his time came and the casket was needed, he was using it as a coffee table in his living room.

I found unusual people wherever I went. Consider the time I went to Bob Wills Day in Turkey, Texas. This is an annual event held to honor the late Bob Wills, creator of western swing, who also recorded one of the all-time best-selling records, "San Antonio Rose." During this celebration held the last weekend in April, more than 20,000 people pack this tiny place of 551 people. If you want to experience a true Texas happening, go to Bob Wills Day. I did in hopes of interviewing some of the surviving members of the Wills band, called The Texas Playboys. They put on an afternoon concert and played for a Saturday night dance.

Well, during this afternoon concert, I met Loyd Cox, a person I first thought must be a part of the sound crew. I surmised this after seeing Cox move all over the stage holding a tiny microphone and a tape recorder during the Playboys' performance. Finally, during a break, some officers led Cox from the stage. I walked over and talked to him. "No, I ain't no fancy sound injuneer," he said. "But I do love Bob Wills music." And he had written some songs himself. He sang one for Jane and me during a break. It was called "False Teeth Security." I doubt if it ever made the top hit charts. But, gosh, what an interesting character Cox was.

And that is my point. Texas is full of people with unusual and strong personalities. The majority of these will never make the newspapers or the magazines or the television screen. But they are there, hard-working individuals who make Texas what it is. You find them everywhere. That is why our state has become such a high interest item for authors and film crews. People admire us for the people who make up our state. There is no mold for our citizens. There is no same cloth. We are all indeed individuals. Proud and interesting and hard working people who make our living in some rather unusual ways like Bob Miller in Fort Worth who buys thousands of cow horns and turns them into beautiful hat racks and chairs and sells them to an international market.

Or consider Laura Butler, an internationally known artist and a native Texan whose paintings are so vivid and real that you swear you can smell the sweat of the cowboys and horses she has created as you look at her work. I talked to this attractive woman in her studio and watched her as she created yet another dramatic scene that when finished would bring in an amount in the five-figure bracket. And she does this in spite of having multiple sclerosis. "Yeah, I got MS," she said. "But it hasn't killed me yet. So I keep on working."

Butler lives in Mingus, a city once renowned for its wild night-clubs sprinkled in the belly of large coal deposits. From 1890 to 1927 Mingus attracted more than 20,000 people from this nation as well as from several European countries to work in the coal mines. The mines have closed. But there still are things to see, like Lovera's Grocery, owned and operated by Albert and Vera Lovera, whose parents came here from Poland to mine coal. Or you can eat at Mary's in nearby Strawn, one of the best Mexican restaurants in Texas.

I say all of this when somebody questions the interest in a collection of my columns, saying, "Hail, nobody outside of your area will be interested in this." I say they are wrong. My people are the same kind of people who make up East, South, North, and West Texas. Their twangs may be an octave or two higher or lower, but they speak the same language and experience the same emotions. They are good people. They are strong people. They are by gawd Texans.

So with that, I give you this book. And I want to say thank you to the people about whom I wrote.

Also, I would like to acknowledge some people who helped me early in my pursuit of becoming a writer. Two of those, Mrs. Nell Bridges and Mrs. Lillian Huffstutler, taught me high school English. Both encouraged me and helped me find my love for writing in the pages of authors like Steinbeck and Mark Twain. God bless both of them.

Another man who thought he recognized my potential was Dr. Ferol Robinson, then head of the journalism department at the University of Sam Houston. He helped me receive two scholarships and offered constant advice and encouragement. He was always there in those often difficult college days. Dr. R, as the students called him, I thank you for helping me find one of the greatest jobs in Texas.

# Chapter 1

# Characters

Finding people with interesting stories was never a problem for me. My problem was having enough time to listen to their stories.

I found my characters everywhere. You can do the same. Go into a small town and look for a livestock feed store, car repair garage, welding shop, a café with several pickups and cars parked in front, or just a good shade tree. All of these are meccas for people and stories. Still others can be found on the front steps of the county courthouse. Or better yet, spot a place like the small bandstand on the courthouse square in Granbury, Texas. Places like that have characters galore assembled there.

I found early in my career that practically everyone has an interesting story to tell. I once told a creative writing class that I taught at Texas Christian University, that if I could sit down with each individual in a group of fifty and spend an hour listening to them, I could find plenty to write about. I still believe that. I am amazed at the stories that have never been told about these people who are in such abundance in our state.

I used to play a game when I left my home early some mornings. Maybe I would have only one interview scheduled 50 miles away. The game called for me to see how many additional interviews I could find just by listening and looking during the remainder of the day. I never came back with only the one interview. Sometimes I would come back with as many as five. When I reached that number, I figured I had won the game.

So I always watched and listened. It was amazing what I heard. And I am still hearing interesting stories despite having retired. Like the other day I attended a funeral of a World War II veteran I had once written a column about. After the funeral, a rancher came to me, shook my hand and said, "Jon, I got a story for you. Quite a mystery, too. I know you ain't writing no more. But I think you will like this one. So just come on down and I'll buy your dinner (lunch really, but few Texans call it lunch; dinner is served at noon and supper is served in the evening) and then we'll go out in them old cedars and hackberries in this ragged old country and fight them horseflies and I'll show you the daggumdest mystery you've ever seen, heard, or read about."

Anyone can find these stories and people. Just look for that shade tree and start listening. The following columns came from people I met that way.

# Charlsie of Mineral Wells

Clients at Charlsie's Hair Gallery and Bargain Store can get everything from a full hair job to a good buy on a piece of junk.

The unusual store with its huge sign does not beat around the bush about the possible bargains inside. Beneath the sign are a couple of used ironing boards with other stuff piled on top of them.

Inside, eight stylists work on hair. Charlsie Sparks, owner, who has done everything from tending bar to styling hair, laughed about her shop.

"I'll sell anything that will sell," she said.

And after a hair session, if the client needs a dozen eggs, well step right over here to this refrigerator. The eggs are fresh from the country.

Sparks is a delight. She has brown eyes and red hair and obviously does not take herself too seriously. Her place is also a delight. On this day, she had a 500-piece jigsaw puzzle for customers to work on if they wanted. If they were hungry, well they could step over to this huge spice pound cake that Sparks baked and get a slice. For free.

If someone comes in just to buy a piece of junk and everyone including Sparks is busy styling hair, she will holler: "Help yourself. If you find something you want, pay for it. The tax schedule is on the cash register."

Sparks took a break to talk about herself and her career.

"I've been a hairdresser for thirty-seven years," she said. "I got my degree from Isabel University of Beauty Culture in Fort Worth in 1961. I've either been a bartender or a hairdresser since."

So how in the world did she begin selling junk?

It was simple. Her father, J.W. Sparks, and her late mother had always collected and sold junk. Sparks did a fair amount of collecting herself. The items had accumulated in piles at her house.

"I brought them down here and they began to sell," she said. "So I began making the garage sales on weekends and buying anything that will sell."

I looked at some of the things she had for sale—old refrigerators, microwaves, used boots, ranch chairs made from rawhide, books, electric heaters, and an old wood stove found in a banker's front yard.

Kay Willmon of Millsap had come to check the junk.

"I love this place," she said. "And someday I just might have my hair done here."

Julia Green voiced similar sentiments after her first visit.

"My friend recommended this place. I'm not disappointed," she said.

So we looked at dolls, snow skis, and a plastic water pistol as we worked our way to the beauty parlor. Evelyn Thomas, who has been doing hair for fifty-one years, is one of the operators. She talked about changes in the business.

"When I first started, hair coloring was done behind curtains so nobody would know whose hair was being colored," she said.

Somebody yelled for help from the bargain section of the shop. Sparks yelled back, "Help yourself."

Then she made a rather startling revelation. She has never lost anything to thieves and has only had one hot check that she could not collect on during her entire career.

That's a pretty good record for hair styling and junk sales.

# Carl Bradley—The Marlboro Man

They say Carl B. Bradley had the looks of this country.

Certainly this country in Knox County held things the late Bradley, one of the original Marlboro cowboys, loved dearly, including cattle and horses.

This region looks like cowboy country. The Brazos River stretches like a finger that has been broken several times through mesquite flats leading to this town north of Abilene. Evidence of the battle with those trees showed in several places where they had been bulldozed and poisoned.

"But they still survive. They are as tough as an old one-nutted bull that hangs out in those brakes," an old rancher told me one time.

Tom Dodge and I had come here to see the grave of Bradley, known as Bigun. The smell of asphalt from a recent paving job was heavy in this town, also known as the home of the seedless watermelon. We stopped at the local newspaper to ask where Bradley was buried.

Stacy Angle Thompson, publisher, said she had no time to talk to us. She was working on the current edition. As we started to leave, she said, "I did sing at his funeral. I sang 'Church in the Wild Wood.' But I can't remember where it was or where he is buried. I'm sorry. I'm in a hurry."

Anne Underwood at the Citizen's Bank was not in such a hurry and talked about Bradley.

"I don't remember much about Bigun other than he was a good dancer and a great guy," Underwood said. "If you'll go across the street and talk to Birdie Helton, she knows a lot about him. They went to school together."

So we stopped across the street at an oil well supply firm and met Birdie Helton, a friendly, attractive woman.

"Oh, yes, I remember Carl B. He was good looking and he always had a big smile," Helton said. "And he loved cowboying. That was his life."

That was what he was doing when he was killed—trying to free a cow from the mud of a stock tank. His horse reared back and fell, killing the horse and Bradley.

"He was chosen as a Marlboro cowboy in the late 1950s," she said. "Carl B. was the most authentic cowboy I've ever known. He got the name Bigun from his little brother. But he was not really a big man."

Then she told us where he was buried. We drove there. As we passed two jackrabbits with long ears sticking up like long, gray slices of potatoes, I thought of what another person, Chandler Dietrich of Fort Worth, a longtime Bradley friend, had said about him.

"Even today, I don't think of Bigun Bradley being gone. He isn't really. He crosses my mind every once in awhile. I can travel around Old Glory and Aspermont, drive through Matador and Guthrie, and he and Sheep Morrow, Mike Shanks, and George Humphreys they just sort of drift back," she said. "He was the best looking man I ever saw and the best I ever saw with a horse."

She met Bradley when she was a freshman at Texas Tech in Lubbock.

"I was the second woman ever to take animal husbandry there. They were just amazed at me," Dietrich said.

But she had always wanted to be a cowboy.

"And I mean cowboy and not a cowgirl," she said.

Her pursuit of that dream led her to be detained several times by campus security because she wore jeans into buildings where women were supposed to wear dresses.

"It was all right for a football player to wear shorts and a jockey strap but not for a woman to wear jeans," she said.

She met Bradley after her only horse died, and she managed to get an invitation to look at the new colt crop at the famed Four Sixes Ranch. She found an animal she wanted.

"She had been ridden three saddlings by Bigun Bradley," said Dietrich. "He took almost three hours to tell about her."

She also remembered Bradley's good looks and manners.

"He was the kind who always took his hat off when he talked to you, and I remember all of the 'yes ma'ams' he used," she said.

The horse she chose was named Reno Dodger, and Bradley helped her load it.

"He wore a white Oxford button-down collar shirt, starched Wranglers, and Tony Llama feedlot boots, black with red tops. He smelled like horses and Old Spice," she said. "And after we loaded her, he told me to be kind to her because he never had much use for anybody that wouldn't be kind to horses."

She kept the animal for thirty-three years until it died a natural death. Both she and Jimmy Lynn, also of Fort Worth, attended Bradley's funeral.

"I was fourteen when he died (May 8, 1973). They said everybody went to his funeral," said Lynn. "I remember how impressed I was. Never seen so many pickups parked in one place before."

Dietrich recalled the scene.

"I hope somebody told you how many folks turned out. Many rode their horses to his funeral," she said. "I also hope somebody told you that there is a special place for real cowboys who are kind to horses."

We easily found Bradley's grave. He was born February 9, 1937. An inscription on the tombstone reads, "Bigun, a cowboy and a man."

Dodge and I sat for a moment under that clear West Texas sky with clouds that looked like white silk. Far off, we saw and heard more jackrabbits loping through the parched grass. About a quarter of a mile away a grove of oaks punched their way from the dry ground. They made an abundant shade, a good place to sit and let the sweat dry off of your shirt.

Some tiny yellow flowers stood nearby, so striking with their delicate appearance in the streams of heat. For some reason I thought of a line from that song by the woman who could not remember where Bradley was buried. It goes, "No spot is so dear to my childhood."

# Coffin Maker from Sand Flat

I've met some characters in my excursions along Texas back roads. I've met people who eat alligator. I've met people who eat rattlesnakes. I've met people who have built houses from railroad crossties and from old cars.

But I have never met anyone who can top Harold Johnston's feat. He has built his own coffin. It sits in his living room waiting for the day he departs. In the meantime, it serves as a coffee table—and quite a conversation piece.

Johnston laughed at my reaction after I walked into his house and saw the casket made of black walnut sitting in prominent display in his living room.

"Well, I always have had a weird sense of humor," he said.

That is obvious. We talked from his home in this community about seven miles southeast of Cleburne on Farm Road 4 in Johnson County. He's short and has a moustache tinged with gray. He is sixty-five and earns his living by overhauling injector pumps for diesel engines, buying and selling cars, and metal art work.

He also won national fame when he spent seven years totally rebuilding a Vultee V1-A airplane once owned by William Randolph Hearst. When he got the plane, a single-engine passenger model built in 1936, it was in pieces. Today, after his several years of work, it is the only one of its kind that is still flying.

But that is another story. This day we talked about the coffin, which is quite attractive. Johnston opened it and inside is a padded lining and a fifth of whiskey near a pillow.

"I don't drink, but I thought it would be a good idea to have that because you don't know where you are going to wind up," he said.

Johnston said memories of his late father, a farmer in West Texas, are what really caused him to build the coffin.

"My dad was a Scotchman's Scotchman," he said. "He did not believe in spending money unless it was absolutely necessary."

He told a story to illustrate his father's frugal philosophy.

"He was the kind that if he had a crew out in the field working and he fell into our well, he would tell Mama to leave him in the well until the crew came in for lunch before telling them to get him out of the well so they wouldn't miss any work," said Johnston.

When his father was seventy-four, he suffered a serious stroke. He figured he did not have long to live. So he went to town to buy a coffin.

"When the funeral home guy quoted him the price, he said, 'Hell, that is too high. I'll just go home and build my own,'" Johnston said.

That impressed the son.

"I decided that I would build my own coffin before I had a stroke," he said.

And there it sits beside the television and beside one of his striking metal creations, a windmill scene cut into an old steel disc from a plow.

Johnston said he has indeed had many laughs from the coffin.

"People walk in. They look at it. They sit down and keep looking at it," he said. "They finally will say, 'What is that? It looks like a coffin.' I tell them they are absolutely right, that it is a coffin...my coffin."

The late Ted Tate, who had gone with me to Johnston's place, shook his head.

"What do your kids think about it?" he asked.

"Aw in the beginning, they thought it was a little weird," said Johnston. "But, it's all right with them now."

The coffin almost ensures that there will be no dead spaces in conversation.

"Say a stranger comes here and we run out of things to talk about. All I've got to do is point at my coffin, and that will get conversation started," he said.

In other words, silence is easily buried when there's a coffin sitting in front of you.

# Essie Huneycutt—Cleburne Hamburger Cook

Getting to talk to Essie Huneycutt at noon requires some planning around her cooking duties at Morris Neal's Handy Hamburgers.

Just taking a guess at the number of hamburgers that Essie has cooked since taking up a spatula in this café located near the courthouse square is impressive.

Somebody figured that she has cooked more than one million. And recently, while I was waiting to talk to her during a noon rush, she obviously was working on that second million.

"I will try to fill in for her for a few minutes," said Pamela Trotter. "But people do love her hamburgers."

One of those is Tom Dodge, author, commentator for PBS, and Cleburne native.

"I've been eating hamburgers here for fifty years, even before Essie came," he said. "The reason is they are good and they have never changed."

We looked at the menu at Neal's, which is located just across from the jail. The smell of frying meat and onions was strong and pleasant. And the prices are pleasant too—$2.20 gets you a jumbo burger.

"I can tell you, the people who eat here don't worry about the fat content," said Dodge, who ordered a double jumbo with cheese for $2.95.

The crowd includes the well dressed and not so well dressed. Practically everyone entering yells, "Hey, Essie, how is it going?"

She smiles as she stands at the huge iron grill, a territory she knows as well as an attorney knows law books. This day she wore shorts, walking shoes, and a red blouse. Our orders came. Dodge's double jumbo was huge.

"Now this is a hamburger," he said.

Shortly afterwards, Essie, seventy-three, joined us.

"The reason the burgers are so good here is that we use only fresh meat," she said.

She believes in what she cooks because for the past twenty-five years, she has eaten one hamburger every day at 9:30 A.M. during her six-day schedule. That is her breakfast and lunch.

"This means you have eaten more than 9,000 hamburgers since you have been here," said Dodge.

"That's right," she responded.

She got her first job cooking when she was about thirty-two. After she and her late husband, Clyde, moved here, she began cooking hamburgers for the late Morris Neal, for whom this place is named.

"I tried other things, like working in a department store and a drugstore. But I didn't like those. So here I am," she said.

She says that working here saved her life.

"When Clyde died a few years ago, I don't think I could have survived if I had not had this job and all of my friends here," she said.

But dealing with the pain of arthritis in her legs sometimes makes her think about quitting.

"But I don't know what I would do. Sit at home and watch soap operas? No, I don't like that idea," she said. "I'd rather be down here cooking hamburgers."

She smiled.

"Besides, I have worn out two spatulas working here. I used them so much that they nearly didn't have a middle left."

Then she asked if it was okay for her to return to the grill. Duty called.

And there she stood, a hardworking, honest person, enveloped in the steaming clouds of cooking meat and onions.

And not too far away is a group of men who have consumed liberal portions of Essie's hamburgers. You can hear about that as well as many other subjects while listening in on a domino game at Club Domino. There is no huge sign proclaiming its existence, but the noise does erupt regularly from the tiny room that has been designated Club Domino off the main lobby of the Greenbrier Inn and Restaurant.

An ancient concrete lion yawns its presence near the front door. The plate glass window is cracked and paint peels from the frame, maybe a result of the blue words flaming from the door.

"Hey, you gripe every play," shouted Bob Milddleton at one of his opponents. "You could make 30 [a high domino score] and you'd still gripe."

Eli Cooper, a tall, slender, white-haired main, smiled at the comments. He wore striped suspenders and looked like a railroad man. He was before retiring from Santa Fe after some forty-two years. He spent many years as an engineer on a steam locomotive.

He mentioned the late L.C. "Blackie" Mansfield, a longtime coach in this town whom everyone knew. He was one tough SOB said Cooper.

"He'd come in while players were showering after practice and say, 'You boys think you are tough. Well, I will show you what is tough.' Then he'd grab a handful of hair from his chest, rip it out, and say, 'Now that is tough. Hail, you boys don't even have any hair on your chest.'"

A just-ended domino game abbreviated his story. The winners pulled money from their pockets and chunked it into a tin cookie can.

"Those are our dues," Cooper explained. "Whoever wins puts money in the pot. We pay our rent with that."

Then Cooper began talking about the late C.C. Cook, a well-known Cleburne doctor.

"They said he removed a man's appendix one time while the man was laying on the hood of his car," said Cooper.

Many people paid their doctor bills by working for him or giving him milk and chickens. An eruption from the table again interrupted Cooper.

"What the hail are you doing playing out of turn?" John Donoho demanded.

One soon realizes that these outbursts are just a part of the game and not meant as true insults.

Really, Noah White said, the games are a chance to get away from the daily routine of retirement or work. White, forty-seven, owner of a concrete-cutting firm, worked seventeen years for the railroad where he met many of the players. Today he is Club Domino president.

"My main job is to find us a place to play so it will keep us out of our wives' hair," he said.

That brought a story about domino players from Carl Glen.

"This circus was leaving town and one of its baboons died. So they threw it to the side of the road. Somebody found it and took it to a doctor to be identified. The doctor looked at it and finally said, 'Well, judging from its red [behind] and the look on its face, I'd say it is a domino player.'"

His story drew several loud laughs followed by a loud demand, "Are we going to tell stories all day or play dominoes?"

They did both.

# Ferris Wheel Builder of Zephyr

People throwing a party often ask for the use of Judy and Eugene Painter's front yard.

That's understandable once you reach their house, which is down a gravel road and about seven miles northeast of this town in southeastern Brown County.

You certainly don't expect to see what is in their front yard. But, there it is...a Ferris wheel.

That's right. Although it's small, it is a legitimate, honest-to-gosh Ferris wheel. There are also a couple of merry-go-rounds and several rather outstanding pieces of metal art.

All have been created by Eugene Painter with help from his wife, Judy. We had driven here after Lucille Roach told us about the Ferris wheel.

"You boys want to see something unusual, then you should go out and look at the Painters' Ferris wheel," Roach told Doc Keen and me on a visit through this part of the country.

So we had gone to Judy Painter's beauty shop here. And she, a friendly woman with a large plait of brown hair spilling down her back, said sure. She would gladly show us the Painter Ferris wheel.

So we went to the Painter place. And, gosh, what an interesting place with antique farm equipment, collected by Eugene Painter's father, Harvey, sitting out front near the Ferris wheel. She told about her husband deciding to build it.

"He saw one when we were at Six Flags," she said. "He looked at it and said, 'I think I'll go home and build me one of those,'" she said laughing. "I thought he was crazy."

She gave the dimensions of the Ferris wheel. It is 18 feet tall, has four seats, and is anchored by 6-inch pipes that are cemented 3 feet deep into the ground. A two-horsepower electric motor with a gearbox turns the 20-inch cog on the end that spins the Ferris wheel.

"You guys want to ride on it?" she asked.

Of course. But first we were shown other things that Eugene Painter has built. She showed us a merry-go-round that is mounted on a car hub and still has the wheel bearings inside. We crawled on and boy did it spin smoothly.

"And he and his dad built that table," said Judy. She pointed to a table with a slab of concrete on top. It was mounted on steel wagon wheels.

She showed us some metal art that her husband had cut from steel. The scene showed a cowboy riding a horse and chasing a cow past cactus and grass.

"I'm real proud of him," said Judy. "He just takes a notion and does these things."

We looked at other metal art. One was a grasshopper made from railroad spikes and another was a huge stinging scorpion made from steel. Open-end wrenches formed its pinchers and were welded to the front of its body.

We walked past some stainless-steel benches.

"They were running boards for a pickup once," she said.

Finally, we were back at the Ferris wheel.

"Our kids don't like to ride it as much as they did at first," she said. "But, we did have the eighth grade graduation party out here. They all loved the Ferris wheel."

She flicked the switch. Keen crawled into a seat. She moved the wheel around for balance and I crawled aboard.

"Okay, here you go," she said.

She turned on the motor and it made a whirring noise as the ride began. And around and around we went. At the top we could see the flat surface of a mountain yawning in the distant ranch land. Down we went.

"Eugene always wants something that nobody else has," Painter had said earlier.

Her words were drowned out by our yelling at each other. Two grown men sounding like, well, kids.

No wonder people want to have their party in the Painters' front yard.

# Norma Wright of Granbury

When Mama Santa Claus requests my presence, I respond.

Particularly when Mama Santa Claus, who is really Norma Wright, is talking about the bicycle program in Granbury in Hood County that each year sees hundreds of youngsters get bikes for Christmas.

Wright is one of those persons whose love for people lies deep in her heart. And when she adopts a project, her enthusiasm is contagious as residents in this picturesque town that attracts thousands of tourists have learned.

"Jon, I've got a couple of youngsters I want you to talk to at Baccus Elementary," said Wright. "They want bicycles, and you know how hard we will work to make sure they get them."

The "we" in this case is the Hood County Christmas for Children group that ensures that youngsters whose families might be experiencing lean financial times are going to get their Christmas wish met.

So I met Wright and Nancy Alana, principal at Baccus. They introduced me to Tyler, six, and Shawna, eight, who told me about their Christmas wishes.

Tyler has a flash of blond hair, blue eyes, and explosions of energy.

"This is Mr. McConal. Did you know that he is a friend of Santa Claus?" asked Wright.

"Certainly, I did," said Tyler. "He looks like an elf."

Then both youngsters said they wanted bikes for Christmas.

"I want a black one like the one they stole from me last year right after Christmas," said Tyler.

Shawna said she wanted a pink bicycle.

"Do you think you deserve them?" asked Wright.

Tyler responded with a long list of reasons that included taking his medicine on time and not getting into a lot of trouble.

"Well, I've kept my room clean and I have helped my parents," said Shawna.

Then Tyler gave a long description of Christmas and how he hopes that they have a tree so fat that they will not be able to get it into the house. And, yes, he wants his mother to get a present.

"I want her to get a robot to play with," he said.

"I want my mother to get a silver necklace with a pendant that can hold a picture," said Shawna. "And some pretty flowers."

"Well, I can do magic," said Tyler. "I can fix toys and I can say 'Abracadabra' and things work or disappear."

And with that, both returned to class. Wright watched and then talked about the Hood County Christmas for Children program.

"The last two years, every child who has put a bike on his wish list has gotten one," she said. "We can get a bike and helmet for $50. Wal-Mart gives us a discount."

Alana said the program means so much to youngsters who might experience a lean Christmas.

"It helps them feel worthy enough to receive a good gift," she said.

Wright said that many people give the bikes to the kids instead of gifts to relatives.

"Then they give a card that says, 'I gave a bike to a kid. Your present is that smile on that kid's face on Christmas morning,'" she said.

She said that the group checks each family to avoid duplications from last year or with other groups that distribute bikes.

"We just want to make sure that a child who wants a bike gets one," she said.

And make Tyler's magic work so that when he says, "Abracadabra" on Christmas, a bike will be there just like Mama Santa has promised.

God bless the world for Mama Santas like Norma Wright.

# Unusual Jurist in Palestine

Shawn Lopez had a quick word of advice for possible drug offenders in this town in Anderson County.

"Don't move here if you plan to mess around with drugs," he said. "This is what happens to you and believe me, it is humiliating."

He pointed to a sandwich board sign that covered his front and back. In huge black letters, it read, "I am Shawn Lopez. I have received ten years probation for possession of drugs."

He also received a sentence to wear this sign for fifty hours as he marched around the Palestine courthouse.

"I've got forty-six hours to go," he said as I walked around the old historic courthouse with him for an interview.

Lopez also received 400 hours of community service.

"That's doing things like cleaning up the public parks," he said. "That I don't mind. But, this, well, it's rough. But my probation officer said that I either wear this sign or I will be wearing prison whites for ten years. Believe me, the judge got my attention with that."

The judge is District Judge Jim Parsons, who said that shortly after he took the bench in 1996, he began studying the results of people pleading guilty and getting probated sentences. He did not like what he found.

"What upset me was that it was too quiet and too closeted. They would plead guilty, be out of the court in five minutes, and then forget about the sentence. I wanted to break that cycle," he said.

Parsons also said he believed that it was too easy for people to receive probation and never incur the public feelings about what they had done. So he began ordering what he calls "placarding."

"I started it in November of last year," Parsons said.

He has been impressed with the results.

"I saw an effect almost immediately," he said. "They had rather do anything than placarding."

And, he said, he has not been discriminatory in his sentencing.

"I sentenced a seventy-two-year-old man who had been indecent with a child to walk around the courthouse square carrying a placard declaring his crime."

He also ordered a man in Athens, who had pleaded guilty to drug possession, to go back to a Dallas nightclub where he had purchased the drugs.

"I ordered him to march around that nightclub with a placard saying that is where he had bought the drugs."

And, in spite of what some of his critics have charged, the judge said he does have a heart.

"But I honestly believe you can't change the direction you are going unless you have a public confession that what you did is wrong. I began this with some trepidation, but I feel reassured with it now. But I don't want people to become accustomed to it to where they have no shame."

If Lopez's comments are typical, that is a long way from happening.

I even felt embarrassed walking around the courthouse with him for an interview.

# Door Builder in Lingleville

Don Weems might just go to his pasture to find a tree to answer the desires of a customer.

Recently a person wanted a door made from mesquite wood. There's not a lot of mesquite wood around, but Weems had been nurturing a mesquite tree for years on his ranch.

"So I cut it, had it milled, and made the door from it," Weems said.

And as a photograph showed, the door was a piece of work, as are all of his handcrafted creations.

He also makes stained and beveled-glass windows, cabinets, fireplace mantels, and furniture. His shop in this Erath County community on Farm Road 8 is filled with the pleasant smells of cedar. He was making twenty-eight cedar doors for a house near Mineral Wells.

Weems is built like a blacksmith, with well-muscled arms and large fingers. His gray hair spirals from beneath his leather hat. He is extremely quiet and unassuming. Getting him to talk is like prying open an old door.

He told how he got into custom woodworking. He was reared in nearby Dublin and served a tour in the Army in Vietnam. When he came home, he began working for an uncle who was a carpenter.

"He was a great inspiration to me, and this is what led me to doing this," Weems said.

We looked at his work in progress.

"I don't have a favorite wood. The favorite is whatever I am working on," he said.

He works with all kinds of wood, like sinker pine, wood that was cut before the Civil War. While being transported to a mill, the logs fell from the load and lay underwater for years. Hence the name, sinker pine.

"A really beautiful wood," Weems said.

He described mesquite the same way. But it is a volatile wood because a soft spot can suddenly appear while the wood is being sawed, causing it to explode when the saw hits it. Jim Leatherwood, a longtime acquaintance, had been listening to our conversation.

"Are you aware of that old bois d'arc that has been growing here all of these years?" he asked.

Weems smiled and led us out the back door. He pointed at a huge bois d'arc tree about 200 yards away, stretching its limbs into the sky.

"That one?" he asked.

He smiled when Leatherwood verified that was the tree. Then he talked about how long it takes him to complete a door.

"About four days," he said. "And that does not include finding the wood, curing it, and making it ready for work."

Many of his doors have his hand carvings in them, and some have exquisite stained glass done by Janine Willingham of Granbury.

When a customer comes in with an idea, Weems will sketch the design until it meets the customer's satisfaction. Then he begins his work. Once he is finished, he backs off, looks at it, and enjoys a feeling of pride.

"It is something I built. Something that I have done on my own. And something that I pretty much have learned by the seat of my pants," he said.

He explained that when he started, he looked for an old door maker to get points about the work.

"I'm still looking," he said. "I'm sure they are out there, but I don't know where."

Someday people will be able to find one of those here at Weems Custom Mill. But it will be awhile. He is in his early fifties.

# Dr. Don Newbury of Brownwood

I doubt that there ever will be another college president like Dr. Don Newbury, now retired but for many years president of Howard Payne University in this city in Brown County. They threw away the mold for college presidents after his creation.

Newbury, a longtime friend, taught me many years ago never to be surprised at his antics. They included such things as putting an old-time popcorn machine inside his home at Howard Payne and popping corn for everyone.

But I wasn't surprised when I saw the popcorn machine sitting inside the residence occupied by him and his wife, Brenda. I remembered how he had once reacted to one of my problems years ago.

I was in the Big Bend area and had to get a story back to my home office in Fort Worth. But I had no car and the closest telegraph agency, which is how we used to send our stories, was in Alpine, nearly 200 miles away.

I didn't know anyone with a car except this lanky guy who was full of one-liners that I had met only the day before. This was Newbury, then working at Sul Ross University in Alpine.

"So you need to get to Alpine," he said. "Well, here's the keys to my car."

I stammered that I hadn't finished writing my story.

"Well, get into my car and I'll drive you to Alpine, and you can finish your story as I drive," he said.

Because of acts like that, probably nobody was surprised when he unloaded the huge old movie popcorn machine and installed it in the chancellor's residence. And many gave things like that credit for his rapport with the students and an increase in the enrollment in this small university during his tenure here.

"How many college presidents do you know who pop corn for you and really talk to you?" asked Brad Miles, nineteen, of Dumas.

Newbury was popping about a ton of corn a year when another idea aimed at establishing rapport with students came to him. That was parasailing. That came not because of his love of a local lake. He had been on the lake only twice despite being reared in this community.

"No, a doctor told me that I needed something to get me away from the telephones. He suggested that I buy a boat," Newbury said.

So he did. He made one trip by himself and decided that was boring. Then he asked students if they wanted to go water skiing. And that led to parasailing, which he had seen on television.

"It looked so relaxing. So exhilarating," he said.

So began his parasailing trips on which he has taken hundreds for free. It became so popular that Newbury had to buy a larger boat. He found a 28-foot craft, powered by a 400-horsepower inboard engine. Then he convinced several local friends that it was a good buy and could be used as a recruiting aid.

They bought it, and the college president used it regularly. I joined him for an afternoon on the lake. Capt. Newbury took the wheel. He wore a wild yellow T-shirt, glasses, and a crazy canvas hat cinched tight by a strap under his chin.

The first parasailer that day was Glenn Petty, Abilene public schools director of instruction. He was strapped into the harness. He nodded and two students hollered, "Go. Go. Go."

The boat roared across the lake. The rope holding the parasail unwound and Petty reached 500 feet in height, becoming a dot in the sky.

Peter Hughes of Brownwood and a Howard Payne graduate helped. His wife, Tiffany, also contributes. She repairs the parasails.

"I think this is definitely different," he said.

Well, it was a different approach to recruitment, though Newbury admitted that no study was ever done to show how many students on campus came as a result of parasailing.

"But I loved it. I liked the challenge and the skill required to drive the boat and to get people in the air," he said. "That's where my reward came from."

He also never had to go out in his boat alone after he began parasailing.

# Politician Elected by Mail in Bremond

The late Herman Yezak's election as a state representative from this town in northern Robertson County is still unbelievable for two reasons.

Not only was he not there during the campaign but he spent only a few dollars soliciting votes. That expense came from buying a few postcards to mail to voters in the community, which is southeast of Waco.

The reason Yezak did not campaign in person was simple. He was a first lieutenant in the Army and was fighting in Italy during World War II.

So he announced his candidacy and his qualifications by sending out a postcard. He wrote, "Since I am overseas in Italy, I am using this card as one way in soliciting your vote."

Then he gave his qualifications.

"I am a Robertson County farm boy, thirty-one, single and a Bremond High School and A&M College graduate. I ask that you give my candidacy careful consideration when casting your vote in the Democratic Primary in July, and if you believe and feel that I am the kind of fellow that you are willing to entrust this office to, then give me your vote and it will be sincerely appreciated.

"Should I be elected, I will be there to serve after having the occasion to face the enemy several times like other Robertson County servicemen had and will before the World conflict is over."

Betty Yezak, his widow and owner of the *Bremond Press*, a weekly newspaper in this farming community, talked about her late husband's campaign in a telephone interview.

"He was fighting in Italy and the war was about over and he was trying to decide what to do. So he decided to run for office," she said with a laugh. "His filing papers got here after the deadline, but the official knew Herman and went ahead and accepted them."

She said that after her husband won the primary, everyone in his troop became excited about his possibility of being elected.

"They tried to take care of him by not sending him out on so many patrols," she said.

He was notified by mail after he won in November 1944.

"He got back to the states in December that year," she said.

21

So why was he able to defeat an incumbent without campaigning in person?

"Well, he was from a good family. People knew them and him," she said.

And being from a small community (1,146), voters probably knew everything about him like his 1938 graduation from Texas A&M and his working on the family farm all of his life.

"I met Herman after he was elected," she said. "But, of course, I knew about him. We were married November 1, 1949."

She said politics was his passion and he was elected to nine terms as a state representative.

"Certainly, he was a Democrat," she said. "We are the kind down here who do not change parties."

She said her husband, a longtime employee of the U.S. Department of Agriculture, bought the Bremond newspaper in 1960.

"I took over running it after he died in 1986," she said. "Our office is in a 100-year-old building. Certainly, I have some files on Herman. People still talk about him being elected and the amount of money he spent in that first campaign."

It is indeed unbelievable in today's ballooned campaign costs.

# Fastest Tire Changer in Texas at Comanche

I hope you never have a flat tire. But if you do, I hope you have it near Bill Ellis' Mobile Station on U.S. 377 in this town west of Fort Worth.

He not only will get your flat fixed in record time, but watching Ellis and his team work is like seeing an action movie in high acceleration.

Ellis has timed himself. So have others. It's fast.

"The fastest one I've ever done is three minutes," he said. "Of course it had a nail that was easy to find."

That time included jacking up the car, removing the tire, patching the puncture, and putting the tire back onto the car. Three minutes. Gosh, it takes longer than that just to put on your shoes.

Ellis talked from his station, which has a sign that says, "Flat City, USA." He took a break, which happens very seldom, for this interview. He's strongly built, has huge fingers, and stands six feet tall. He has thick hair and kind of sleepy blue eyes. He smiles frequently, making a grin that comes from the right side of his mouth. (He was twenty-nine when I did this interview in 1990.)

"I started fixing flats when I was six," he said. "My dad owned a service station and that's where I started."

His philosophy about flat-fixing has always been to do it fast.

"Let a person stand around here for about an hour while you are working and you are losing business and money," said Ellis.

He probably would be faster, he said, if he didn't have a crooked right arm. That came from an accident when he was fourteen. He was fixing a 15½-inch tire that was mounted on a 16-inch rim. He didn't notice the size difference and kept trying to air up the tire. It exploded.

"Knocked both of my arms up into my face," he said. "Broke both of them. Made my head swell up so much that my right eye was closed."

The explosion sent the tube to the top of some power lines.

"My dad started outside to where I was, and by the time he got to me, the rim fell near him," he said. "That's how high it blew it."

He was hospitalized for eight days. But he was not afraid to go right back to work at changing tires and fixing flats.

"Naw, I guess I'm too ignorant," he said.

He pointed to his right arm, which has a huge scar on the elbow.

"I tell people if it wasn't for that, I could do tire changing a lot quicker," he said.

He says people are constantly amazed at how quickly he and his team can change a tire. He's not.

"I always tell them I'm sorry it took so long," he said. "They get about halfway to their car and start laughing."

So is anyone faster than he? Well, he has heard about a man in Mansfield who is supposed to be pretty fast. And that man is so strong, they say that he removes the valve stems with his bare hands. So would Ellis challenge him?

"I might to changing tires," he said. He smiled. "But I sure wouldn't want to challenge him to anything else if he can pull those valve stems out with his hands."

He said many people stop for gas and ask for him to air up a low tire.

"We tell them we will do it," he said. "But we also tell them we can have that tire off and fixed in five minutes for $4 and then they won't have to worry about it anymore."

Ellis used to work seven days a week. But now he takes Sunday off.

"I was saved last year," he said. "So now we give Sunday to Jesus."

A customer arrived outside. Ellis leaped to his feet and began hollering at his help.

"Come on boys...get out there and get with it. Now!" he shouted.

The men ran to the front and quickly began their duties.

After all, the fastest flat fixer in the west had spoken.

# Family Firefighters in Gordon

The chances at one time were darn good that when a fire or ambulance call was made in this town, one of the Bill James family would be on the scene.

Bill, the father, had been the fire chief for twenty-five years when I visited here a few years ago. And as many as ten James relatives had been on either the volunteer fire department or ambulance staff at that time.

I checked in at the James residence, which is smack in the middle of this town of 516 residents in Palo Pinto County. The house can't be missed. There's a huge Premier gas sign in the front yard. And next door is one of two fire halls in this town off Interstate 20 west of Weatherford.

Joyce James, Bill's wife, greeted me warmly. She told about the family's involvement with the fire and ambulance departments.

"I was a dispatcher until I had a stroke," she said. "And, yeah, we have quite a few in our family doing it. Let's see, we have two daughters and a son."

She began reciting a list of names that even included a grandson.

"If you want to find Bill, go out the door, take a right, and go down to a gravel road and take another right," she said. "He's down there on a controlled burn."

I found him. He is sixty-five, a short, thickly built man with eyes nearly hidden by pockets. His first words:

"Call me Bill. I may be fire chief, but I am not a formal person."

He explained the controlled burn he was watching.

"They are burning some brush so they can put a trailer house here," he said. "So I figured we should have a fire truck here in case a fire started. It's pretty dry right now."

As we walked to our vehicles to go to city hall, I asked why he had been involved so long in a job that offers no pay.

"Well, when I was a kid, we used to fight grass fires by hand. We'd wet a tow sack [burlap bag] and start swinging," he said. "It is just something you grow up with and realize that it's your duty."

We drove to city hall. Inside were Barb Venable and Judy Cathey (James' daughter), both members of the ambulance force, and Kenneth Epperson, a city employee and volunteer firefighter. They talked about some of their recent calls.

"We went over to Ranger and helped them when all of those fires were set recently," James said.

They also talked about some of their problems.

"Like, we have a railroad track that runs through the middle of town. That means that sometimes a train will be stopped, and if we only had one fire station, we could not respond immediately to somebody living on the other side of the track," Epperson said.

They solved that by building a fire station on the east side of the tracks. But the main fire hall is on the north side of the tracks. It is also used for town meetings and fund-raising efforts such as pie suppers, biscuit suppers, and stew suppers.

"We can seat 250 in there without any problem," Venable said.

Then he cited a drawback to serving as a volunteer fireman in this city. That is you know practically everyone in the area, which means when a volunteer responds to a bad accident, they will know the victim. That hurts, particularly when there is a fatality.

"It just jerks your heart out," Venable said.

And there's the problem of having to respond to calls immediately.

"I've had to crawl out of my bathtub and go when I still had soap suds in my hair," Venable said.

Cathey began yawning. She should have. She had responded to five calls the night before and had reported to her job at the local school at 7 A.M.

That's just part of being a James and a volunteer.

# Windmill Repairman in Montague

Edward Fenoglio hands out two cards. One says he sells complete water systems and buys, sells, and repairs Aeromotor windmills.

Then he smiles and hands you the other card. It says that he designs septic systems and issues permits for their use in Montague County.

"I tell people, if you want to take a drink of water or flush your commode, you have to contact me for approval," he said.

He's a friendly, strongly built man with a graying beard. He chews tobacco. His place is on the edge of this whisper of a town. He talks in bursts of words like wind catching the blades of one of the many windmills standing there. He pointed to a wooden tower for a windmill that he builds.

"It takes 350 bolts to bolt one of them together. I charge $1,200 and I don't make that much. It costs me $300 for the wood, $100 for the bolts, $185 for the stub tower and legs, and two hard days of labor," he said.

But you get the impression that he likes it, even though there aren't many people doing the work.

"One reason, it's expensive. The other, well, it is hard work," said Fenoglio. "We've got a motto here, 'The only thing free about a windmill is the wind.'"

He charges $45 an hour to work on windmills. Since he is one of a few doing the work, he stays busy without advertising.

"I've got one ranch in Oklahoma and they've got twenty-six mills. They use them because they don't have electricity and they want their cattle to get fresh water," he said.

And, he has just received a call from a ranch in Turkey, Texas, about 200 miles away.

"They got seventeen mills. Heck yeah, it will cost them. When we leave at 7:30 A.M., that's when the time starts. And it doesn't go off until we quit at 7 P.M. We charge them for everything but sleeping time," he said. "But, they want somebody they can depend on."

And there are lots of people who will tell that you can depend on Fenoglio, who has been working on windmills since 1981. Before that he taught school and built houses.

"Let me tell you something about a windmill," he said. "Other than it being dirty, nasty, and hard work, it doesn't take a genius to work on one."

He sells a completely rebuilt Aeromotor with an eight-foot blade for $1,300 including exchange of the worn-out mill.

"An Aeromotor is like a Caterpillar 'dozer...you can rebuild them forever," he said.

Then he led us into his shop. There is an abundance of windmill parts and pieces, old tractors, and antique farm machines that he exhibits at tractor shows. He showed us an old Monitor pump jack with a massive single-piston engine that explodes with a "pow, pow" when running.

"I'm going to take that to tractor shows. I'll show people how cornmeal and flour is ground. I'll even sell them some," he said.

He could add that to another card and change his line. It would go, "If you want to take a drink, flush your commode, or buy a loaf of bread in Montague County, you've got to get approval from Eddie Fenoglio."

# Watermelon Thumper in Desdemona

Anybody who claims to be able to determine a watermelon's ripeness by the way it sounds when it's thumped is singing the wrong tune.

At least, that was Clyde Hodges' feelings. He got downright ill tempered when asked about thumping melons with one's fingers or knuckles to determine their ripeness.

He scowled and spat tobacco into his spittoon fashioned from a Clabber Girl baking powder can.

"I never thumped one in my life," he said. "I can look at them and tell when they're ready to pull. They get a cast to them. These fellers who thump them...hah. They don't know what they are doing."

Hodges should know what he is doing when it comes to watermelons. He raised them on farmland in this area in Eastland County for most of his ninety-one years. He retired from farming a few years ago, but still has a love for his knowledge and stories about watermelons.

"I was a watermelon raiser that nobody could beat. I was the watermelon king of De Leon. Everybody wanted to buy their melons from me. The reason—I raised good melons. I contracted with a guy down in San Antonio and I never had to replace even one melon," he said.

I had talked to Hodges at his place in this small town about 25 miles west of Stephenville just before melon planting began. He was ripe with watermelon stories and told about raising a crop of black diamond watermelons. A potential buyer came to look at them. The man pointed to a 40-pound melon and said it was ripe.

"I told him it wasn't," said Hodges. "I told him that there was just a little red around the seed. He looked at me like I was crazy."

So Hodges proved his point by pulling out his pocketknife.

"I'm going to show you what I mean," he told the buyer. "He tried to stop me. But I went ahead and cut that melon. Sure enough, there was nothing but a little red around the seed."

Hodges, a small, lean man, blinked his eyes, spat, and continued.

"I've seen a lot of melons at the market and knew not over half of them were ripe. Boy, somebody sure got stuck on them melons."

He laughed then continued telling more watermelon stories.

One concerned a man named Uncle Billy Preston who bought melons and took them to other towns to sell. He bought some from Hodges and tried to sell them at Stamford.

"The man asked him where those melons were from," said Hodges. "Uncle Billy told him and the man said he didn't want any...that De Leon watermelons were white-hearted [not ripe]. Well, Uncle Billy listened and said, 'Just let me leave you a few and you try 'em.' He did."

Uncle Billy then stopped on his return. The man said, "I want to buy all of them melons. They are the finest I ever ate."

Hodges frowned.

"What happened was a couple of fellers from Weatherford had come through there and sold that man some melons. They were white-hearted. They had told him they had come from De Leon. Hmmmph. White-hearted melons won't make good hog feed."

Hodges said his melons were never irrigated.

"A watered watermelon is not as good as a dry-land melon," he said. "They don't keep as good. They don't eat as good. No sir, watered watermelons aren't as good as dry land melons."

He said if the ground is prepared right and the melons are spaced right, they'll make on a small amount of rain.

"I had one year when I never got a drop of rain after I planted them," he said. "But boy they were good watermelons."

People could always tell which melons were his. They'd be the ones all of the judges in watermelon contests would be standing around and almost fighting to get a bite from.

And nobody had to thump them to see if they were ripe. They knew Charles Hodges never brought in green watermelons.

# Fighter from the Past from Midlothian

The memories of Donnie Fleeman's strength came flooding back when I saw him hoist a steel anvil over his head several times.

My friends Tom Dodge and John Tushim, who had come to listen to Fleeman's stories, could barely budge the anvil. I had not even tried. But Fleeman easily lifted the anvil that day. He calls the

85-pound piece of steel that has been with him fifty years "the anvil" like it is a person. He used to hoist it over his head twenty-five or thirty times with either hand. No wonder he could knock fire from a boxer.

He did that for years as a heavyweight. He may be the only man to have fought three men who became or were world champions.

He whipped one, Ezzard Charles. And he might have whipped Muhammad Ali. But Fleeman had a busted sternum when he fought Ali. Most people with this injury could not lift themselves out of bed, much less crawl into a ring and go seven rounds with Ali.

We met at his home in this town in Ellis County, east of Midlothian where he attended school and where I as a junior high student had watched in awe as he downed football running backs with exploding tackles. He was still lean and looked like a fighter despite being in his late sixties.

And he still has those huge hands. Shazam, look at them, said Dodge, who had seen Fleeman fight.

"How would you like to have one of those coming to your face?" Dodge asked.

Fleeman grinned slightly. He does not flail the air with boasts. You have to really push to get him to talking about his days as a heavyweight fighter.

But he finally talked of his 47 professional fights. He had 37 wins, 22 by knockouts.

So why did he fight? Well, he grew up with older boys picking on him. So one day a principal told him to bring some boxing gloves to school. He did. The older boys quit picking on him. They didn't like him smashing them in the face.

He got into shape by running to and from school. Then he began hoisting the 85-pound anvil. He figured doing it with one hand would be good for him.

It must have been. He won so much in Golden Gloves that he has forgotten many of his triumphs. But he did win the state heavyweight title and fought in the national Golden Gloves tournament before turning professional.

"I was never knocked out. But Sonny Liston hit me so hard that if I had not got tangled up in the ropes, I would have been knocked out," he said.

That happened in Chicago where he had gone to compete in some club fights. He recalled going backstage and sitting beside this huge man, waiting for his turn to fight.

"I didn't know who he was except he was a monster, and I felt sorry for whoever was going to fight him," said Fleeman. "Then I go out and see my opponent. It was him. I lost that fight sitting beside him."

So how about the fight with Ali on February 23, 1961, in Miami?

"I had fought Pete Radamacher before that. He had fractured my sternum. My doctor said I should not fight. I could barely raise my left arm. But I had a guarantee of $3,000. So I went ahead and fought," Fleeman said. "I'm not taking anything away from Cassius. He was quick and after seven rounds, I quit. That was the only fight when I was ready to get out of the ring."

He told about fighting Mike Holt, heavyweight champion of South Africa.

"I knocked that rascal down, but I went to the wrong corner," he said. "They had started counting but stopped and sent me to the right corner. Then they started counting again, and he got up and finished the fight."

He shook his head as he showed a picture of Holt after the fight. His left eye was closed. His face looked like a busted tomato.

"They gave him the decision. But if you are in another man's backyard, it is hard to win a decision. The only way you can win is by knocking him out," Fleeman said.

That's what he did to Bo Myers, once considered the toughest man in Cleburne. Dodge saw that fight with his buddy Bill Shehorn.

"I'd never seen anybody hit that hard," Shehorn said. "And do you remember us going back to the dressing room after the fight?" he asked Dodge.

They told about getting there just after Myers had been revived. Myers' little brother was standing by his side, checking on him.

He asked Bo if he was all right and if he knew who he (the little brother) was. Myers eyed his brother and said, "Yeah, you're the little kid who lives down the road from me, aren't you?"

Fleeman flashed a faint grin at the story. Then he invited us to look at his garden full of onions, watermelons, squash, and tomatoes.

"Look at them tomatoes. Aren't they pretty?" he said.

They were with their big, red faces that looked like the opponents Fleeman used to hammer.

# Paulino Rosales from Fort Worth

I've always considered Paulino Rosales a truly neat person with an unmeasurable heart when it came to helping others.

So it was with sadness that I read about his death in the *Star-Telegram*. I immediately recalled his efforts at helping a young girl in Monterrey, Mexico. That had led to our first meeting.

He had called me at our downtown office. He spoke in bursts of words saying:

"Mr. Jon McConal, I need some help. I've found out about this little girl who lives in Monterrey, Mexico, who had polio when she was a baby, and she is now six or seven, and the only way she can walk is by dragging herself around.

"Her father came up here illegally and tried to make money so he could buy some braces for his daughter. But he was caught and sent back without any money. Can you help me? Her name is Elida Valderas."

So I wrote a story about Elida. As a result, a local service club adopted her as a project. The club established a fund to finance operations to straighten her limbs and buy her braces.

After this, Paulino suggested that I go to Monterrey with him to visit Elida. He also invited Dave Poindexter, a representative of the service club.

The trip sounded great to me and Poindexter. However I think he began to have doubts when he saw that we were going to Monterrey in Paulino's rather beat-up pickup that had a camper shell.

"I just put in a mattress so we can take turns sleeping," Paulino said.

Poindexter looked at the pickup and asked, "Jon, are we really going down there...in that?"

Paulino answered for both of us.

"Sure, Mr. Dave. It will make it. It's made it many times," Paulino said.

We left about midnight. Paulino and I began sipping beer and singing. The more miles passed, the better we sounded. Or so we thought, even though Mr. Dave did not join in the serenading.

I finally grew tired and got in the back for some sleep. Paulino said his dogs had slept on the mattress but that it was clean and free of fleas and ticks.

Two hours later it was Poindexter's time to sleep. So he crawled inside the camper.

Paulino and I continued driving. We were soon singing again and telling loud stories when we heard pounding on the back window. It was Poindexter. He wanted to get back up front with us.

"That mattress is, well, a little uncomfortable," he said.

We made it to Monterrey by daybreak. We checked into a hotel, cleaned up, and then headed to see Elida.

Her family lived in a poor section of town. They had no running water and no indoor facilities. But they were so glad to see us. Mrs. Valderas almost immediately began to prepare a meal.

And we met Elida, a beautiful child with long brown hair. She held our hands with her slender, almost elegant fingers and said in a soft voice, "Gracias, señores. Gracias."

We ate the meal of scrambled eggs with hot sauce and flour tortillas. We drank strong boiled coffee into which Mrs. Valderas had poured milk and sugar. Everything was delicious.

We spent about three hours with the family. They thanked us repeatedly. Poindexter and I flew home but Paulino stayed a week before returning.

Paulino and I kept in touch for several years. He'd call and would always say, "And how is Mr. Jon doing?"

He also kept in touch with Elida. Once he showed me photographs of her. She had matured and could walk with her new braces. She also had a job.

I always thought of how this little girl had been aided by a man who worked hard and had little money but had a heart so big he never thought about himself but rather how he could help others.

So when I read of his death, I said, "God bless you, Paulino Rosales."

My eyes were wet when I said it.

# Chapter 2

# Towns with Unusual Names

I'd bet there are people who have gone on to the great beyond who are laughing at folks today who try to find reasons why certain towns got their names.

Indeed, there are many towns with unusual names as I discovered during my twenty years of looking for columns. When I stopped and spent a few hours talking to people who lived in these unusually named places, I discovered that many of the names seemed appropriate, particularly from a common sense viewpoint.

But in stopping and trying to find out why these towns were so named, I developed an appreciation for the imagination and humor of our ancestors. This section is about some of those unusually named towns.

## Snake Den/Weeping Mary

When warm weather comes, snakes begin crawling around this community in Stephens County.

Without a doubt, this village along with Weeping Mary, which is nearly 300 miles from here in East Texas, are appropriately named when considering their history.

But first consider Snake Den, a tiny settlement about 17 miles northwest of Breckenridge on U.S. 183, which came by its name honestly.

In his book *Discovery Well*, Charles R. Lewis, says C.L. "Pappy" Morales told him that name came from the abundance of rattlesnakes in the area.

"I killed twenty-eight in one day," Morales told Lewis.

Morales also lost two children from snakebite. So considering that, the place seems well named.

Betty Hanna, a Breckenridge native and longtime writer of history in this area, had an aunt who taught at the Snake Den school.

"It was a little one-room schoolhouse," Hanna explained. "At one time we had forty-eight such schoolhouses in this county."

That reminded me of a bit of history I heard on earlier travels when an old-timer said a school was built every six miles in an effort to make education available to everyone.

"They could either walk or ride their horses that distance," he had said.

Regardless, Hanna gave us directions to the community.

"Snake Den is not too far from Crystal Falls, one of the first settlements in this county," she said. "If you go there, be sure and look at the little square concrete building. That used to be the bank vault."

So we headed to Snake Den. When we topped a hill, there was Pioneer Cemetery with a gate that features a welded-iron sculpture of cowboys, cattle, and horses. No snakes, however.

As we walked into the cemetery, I kidded my traveling companion, John Tushim, about the possibility of snakes crawling in the warm weather. He's a Pennsylvania native and definitely does not like snakes.

So as he walked behind me, I found a marker dedicated to the memory of pioneers of Snake Den. It read, "To those who in 1887 despite roaming Indians and gunfighters and a few buffalo were determined not only to build a cemetery but to erect a school to make a better life. Will Stouard, Felix Morales and others gave of their time and land for this purpose. The cemetery is the resting place of S.M. McClenny, the first known teacher of Snake Den School in 1901."

The cemetery had cedar elms and mesquites that were trying hard to awaken from winter on that day but were having trouble because of a drought that had hammered them so hard. The mesquites had trunks with deep gashes in their bark, similar to scars on wet leather left lying in the sun.

We found the grave of McClenny, surrounded by hand-shaped limestone blocks. On one side was a mesquite tree with blossoms trying to burst out of knots that looked like the ends of frayed shoelaces.

Nearby was an old marker with the writing erased by time. Lichens had formed a beautiful rainbow of green, yellow, and light orange colors on the stone.

A strong wind cut through the trees' branches, causing a mournful echo—perhaps re-creating the grieving cries from those early settlers over the loss of family members.

I looked at the marker of Cecil R. Sanders. A tribute read, "Oh, heavenly father, we pray that you will guide us in the arena of life as we take that last inevitable ride up there where the grass is lush and green and stirrup high."

A wooden cross with a rusting horseshoe was on the grave. A pile of brush with a huge twisted log that looked like a broken nose lay just beyond a barbed wire fence.

That site reminded me of many I saw when I visited Weeping Mary.

Once I saw the name of that East Texas community, I knew I would return.

Jane and I spotted it two years ago on one of our East Texas trips to see the Caddo Indian mounds.

"Knowing you, I'm sure we will return," she had said.

So we did. We used Texas 21 that leads from Alto to Crockett. After a few miles past towering pine trees and beautiful farm scenes, we reached County Road 2907. A sign said, "Weeping Mary."

We drove past a site where Zebulon Pike, for whom Pikes Peak in Colorado is named, had camped on June 23, 1807.

We followed a tiny road lined with trees. We crossed two old wooden bridges that creaked as if an old man were clacking his false teeth. There, near a creek that looked like a ragged ribbon of brown, was Weeping Mary Baptist Church. The white-frame structure sits on the edge of the main street of Weeping Mary. Frame houses and mobile homes flank the road.

We stopped at a car repair shop owned by Cherry Jenkins. Jenkins has left Weeping Mary several times but has always returned.

"But I'm not sure how it got its name. Go talk to Uncle William. He might be able to tell you," he said.

Uncle William Skinner used to own the garage now owned by Jenkins. As we looked for his place, which was across the road from a wire pen with a hog sleeping happily in a mud waller, a young man walked up.

"I'm Cherry Jenkins Number Two," he said, flashing a slight grin. "I used to live in Dallas. Moved here to relax and get away from that pressure in Dallas. And, yeah, this is certainly different from Dallas. But I like it."

We walked across the street to where Skinner dug in soil with a huge hoe.

"Getting ready to plant cabbage," he said. "Yeah, I have lived here all my life. I'm eighty-one. Born over there in them pine trees."

So how did the community get its name?

"I don't know. Too many people come here asking that question. You need to ask the oldest man here. But he took sick and they took him to the hospital yesterday," Skinner said.

He returned to digging. End of interview.

We visited Jenkins again. He related one story that he had once heard about how the town got its name.

"There was a black woman who had some land here. Some man stole her land some way. She cried until she died," he said. "Her name was Mary. So they come up with the name, Weeping Mary."

He talked about life. He is happy to be alive. Every morning when he wakes up, he says, "Thank you, Jesus."

He looked at us.

"The grass grows under my feet. The sun comes up and shines on me. That's the same grass that grows under your feet and the same sun that shines on you," he said. "And, the same Man up there takes care of both of us."

Well, Jenkins does have somebody else taking care of him. A 165-pound Rottweiler named Desiree.

"She is the gentlest thing around," he said. "But don't holler at me. She ain't so gentle then."

We shook hands and said goodbye.

We drove past houses with the morning wash hanging on clotheslines, and a house with a purple fence.

We watched a hawk that was circling overhead spread its wings, hit an air current, and sail away so fast and graceful. A nice scene in Weeping Mary.

# Gunsight

Catch the scene just right as the sun comes through two hills and you know how this once-lively town got its name.

I got word of the community from Olene D. Spill of Clifton. She lived here in 1920 when she was four.

"Enclosed is a picture of Gunsight taken in 1920 when new oil wells were flowing," she said. "My father bought a tiny business and sold oilfield workers tobacco, candy, fruit, sugar, flour, and a few canned goods. For me, life there was interesting. Why don't you visit the place?"

So I did along with my buddy John Tushim. The community is in southern Stephens County. We drove down a gravel road lined with bare mesquites with thick clumps of mistletoe sucking their limbs.

And there was Gunsight. A historical marker said it was established in the 1870s as a stage stop.

"It was boosted by an area oil boom in the 1920s. But the town began a steady decline after WW II and today consists of a few houses, a few buildings, and this cemetery," the marker read.

Two white-framed church buildings with tin roofs remain. A rope hung from a light near the entryway of one. Tushim pulled it. A bell boomed, making lonely echoes. Inside were the smells of age, old Methodist hymnals, and a wooden floor that made sounds like the rasping coughs from a longtime smoker's lungs as we walked across it.

It was in one of these buildings that Spill saw an unusual Christmas event. The building had filled with parents and children. Then in came Santa Claus.

"He began taking presents off the tree and calling the names of the recipients," she said. "But his beard caught fire and flamed up. A woman helper rushed him out the side door. He soon returned with a jolly 'Ho, ho, ho' and finished giving out the presents," she said. "But, his beard had kind of a singed smell to it."

Across from the building is the cemetery. A barrel of plastic flowers sat near the front gate.

A long snakeskin lay near an 18-inch-high wall, which had been hand-fashioned with native stones stuck on top like pieces of a glass puzzle. We found the first grave where Lewis B. McClesky was buried. He was born March 9, 1875, and died January 27, 1877.

Acorns crunched under our feet as we walked past graves. They sounded like the dull thumps of a fistfight. Spill recalled one such fight.

"Two oilfield workers decided to have an argument in front of our store. When they were about ten feet from each other, one bent over, picked up a 9- or 10-inch piece of pipe and kept walking toward the other man. Then my mother grabbed me and I missed the action and words," she wrote. "But later one of the men came into my father's store with bandages around his head and explained his side of the argument."

We looked at some deep deer tracks and then drove to Dale Griffin's house, which was nearby. He was working with cattle. He had the smell of work and chewing tobacco about him.

"Yeah, I know how it got its name. Look at them two hills just right down that road. Catch the sun just right and it looks like you are looking down the front sight of a gun. That's how they named it."

We looked. By gosh the name didn't sound so crazy after all.

# Democrat

Only once that anyone can remember did anyone vote for a Republican in this community in northern Mills County.

"That was when Eisenhower was running," said Josephine Johnson. "Somebody voted for him. They made a big story about it. Wrote it up and put it on the front page of the newspaper. It said,

'Democrat Has Gone Republican.' But, shoot, there was only one voted Republican. And we never were sure who that was."

So one might say the approximately sixty registered voters are a Democratic stronghold in this tiny community. We sat in the Johnson's home. Her husband, Leroy, and her sister, Elizabeth Aldridge Hodges, 79, and Hodges' grandson, Sam Shelton, 32, all were there. We were waiting for their brother, Dudley Aldridge to arrive. He's 89. Still works cattle. Still rides a horse. And still votes Democrat.

"Everybody in here was born right here," said Johnson, 77.

"Matter of fact, Sam's three children are the sixth generation to live on this land that has been in our family for over 100 years," Hodges said.

They told about J.H. Dudley and J.D. Aldridge coming here in 1886 and buying several sections of land.

"But they went back to Arkansas where they had a sawmill. They ran that mill until they had the land paid off," Shelton said.

"Yes, and when they moved here they brought a wagonload of lumber that they built their first home with," Hodges said. "And I've got part of that lumber in my house."

Then Uncle Dudley arrived. He's a lean man. Uses a cane to walk but is strong looking. He has a red face. His boots are scarred heavily, probably from riding past mesquite limbs full of thorns as he chased cattle.

"So Uncle Dudley, do you know why they named this Democrat?" asked Shelton.

He didn't. Neither did the women. But Johnson had an idea.

"Probably because everybody voted Democrat," she said. "Makes sense to me."

Uncle Dudley smiled at that. Then he talked about the Democrat store that Aldridge and Dudley had started. It had a barbershop, dry goods, blacksmith shop, and icehouse.

"And they bought eggs and meat from everybody," he said. "The people brought eggs in buckets. Me and Grandpa would test them and then put them into crates."

They had a Democrat Common School District, a Democrat Woodmen of the World lodge and of course, a Baptist church. But it was called the Rock Springs Baptist Church.

"That's where we vote today," Hodges said. "I help with the elections in the old church building. We call it the Democrat community."

Not too far from that, the Johnsons once had a store and café they called the Democrat. They sold hamburgers and old-style meals for a quarter before closing in 1957.

Then Uncle Dudley and Shelton invited me to see what's left of Democrat. As he drove, Shelton told about Uncle Dudley's teaching him how to ride horses and work cattle. Uncle Dudley smiled. The sun caught several gold caps on his teeth.

"He's a good hand," he said. "But that boy, well, it takes one feller carrying water for him. Drinks more water than anyone I've ever seen in my life."

"Aw, Uncle Dudley," Shelton said.

He turned east and drove about a quarter of a mile and stopped. Two cemeteries edged the road. One is the Dudley family cemetery.

"You have to be a member of the family to be buried here," Shelton said.

The other cemetery is the Democrat Cemetery. You don't have to be a Democrat to be buried there. But I kind of got the impression that it sure would help you some to be approved for burial here if you were a Democrat.

# Cool

As temperatures boil past 100, folks in this tiny city don't get heated up over the soaring mercury.

The town's name tells why. This city, which is 12 miles west of Weatherford on U.S. 180, is from four to six degrees cooler than any other town in Parker County, residents claim.

I had long wondered about this name while passing through it. The town has a Phillips 66 station and store, Cool Church of Christ, and a huge stock tank that looks inviting for a quick dip on crackling hot summer days.

So I visited Sam Davis, the man given credit for the name. He sat on his front porch beside Johnny's Truck and Auto Salvage. He's a slender man with short gray hair combed straight back. He rolls his own cigarettes, which he smokes until ashes touch his lips. He's seventy-eight.

"My wife and I bought land here in 1937. They were just building that highway," he said, gesturing at busy U.S. 180.

"There wasn't anything here then. Well, I take that back. We had a good crop of copperheads [snakes]. Almost any rock you picked up then had a copperhead from six inches to a foot long under it," he said. "I never got bit, but I did eliminate a lot of them."

He rolled another cigarette, lighted it, and talked about the name Cool.

"They nicknamed it about everything then," he said. "It was called Tile City because most of the houses were built from tile made in Mineral Wells."

Then Marvin McCrackin moved here. He was a good fiddle player.

"So they started calling it Fiddler's Ridge," Davis said. "Old Marvin could really play the fiddle. I used to play with him with my guitar."

He flipped his cigarette into his front yard. One could just imagine his long fingers flying in runs down a guitar neck.

"Then me and Marvin and old Joe Tidwell put on a celebration one year. It was July Fourth and about 1942 if I remember right," Davis said. "It was quite a big deal. Everybody came. And after we got through with the watermelon cutting and the ice cream making, we had a heart-to-heart talk about what to officially name our city."

Tile City was suggested. So was Fiddler's Ridge. Then somebody in the audience shouted, "Why not Cool? It is cooler here than any other place in the county."

Davis smiled.

"You know he was right," he said. "I don't know why, but it is cooler here. Maybe it's because we are on a hill or something. Heck, I have only had my air conditioner on for about two hours this year. And sitting out here...don't you feel cool?"

I did.

Well, that fact sold folks. Cool won by a landslide.

Davis rolled still another cigarette and mused about the name.

"It seems more appropriate than Tile City," he said. "And you've got to have a reason to move to a place like this. So maybe the name attracts some people."

There's no doubt that Davis likes the place. He and his wife once had to move away because of a severe drought in the early 1950s.

"We had credit at our store, and the drought hit and those folks couldn't pay," he said. "So we shut down and moved to Midland where I became a boiler maker. We lived there until 1970. We came home. Cool sure looked good to me."

Well, two other people have found happiness in this tiny town and have turned fifteen acres of what once was raw, ranching country, into a landscaped elegance that attracts visitors from all over the state. Those people are Max and Billie Clark, and a visit to Clark Gardens is a must if you come to Cool.

Billie led us on a tour of the surroundings that include irises, azaleas, and day lilies, all planted in flower boxes that Max has made in his workshop.

As we walked, we heard the crazy chatter of guineas.

"That is our bug control. We don't poison anything except fire ants," she said.

We walked past impatiens with wild splashes of red, white, and pink and onto a carpet of St. Augustine grass. She pointed to a tree house that Max built. It is surrounded by azaleas and huge trees with vines that look like they have been plaited around the trunk by hand.

"Max never does anything halfway," she said.

As we continued, the echoes of locusts and birds hit a high volume.

"That is another reason we don't spray," she said. "Every morning we wake up to their sound."

We stopped as a peacock screamed at us. We looked at a small pond where black swans swam. We stopped at her herb garden.

"All I really wanted was a small one. But look what Max did," she said.

There is box after box of rosemary, thyme, horseradish, basil, and leeks.

We walked past hundreds of irises sent to them by the National Iris Society in 1990 and past huge clumps of pampas grass.

"This is where our money goes. Instead of for boats or whatever, we get our kicks out here," she said.

Out here in Cool, Texas.

# Ohio

So here we were fulfilling a desire of mine since I had first been told about this community and one to the north.

"Jon, did you know that you can visit Ohio and Ireland within 30 minutes of each other?" asked Bill Snell of Hamilton, county seat of Hamilton County in which this community is located.

Well, I didn't until he showed me these once-thriving small communities. And on a Saturday, a group of us crawled into Fred Massingill's motor home and headed first for Ohio.

We drove south of Hamilton on a day with sunshine spilling liberally from blue skies. Trees along the road were just being nipped by fall. Some appeared almost embarrassed about the changing of their colors. Then came the sumac. It exploded in blasts of oranges and crimsons.

Alvin Wood watched the countryside. He's a western-looking man with a strong build and has lived in Ohio for many years. He was seventy but everyone agreed that he didn't look it.

"It's the water in Ohio," he said. He smiled and then told how the Ohio residents have fun with the name.

"A neighbor would move and people would ask about him and we'd say, 'Oh, he's not our neighbor anymore. He moved south of Ohio,'" he said.

We drove past mesquite flats still heavy with green. We looked at post oaks and cedars dripping rainbows of color. Massingill, fifty-two, told about being reared north of here.

"I went to school at Gum Branch my first year," he said. "Sometimes I would ride a horse and sometimes I would walk. It was about eight miles and I'd take off my shoes. The teacher always made me put them back on before letting me in school. Gosh, they hurt my feet."

We drove to Parlsey's Crossing, which leads across Cow House Creek. Massingill laughed.

"Been more lies told here than anywhere in the country," he said. "This was the place where young couples used to come and park."

A person prowled among the rocks on the creek bank.

"He's the local rock hound," said Wood. "He's got names and meanings for all of them rocks. But they're just rocks to me."

A hawk sailed through the sky, like a soldier keeping a lonely vigil. Huge elms hung over the creek that was still and green like the fading color of aging Astroturf.

"This is the longest creek in the state of Texas," said Snell.

We continued south. The sun bounced off a suspension bridge like a dusty penny caught in a burst of light.

"We are nearing Ohio," said Snell. "I tried to buy the store here once. I wanted to be able to say I owned my own town."

Massingill stopped the motor home. All that is left of Ohio today is a vacant two-story rock house. We looked at it as Massingill told about coming to Ohio one day and seeing a naked woman floating down the creek in an inner tube.

"She was drinking wine. All she had on was a straw hat," he said.

So what did he do?

"I got in my truck and went home," he said.

We listened to the wind rustling the dried leaves. A raw outdoor smell filled the area.

"Well, let's head on to Ireland," said Massingill. "It's about twenty minutes from here, right on the edge of Coryell County."

We drove on Farm Road 932. We passed green grain fields and an old vacant two-story single wall plank house. It looked as thin as an old woman hunched over her churn. Wood told of living in such a house in the Panhandle.

"It had openings between the planks. One night I went to bed when it was snowing," he said. "I woke up and there were strips of snow on my quilt where it had blown in."

We arrived at Ireland, a town founded in 1911 and named after Texas governor John Ireland. We stopped at the old First Methodist Church. Janice and Kenneth Ganske greeted us. They had bought the old building and were rebuilding it for their residence.

Both said it was love at first sight when they saw for sale signs on the church.

"We knew we had to save it," said Kenneth.

Both were reared in Hamilton County. But neither ever dreamed that they would one day live here.

"I had lived fourteen years in Detroit before coming back," said Janice. "Nobody was more amazed than me that I would do this."

Living in the church during the remodeling has been hard.

"The first winter, we lived in the balcony," he said. "Gosh, it got cold. Then we bought an old mobile home and lived in it. We hauled water for over a year."

They led us through the building, which has about 5,500 square feet. We walked up aching wooden stairs to the attic where a spare bedroom and sewing room are planned. Faint wind noises skipped around where once-booming gospel hymns echoed.

They talked of the work. Of hauling away seventeen loads of trash. Of adding insulation and a hot tub in a Sunday school room.

"I want my great-grandkids to be able to go through here and say, 'This is 150 years old, and if it was not for my great-grandmother, it wouldn't be here,'" she said.

Then she laughed. "Here we are living in a Methodist church," she said. "We both are Baptists."

We walked outside and said goodbye. As we drove away, Snell said, "Well, you can now say you've visited Ireland and Ohio in a couple of hours. That's a kick."

It was indeed.

# Hazel Dell

You won't find this tiny whisper of a town on any maps. Only a cemetery and a wind greeted us on the day of our visit.

But what a town it once was. It was called the roughest, meanest, toughest town in Texas. Its birth came during rugged times in this country in southern Erath County. The location for the town is in raw terrain, and the tiny Hazel Dell Cemetery lies on a hilltop, surrounded by cliffs with rocks punched in them like ragged scars left from a knife fight.

The town began officially in 1867 when the Rev. William "Choctaw Bill" Robinson opened a sawmill here. He knew how to handle the rough nature of the town. When he preached, he leaned a rifle on each side of his podium and two loaded six-guns near his Bible.

History has it that people once considered naming the town after Brother Robinson and calling it Robinsonville. But instead they chose Hazel Dell because the soil had a hazel-brown color and the village was in a dell.

It soon achieved its reputation as Texas's toughest town because of its bloat of saloons and other nests of sin.

So while Robinson, who had received the calling to be a Baptist preacher, preached against sin, sin abounded in Hazel Dell.

But in its first days there was a problem. They didn't have a cemetery. After hours of drinking and debating, the town leaders came up with a solution.

A trapper whom nobody knew had camped out in the town.

"So let's just kill him and start our cemetery," reasoned one Hazel Dell resident.

They did, and Hazel Dell had its cemetery. That is all that is left of the town. A tiny clot of land clinging to a hilltop with many graves. One huge marker reads, "Leona L. Rowe. Born Sept. 30, 1872. Died May 25, 1873."

There are many other youngsters buried here.

"Diphtheria took a lot of kids then," said Wade Cowan of nearby Dublin. Cowan, who had brought me here, has long studied the town's history.

We walked through graves to reach an old crumbling concrete vault, cracked like the lips of an old man who has done without water for days. Nearby was a grave of Arthur A. Hughes. The stone read:

"Farewell, dear son, farewell." A photograph inside the marker shows a proud-looking young man. He was wearing a tie and had long curly hair.

One stone reads simply, "The Fraley Brothers."

Ah, the poor Fraleys. They found out how mean Hazel Dell was. History has it that the brothers became disenchanted with those ruling Hazel Dell. They planned to take action, but Hazel Dell citizens stopped them.

They arrested the brothers and chained them together, charging them with stealing horses. They held them in the general store while somebody went for the sheriff. The mob didn't wait.

They carried the Fraleys to a large live oak tree north of town. The older brother begged for his younger brother's life. The mob didn't listen. They hanged them and then buried them in a single grave.

Near the grave stands a twisting oak with limbs that look like someone wringing his hands in sadness. Yellow wildflowers that look like yellow paint dashed haphazardly on them grew in abundance.

We listened to a mourning dove sound its lonely echoes. We heard the wind growing down in the tiny valley.

"Yeah, about the only thing left of this town is the graveyard," said Cowan. "The graveyard and the wind."

I remembered a postscript written about Hazel Dell that Cowan had shown me. It had said:

"It was known all over the state and many tall tales have been told about the meanness and the horrible crimes committed at this little place. It is said that of the first ten citizens, all died violently but the Reverend Robinson."

Maybe that's why the wind gathering in the mesquite and live oak thickets seemed to be moaning that day. Those same lonely echoes can be heard in Cottonwood, another frontier town that was known for its meanness. This Callahan County town once was known for people settling arguments by killings.

Buried in its cemetery is a man killed when beaten to death with a breast yoke from a wagon. Another died when a friend chopped his head open with a hoe during a fight in a cotton field. And still another was killed after he left his neighbor's gate open.

And then there were the two close friends who got into a gun battle after arguments over a woman. One was killed immediately. The one who survived briefly asked that he and his friend be buried together in the same grave.

"No frontier town in Callahan County was the scene of more gun battles than in the early day town of Cottonwood," reads the book *Early Days in Callahan County* by B.D. Crisman.

Jim Williams of Fort Worth, who was reared near Cottonwood, which at one time had two cotton gins, a hardware store, two blacksmiths, four physicians, and a newspaper, shared Crisman's book with me.

"The soil fertility and the availability of wood—blackjack and post oak—and the fact that water could be hit at 12 to 25 feet made it superior for settling to any county in the state," Crisman wrote.

We had arrived at Cottonwood, which today is practically a ghost town. A historical marker said that the town was founded in 1875 and at one time was the largest in Callahan County.

We talked to R.T. Peevy, who lives close to the cemetery. His mother and father were born near the town. And so was he.

"But let me tell you about another double killing. There was another that involved my great-grandfathers on both sides of the family," he said.

The men got into a knife fight. After one stabbed the other to death, he hid out in the woods.

"My uncle carried him food for three days. But on the third day, he found him dead. He had killed himself. Couldn't stand to think of what he had done," said Peevy.

Then he looked at gathering rain clouds that looked like giant purple-colored turkey eggs. Or maybe like the bruises on the faces of people who once lived in Cottonwood and fought to settle their arguments.

# Exray

I discovered the name of this town on some old Erath County tax rolls. I had never heard of it and then I met J.W. Burris, who had once lived in Exray in northern Erath County.

We sat on the front porch of his home, which is about five miles west of here and about nineteen miles north of Stephenville on FM 108. He was eighty-two, a sparely built, red-faced man with short sandy hair. He swatted flies with a swatter as he talked. His dog, Blue, lay at his feet.

"Yeah, I was born in Exray," Burris said. "So how did it get its name? Well, I always heard that you could stand right in the center of town and see all the way through it. So they named it Exray."

He smiled. Blue bit at some ticks.

"I was delivered by a man named Dr. McDonald. Don't know if he was a doctor or not," he said. "But he owned the drugstore in Exray. He mixed all of those old drugs and did some doctoring."

Back then Exray had two grocery stores, a gin, and a store that sold wagons, buggies, cultivators, and clothes.

"I went to school there. It had three teachers," he said. "Then it shrank to one teacher and finally closed, and the school moved to Huckaby."

He swatted at a fly and tapped his foot.

"I was so far behind I couldn't find the classroom," he said. "So I quit."

But Exray continued thriving. It had a cotton gin and a dipping vat for ticks that caused Texas tick fever.

"I worked that vat. I used to drive cattle through it," he said. "Back then it took half a day to go to Stephenville. Then if you didn't spend too much time there, you could make it home by dark."

He recalled when his father suffered a ruptured appendix. The old doctor in Exray could do nothing. So they put him in a wagon and hauled him over rough roads to Gordon.

"They put him on a train and took him to Weatherford," Burris said. He shook his head. "He was dead by the time he got there. Yeah, times were tough back then."

Then came 1919 and a kind of boom as a result of oil found in this area. They built a café at Exray. Cotton sold for forty cents a pound.

"Pretty good year," Burris said.

We left and drove to the town site. We looked at the cemetery that is well kept. The grave of Warren J. Wilmoth is there. He was the coach for the Texas Amateur Wrestling Hall of Honor.

Johnson grass browned by summer surrounded the burial ground. Nearby was a whitewashed concrete block church. And down a hill and inside a draw, a person can still see where the old dipping vat stood. Blood weeds badly in need of a rain stood like withered guards.

We set up a table in the shade of an old tabernacle, an open structure with a tin roof used for summer preaching.

Blister-bug weeds grew on the edges of the shade. Wasp nests clung to bailing wire in the rafters, and their occupants made faint echoes as we made sandwiches.

"Well, look here," said Doc Keen, a friend who was with me. "Here's a dog."

A brown and white mixed pit bull female dog walked up. She was friendly. She had several huge seed ticks on her side.

We pitched her pieces of our sandwiches.

"Hey are you the Queen of Exray?" I asked.

She ducked her head and looked down the street. I looked the way she looked. By gosh, you could see right through Exray.

# Energy

I had heard several stories about how this town got its name.

But when I asked Bill Snell, a former county commissioner in Hamilton County in which the town is located, he suggested we drive here and talk to Cecil McPherson.

So we drove through pasturelands of mesquite trees and fields of tall bluestem grass and milkweeds bonneted in white bursts of flowers.

"My grandfather was a Methodist circuit preacher, and he preached at Energy," Snell said as we reached the post offices where McPherson and Anne Fuqua were sitting on wooden benches.

The post office is inside an old store where folks can still get gasoline from two pumps operated under a key system. The customers are assigned keys, draw their own gas, and are billed monthly.

Fuqua and McPherson showed us inside the post office. A sign on a wall said, "There is no limit to the good a man can do if he don't care who gets the credit."

Then we sat in the shade and listened to McPherson talk about his life in Energy. He was born here some eighty years ago.

"As for the name, well, one story I heard was that some people were visiting here one time and they saw these children really playing with vigor," he said. "One of them said, 'I've never seen any young people with that much energy.' So they named the town Energy. Pretty simple, huh."

McPherson lived in a house that had some of the lumber from the original post office. He attended school here, played basketball for the Energy Eagles, and played baseball on the summer team.

"We were the smallest community in the league area here," he said. "But we won the Cow House League Championship two or three years."

McPherson remembered when there were no paved roads leading to town. He and other boys would watch for the mailman to come from Gustine.

"When it rained he'd get stuck up on that hill, and we'd walk up there and push him out," he said.

He pointed across the road to an area with some huge trees with thick masses of vines knotted around the limbs.

"That used to be a well and had a bucket you pulled up for water," he said. "One day two men rode up and got themselves a drink. They didn't say hardly anything and left. The next day a group came into town and asked about the men. They were told their description and they said, 'You boys know that was Frank James [Jesse James' brother]?'"

McPherson then told about climbing under a house that belonged to a woman called Grandma Moore. Her husband, John, had fought in the Civil War.

"I found this old pistol way back there and showed it to Grandma Moore. She said it was the pistol that John had carried in the war and told me to put it back. I did. No telling what that pistol was worth," he said.

Fuqua, then secretary-treasurer of the Energy Volunteer Fire Department, invited us to look at the community center where the Fire Department keeps its equipment.

We drove to what had once been the Baptist church. A person could almost hear one of those old preachers shouting at the Energy kids for holding hands under those live oaks in the moonlight and dooming themselves to a life of hellfire.

And there in a shed on the side was the Energy fire wagon. It was mounted on a steel frame that had four wheels and a square tank. A gasoline engine powered the pump.

"Whoever gets here first in their pickup hooks onto the trailer and takes it to the fire," Fuqua said.

And with that, and a lot of energy, they fight fires in Energy, Texas.

# Goat Neck

Yes, there really is a place by this name. And it gets as full as a goat's neck when they have the Goat Neck Open Chili Cookoff and Horseshoe Tournament here.

I visited here on the twentieth such event. Lewis "Snooks" Moore of nearby Glen Rose warned me about the crowds.

"Our chili and horseshoe contests get pretty spirited and draw a bunch of people," he said.

As we drove to this once thriving community in southwest Johnson County about twenty miles from Cleburne, Moore told stories about the area. He attended school in the two-room school that closed in the 1940s.

Moore, seventy-three, a large solid man, pointed out noted landmarks like Five Oaks.

"Those trees were big even seventy years ago," he said.

We turned at the five trees and passed Freeland where New Hope Baptist Church stands.

"I was saved right there in a brush arbor," he said. "They had some real high-powered talking preachers back then. They put it [the gospel] on you pretty strong."

So he and other saved souls were taken to nearby Camp Creek and baptized.

"I got a picture of that place showing about 100 people being baptized," he said.

We continued. He pointed at a grove of live oaks in a pasture. He was born there on April 10, 1924. It's not far from the old Goat Neck baseball field where evidence of the toughness of the people flashed regularly.

"My uncle Roger got into an argument one Sunday with another player, and that guy nearly bit his whole ear off during a fight," said Moore.

We drove down a line of trees. And there under the shade of giant oaks sits Goat Neck and its community center, which was once the schoolhouse.

"Bunch of us organized and we got this old schoolhouse and decided to fix it up," he said. "Every window in it was busted and the floor was gone."

Now, the white frame building is in good condition. On the front is a wooden sign made by Moore that says, "Goat Neck." There also is a sign that says "Hiland," which should be Highland, the real name of the community.

"But back then everybody and every place had a nickname," said Moore.

There are several stories of how the name of Goat Neck came about.

"One is that one of the first families to move here had a bunch of goats," said Moore. "The other one is when they drew a map of this country and saw the way the community was cradled in the arms of the Brazos River, somebody said, "That looks just like a goat's neck."

We walked into what used to be the school.

"I started here in 1931 and quit in 1940," said Moore.

We looked at the wooden window sills with initials carved deeply into them. The edges have been whittled so much that they look like mountain slopes.

Outside, Moore shook hands with an old-time friend. They shared some stories that brought deep, wheezing laughter from them.

"The outdoor toilets...they had billies and nannies on them to let people know which one to go to," he said.

But they are uptown now. They have an indoor toilet in the old school building.

Gosh. What is Goat Neck coming to.

# Necessity

The way A.J. Jensen sees it, it was the only decent thing to do.

"I'll tell you what I think. When a person is put into the ground, that place is special," said Jensen. "That place should be reserved. If our generation doesn't think this, then the next one probably won't either. But a person's grave is his or her special place."

In this case, the special place is the gravesite of Mrs. I. Williams. And the location of the grave of Williams, who died in 1888, is indeed in a rather special place...smack-dab in the middle of a road near this once thriving community eighteen miles northwest of Ranger.

Had not the Necessity-Bradshaw Cemetery Association and the Stephens County commissioners taken some action, that grave might well have been graded and paved over. Jensen was one of several who helped see that didn't happen.

"We thought if we didn't do something, it [the grave] would be a forgotten deal, just graded over and forgotten," he said.

That would have bothered him and others. Because the grave of Williams anchors a bit of history. There are different versions as to what actually happened to her.

According to one story told to Elsie Hope Sturgeon, Williams and her family were traveling from East Texas to the west when she died in childbirth. Her baby also died and shares the grave.

Another story says that Williams and her family were going west for her health when she became ill and died in a camp near Necessity.

At any rate, Williams was buried near the town, and a small marker was erected. Eventually the grave ended up in the middle of a road. In 1933 County Commissioner J.W. Ramsey had the grave covered with native stone set in concrete.

But in the ensuing years, age and wear from traffic took its toll on the grave.

"I can remember it when it was just a rocked-up wall with a concrete slab," said Jensen, who moved here in 1952. "The road went around it. I asked an old man who saw it when he was a little boy, and he said he remembered when it was just a pile of rocks."

As the marker deteriorated, Jensen said more people thought something should be done about it.

"I had been contacted by two different people about it," he said. "One was a paraplegic from Austin. He stopped by here one night and told me that we should place a historical marker over the grave. And then one time I talked to a petroleum land man. He's one of them fellers who look for oil leases. He had the same feelings."

So the cemetery association contacted the county commissioners. And in September of 1989 something was done. Workers put in a new marker and built a pipe fence around the grave.

"You know if anybody was ever going to go back and check on their family tree, they might find this," said Jensen. "Go down there and look at it and you will see what I mean."

He gave directions to the grave, which is about a mile from his home. We drove there. And the grave does indeed sit in the middle of the road.

Mesquite flats flank the white pipe fence that protects the marker. The mesquites have gray eating at their trunks like stubble from an old man's beard.

On this day, clouds heavy with rain hung overhead. A road grader echoed in the background as it dug at the wet roadway.

"This monument is given in memory of Mrs. I. Williams. Died in camp at this place, July, 1884," reads the marker.

Flat-topped hills that looked like the flattop haircuts of the 1950s stretched in the background. A huge truck, heavy with the smell of diesel, roared around a curve in the road. The driver slowed as he approached the grave, honked his horn, and sped on.

We left soon afterwards. We were fifty miles down the road before I realized I had not asked how Necessity got its name.

# Vinegar Hill

The evils of dancing brought a sour name to this community in Hood County west of Granbury.

And some believe that dancing also brought a plague and the destruction of the community cemetery.

All that remains of Vinegar Hill, originally called Bethel, are words in aging diaries and references in family stories.

Some of those stories say that tempers boiled so hot after a dance was held in a church shared by the Methodist, Baptist, and Christian church members that the Methodists demanded the floor be ripped up and burned.

"I'm sure the story has been embellished as years have gone by," said Janet Saltsgiver of Fort Worth. "But it did cause some hard feelings."

Saltsgiver, whose relatives were involved in the controversy, showed me the way to Vinegar Hill. We drove through the beautiful Paluxy River bottom filled with majestic pecan trees and populated by grazing cattle. We reached a private road, barricaded by a gate with a heavy lock and log chain.

"Vinegar Hill is about a half-mile up that road," Saltsgiver said.

She told the story of what ripped the community apart.

"When the first settlers came here in the late 1850s, they were hungry for knowledge," she said.

In those days, dance masters worked their way through the country.

"They were pretty much like itinerant preachers. As long as people would pay and feed them, they would stay and teach music and dancing," she said.

That is what happened here according to an article published in the *Stephenville Empire* on October 17, 1947. In that account, Mary Lou Cowan Williams, one of the original settlers, said the community had thrived until two dance masters began teaching square dancing.

"The church people objected to the dancing," she said. "Some objected violently."

Baptists, Methodist, and Christian churches shared the building on alternate Sundays. Williams said the Methodists became so upset over the dancing on the church floor that they wanted to tear up the floor and turn it over to purify the building.

Instead, the three churches split. The building was moved two miles away, leaving only a cemetery at Bethel.

"The amused local wags then named the place Vinegar Hill because of the sour feelings that had been stirred up," Williams said.

Then the plague (probably a flu epidemic) hit, killing most of those remaining in the community. Later, the land containing the cemetery was sold. Then somebody pushed most of the tombstones into a stock tank.

The final indignity occurred about twenty years ago when a man bought land and used the remaining tombstones to underpin his mobile home.

About two miles from the spot is the grave of Saltsgiver's great-great-grandfather, Lorenzo D. Wood.

"He was what you call an exhorter. He would get up and tell about good and evil in the church. He probably really raised Hades about the dancing," she said.

His grave is beneath some huge cedars. Their smell is powerful—almost as powerful as vinegar.

# Chapter 3

# Looking for Goodnight and Route 66

$F$rom my early childhood I began hearing stories about the famed Texas rancher Charles Goodnight and Route 66, that equally famed highway that sliced through the Texas Panhandle and became the road to new lives for thousands during the Depression.

But first my fascination with Goodnight came because of my being reared in the ranch country of West Texas. I began riding horses and working cattle by the time I was eight. My father was a well-known cattle trader in the area around Kermit, Midland, and Odessa. As a result, he frequently had cowboys helping him who had worked for Charles Goodnight.

"He was one of the toughest S.O.B.s you ever came across," the late Billy Pee, a short and spare cowboy told us one time over the coals of a branding fire. "But he treated his men fairly and never asked any more of you than what he could do himself."

That was a bunch as evidenced in the book about his life, *Charles Goodnight*, written by the late J. Evetts Haley. Many people are unaware, but Goodnight and his partner, Oliver Loving, were the two main characters in the popular novel *Lonesome Dove* written by Larry McMurtry and which later became a hit movie.

After that came out, I reread Haley's book. Then a friend, Doc Keen, a Fort Worth veterinarian, and I decided we would go to Goodnight, Texas, and look for Goodnight's grave. We camped out along the way, probably making camp near where Goodnight and Loving may have once pitched their bedrolls.

We did the same thing when we decided to retrace the route of Route 66, which began in Chicago and ended in Santa Monica, California. Gosh the stories this pavement ribbon left during those years of the Depression. I was amazed at the number of people still living along the route who have memories of those tough times.

So here's my experiences in looking for Goodnight's grave and retracing Route 66.

# Colonel Goodnight

We left on a Sunday and were driving near Palo Pinto Lake. It is scarred country with trees weeping rain and humidity. Wind echoes through the trees that look like lonely sentinels made by God. Not too far away from us is where one-armed Billy Wilson once lived and died. God what a man he was.

He worked for Goodnight and was the one with Loving when they became pinned down by Comanches while moving a herd of cattle to Fort Sumner, New Mexico. After Loving was wounded, Wilson walked barefooted for ninety miles to find Goodnight. He gave him a short message, saying, "Loving's yonder, pointing to the west."

The trees have edges of reds and yellows, just tipped by fall, like colors made by a kid strumming through a giant coloring book and had just thrown colors at pieces of pictures.

We pass a marker of George S. Slaughter, another famous rancher. Old broom weeds and dead mesquites with aching arms stretch to the sky, their trunks looking like the knurled hands of cowboys that once worked for ranchers like Goodnight.

As we drove, Doc reviewed some of the history of Goodnight. He quoted from Haley's book: "Charlie Goodnight rode bareback from Illinois to Texas when he was nine years of age. He was hunting with the Caddo Indians beyond the frontier at thirteen ...launching into the cattle business at twenty, guiding Texas Rangers at twenty-four, blazing cattle trails nearly two thousand miles beyond the frontier at forty, and at forty-five dominating nearly twenty million acres of range country in the interest of order."

"Gawd, what a man," said Doc.

We were driving past some old stone corrals north of Graford. Goodnight and Loving once used these to work their cattle and horses. A thunderstorm blurred images on the highway with its driving rain. I slow down. We are now in a country that as far as you see, there are no cross fences, no grain fields. Just wide-open pastureland and every so often a lonely house that looks like the whiskers just beginning on a young man's face.

We pass our first tumbleweeds, round, rusting, misshapen wheels that go dancing across the land and hang up on wire fences. And if the owner does not remove them, in a year or so his fence disappears beneath waves of blown sand.

We reach Matador, county seat of Motley County. There is an old two-story sandstone jail here built in 1891. Old bars still are over the windows. You can almost hear the yells of cowboys who had drunk too much, yelling for relief from those blistering ovens called cells. A stone fence around the structure is leaning. But somebody has hammered some steel posts into the ground, tied ropes to them and then to huge limbs of a fruit tree inside the fence. Call it cowboy engineering.

We stop at White Flat. There is a deserted two-story red brick school building with rotten wooden windows hanging out like somebody's busted lip. It was called White Flat due to large fields of needle grass. It was established in 1890. The school closed in 1946. The last retail store closed in 1968. Goodbye White Flat.

Then we reach Paint Rock Canyon and definitely Goodnight country. The sun sets in a blizzard of reds and yellows. We build a campfire from mesquite wood. The smoke and smells of our cooking causes Doc to say, "It is the smell of the old vaqueros and cowboys sitting around the campfire."

The campfire eats into the night. We talk about Goodnight. Then we are quiet. And far off comes the mournful wail of coyotes. Are they howling because they want to howl? Or are they mad because the moon's neon-like brightness has irritated them?

I look at the moon and those stars that look like somebody spilled a box full of diamonds up there. I think I know why Goodnight loved this country so much. I crawl into my sleeping bag. I dream of bawling cattle that have just been branded.

It is colder than hell the next morning. Hunks of rain clouds are in the sky. Doc builds a fire. I make strong, boiled coffee, black as a patch of midnight. The temperature is near thirty. We cook bacon, eggs, onions, and tortillas. We gobble them quickly. They are already cold.

We look at the canyon. This is the kind of country where Goodnight had his JA Ranch. Red, maroon, gray, and white rocks are in abundance. Their colors are always different like a crazy artist has been turned loose with a jet nozzle. The small gorges and draws are orange and red like lipstick applied by a woman who is in a hurry. A marker tells us that their origin goes back eons. This was once an ancient sea. My fingers suddenly are ice cold. I blow on them. A mule deer loping by stops and looks at us. She snorts and then is gone.

We eventually reach Goodnight. But it is getting colder so we chicken out and camp out in a motel in nearby Claude. The next morning we walk to a Shamrock station where several old-timers sit smoking cigarettes down to the filter.

One is Lynn Friday Sewell. He is seventy-seven and retired from ranching. He has brown eyes almost hidden by pockets. Nicotine stains his fingernails. He moved to Goodnight with his folks when he was two. His father had a general store.

"My folks and Mr. Goodnight were good friends. We'd go over to their old house and sit and visit. He was tough but he was good to his men and to us kids. We'd ride out there on our horses, and he'd let us ride anywhere except on the buffalo section."

He said Goodnight was a tall man. He loved to raise different animals and birds. He had a lot of peacocks that he kept at what he called the old red house.

"After they moved to Clarendon, I used to deliver milk to them. I had my own cow and took them a quart a day," he said. "The funeral ...yeah, I remember it. My dad went to it. But it was not as big as you might think. By that time there were quite a few people around here who didn't even know him. It was kinda' sad."

We walked across the street and talked to a woman who was a relative of a woman who once cooked for Mr. Goodnight. She insisted that her name not be used. She said the woman who cooked for Goodnight said one of his favorite things was Sonabitch Stew, cooked from the heart and other things normally thrown away with plenty of onions.

"He also loved pecan cake, my friend said. She'd make the icing from one pound of butter and pounds of pecans, mashed and broken, and then after putting that on the cake, she laced the icing with other pecans," she said.

We said our goodbyes and drove to the Max Baird House, built in 1913 by the then banker of Goodnight. Baird's hair is combed straight back with a dusting of gray. He has a large nose. He is friendly and says, "I was born the same time that Mr. Goodnight departed from this earth. That's right, nearly the same minute, so I understand."

Baird is a country preacher. He surrendered to God in the summer of 1959. He still farms and ranches and has a way of putting his hands together and roaring with rasping laughter.

"I've heard a lot of good about Colonel Goodnight, and I've heard some bad," he said. He roared. "But you know that is how it will be with all of us."

His wife is Betty. She talked about their old house and how it is pretty cold on days like today with that north wind pouring through three huge windows like water from a well. They've tried to stop the cold by nailing sheets of plastic over the fronts of the windows.

As we started to leave, Baird asked us to join hands and Doc to lead us in a word of prayer. Baird echoed Doc's "amen" with another loud snort. Then he led us outside and pointed to a cemetery about a half-mile away.

"That's where he is buried," he said.

We leave and go to the cemetery.

It is stuck on top of a hill. There are a few squat cedars. The north wind is numbing and brings instant watering to our eyes. The grave of Goodnight is not garish or expensive. Its elegance is in its simplicity. The marker is about three feet tall. All it says is "Charles Goodnight." It lists his birthday as March 5, 1836, and his death as December 12, 1929.

His wife, Mary Ann, is buried next to him. She was born September 12, 1829, and died April 11, 1926. At the top of her marker, it reads, "One who spent her whole life in the service of others."

I walk around and look at other graves of the Vaughans, Crains, Kestersons, and Justices. Far off I hear the lonely aching whirl of a windmill. The wind spins its blades so fast that they are out of focus.

I pull our cooking stove from the van. I light it and put on the coffee pot. I have filled it with water and poured nearly a third of a can of coffee into this. We wait for it to boil.

I look at the highway about a mile away. A big semi-truck, its trailer loaded with cattle, is heading north.

The coffee boils. I get two cups. I pour Doc one and myself the other. It is strong and thick. We drink and I say, "Here's to you, Charles Goodnight."

The coffee is so strong it could howl. Goodnight would have loved it.

# Route 66

## Day 1

We left on a blistering summer day to retrace part of Route 66. We headed west to Copper Breaks State Park, which is south of Quanah. The temperature boiled at 107. We cooked hamburgers, and the meat's grease sent spirals of yellow flames spitting back at the grill.

We watched the sunset with pieces of clouds with the sun blasting behind them, making them look like blisters on the working hands of people hoeing cotton. Another cloud looked like a wolf howling said John Tushim, making the trip with Doc Keen and me. Keen had made the trip with his family as a youngster during the early 1930s. He frequently relived some of those moments as we drove and camped.

He had smiled at Tushim's cloud description.

"Yeah, that cloud does indeed look like a big wolf howling or moaning from hunger, like the thousands of people who traveled Route 66 during the Depression, seeking work and hoping to make California," he said.

We slipped to sleep amidst clouds of mosquitoes. We thought of tomorrow when we would officially begin our trip on the edge of Oklahoma in the tiny town of Erick.

# Day 2

We wanted to reach there before the heat had really clamped down. We drove past closed stores like Frank's Shoe Machinery and Leather Shop. We headed on west across almost flat pastureland and farmland packed with huge round bales of hay. We stopped at Texola. A sign on a beer joint said, "No place like Texola. There is no other place like this place anywhere near this place so this must be the place."

We go into Pat's Beer to Go. Gina Blake is running the place. She was reared in Arlington, Texas, but moved here because it was so peaceful and quiet.

"I like it," she said.

We talked to Linda Matthews, a tall, rangy, instantly friendly woman. She remembers when Route 66 was bypassed by I-40.

"It was such a big deal to drive on those four lanes," she said.

Her miniature Dachshund looked at us. He is eight years old and is called Chili Dog. He's half dachshund, quarter cocker, and some Pekingese.

"This dog is a tough little booger. He's been rattlesnake bit twice, been run over by a Lincoln town car, and been torn up by other dogs three times. Oh yeah, he has been poisoned and stolen. And when he was stolen, I drove 740 miles to bring him home. Then he got bit in the head in a fight and his head swole so much he looked like an elephant dog," she said. "You know, he reminds me of those people who come down Route 66 during the Depression. They were tough, just like him."

We said goodbye and drove past the old jail in Texola. It has two barred windows and a towering elm tree for air conditioning. A rusting 1934 Ford sits nearby, the kind that made that trip to California, crammed with people and their belongings. It's covered with rust that looks like icing on a chocolate cake.

We drive into Texas. Gosh, what a panoramic view. I think of those early people on Route 66 in those old cars looking out across that scene and what they must have thought.

We stopped in Shamrock where the now closed U Drop Inn once fed thousands. It was built of cream brick at a cost of $23,000. It has a tower with some things that look like replicas of loaves of breads. Its top is painted green.

Just down the road is the Lewis Camp, which Inez and Howard Evans say they are in the process of repairing.

"We bought this for its historical value," she said. "We've had it ten years and want to get it to looking good."

He has traveled the old Route 66 from Oklahoma City to Chicago dozens of times, he said. He smokes. She does too. They both light up.

"One time, so a feller across the street told me, there'd be cars backed up two blocks to buy gas and git in here. Bonnie and Clyde [Barrow] stopped here once to get their tires fixed. The owners looked in the back and saw all of their guns and said, "You don't owe us nothing for fixing that flat."

Howard is a tall slender man with huge hands. Said he once sang with the Stamps Brothers Quartet. He has wildly tasseled hair like he has been standing in front of a powerful fan.

"I started out singing tenor. When I got older, I sang alto," he said. He laughed. "Some said I sounded like a woman."

He recalled the Depression.

"I seen those little kids go to school with holes in their shoes and patches on their pants and hungry looks on their faces. I seen cattle sell for $12 a head and wheat for 25 cents a bushel. It was pitiful and bread brought a nickel a loaf if you could get the nickel," he said. "Them danged Republicans cuss Roosevelt. Let me tell you, Roosevelt is the greatest president who ever lived in my time."

His voice cracked. He rubbed his eyes. Inez waited and then she said that they sometimes get people coming back from California and headed home.

"They stop and ask if they can sleep on the ground just like they did in the old days and I say, 'No, just come on in and sleep inside and let us feed you,'" she said.

We camped that night at McClelland Creek National Grasslands. The temperature was still in the lower 100s. Flies were thick followed by equally thick storms of mosquitoes that hit almost as soon as darkness replaced the sun.

We watched two wild turkey toms, walking with their whiskers sticking out of their chests like shaving brushes. We could imagine those people of the 1930s seeing something like that and catching them and digging a cooking pit and filling the turkeys' chest cavities with sweet potatoes and cooking them.

We don't have turkey. We do have hobo stew cooked by Doc. It is filled with potatoes and the remainders of a hamburger we had cooked but not eaten. It was good.

Later as the moon crawled high above us, Doc began talking.

"We'd get some old beef bones and go to the produce area and see if there were any old wilted potatoes they were going to throw away. Then we'd go to the back and try to find an onion or two in a sack that they were about to throw away. And you can always bum them out of some pepper. Put all of it into a big container and cook it long enough and it tasted good," he said.

The sun had gone. The moon played hide and seek with some clouds, reminding a person of a white cat hiding from a dog until it was sure the dog was gone and then the cat flashed its presence quickly and boldly.

# Day 3

The next day we drove toward McClean. We passed a small town with old closed stations and a place shaded by a tree with sheet iron nailed over its windows. It had been the Magnolia Café. Two dogs watched us. They were lying near fresh-looking gourd plants that had huge, beautiful yellow blossoms. They smelled awful.

We stopped at the Devil's Rope Museum in McClean. It's packed with a history of barbed wire. They also have a Route 66 museum. Both are inside a building where they once made brassieres for Sears.

"They worked about eighty women here. They came in from all of these little towns," said Ruth Trew. "We still find needles in cracks in the floor and lint from the machines."

Sears gave the building to the city after the factory closed. It stood vacant for twenty-one years and then Ruth's husband Delbert Trew approached the city council about a possible museum. They rented the facility for $50 a month. With volunteer work they eventually opened the museum.

"No grants from the state or federal government, either," she said. "We did it on our own."

They have up to forty volunteers who help today.

"There is another barbed wire museum in Kansas run by the chamber of commerce. But this is the largest barbed wire museum in the world devoted entirely to barbed wire," she said.

And since they have opened, sales tax revenues have been up in every quarter except one. And their little souvenir shop grossed $20,000 last year.

"All of this in a town of 850 people. I think it's because of us combining the Route 66 and the barbed wire stuff. Nine of ten stop to see the 66 Museum, but they become fascinated with the barbed wire part," she said.

Well, it is interesting with its collection of barbed wire and its post hole diggers that number about 200 and wire stretchers. They also have some unusual things made from barbed wire like a replica of a western hat.

Of course what can you expect from a product that has more than 600 patents held on it We finally ripped ourselves away and headed back to Route 66. We passed an old Burma Shave sign that said, "Don't stick your elbow out so far, it might go home in another car."

We passed one of the many former attractions on the old route. This one was a sign that read, "The Regal Reptile Ranch." It had a huge, plastic snakehead, painted a garish yellow and red, and a sign said, "The locals were not so fond of this tourist trap. So they brought dead rattlers and left them on the road near the snake farm to give the impression some might have escaped."

We headed on for Amarillo through rolling country where maybe you can see fifty miles ahead. You can see so far that blueness comes into the distance and things get out of focus. At Groom, the Golden Spread Motel is closed. It is right across from the grain elevator. Nearby is an old green and white four-door Edsel with bullet holes through the windshield.

We reach a large roadside park and stop for a break. A family is parked near one of the tables. The children are running through water coming from a sprinkler.

"We live in Juarez," said the mother. "There are eight of us. We are going home. We have been visiting our family in Kansas. *Bien Vieja.*"

Nearby a man was walking a gray parrot with a red face. The man looked at his watch. He swore at the parrot like it was his fault, saying, "Sheet. We've got to get back on the road. We've fiddled around here too long. Don't you know this?"

The parrot just looked at him.

We drive on to Amarillo and stop at the Big Texan where if you can eat a 72-ounce steak in one hour with no help from anyone, you get it free. If you don't eat it, then you have to pay $50. Some 22,568 attempts have been made. There have been some 3,736 winners. None of us opted for a chance.

We stop at the Marsh Cadillacs buried at a slanting angle in some concrete. You can't help but see these old fin-type Cadillacs lying about a quarter of a mile from the interstate.

We look as other people stop and walk up to join us. People have painted an abundance of graffiti onto them. As we look, dust devils, skinny spirals of dust like spinning shoestrings, skip across the land.

We drive on and pass a sign in Adrian that reads, "Luck favors the backbone and not a wishbone." Sand comes from the fields like dust flying from somebody sanding wood.

We finally camp at Ute Lake. I make my famous skillet hominy casserole. Put in a can of hominy, a can of pinto beans, three strips of fried bacon, an onion, several jalapeños, and some cheese. We eat it with corn tortillas. I figured that cost $3.19. That plus $7 for camping means, well, damn, we are living high on the hog, boys.

# Day 4

We reached Tumcumcari before noon. This city of some 6,765 population and some 4,096 feet in elevation has long been a landmark for travelers along the Canadian River. Lodgings like the Pow Wow Inn and the Pony Soldier Motel sit in a blast of neon signs advertising for overnight customers. They advertise with such slogans as the Best Little Snore House in New Mexico. We finally stop at the Blue Swallow, and there is Mrs. Lillian Redman.

"Certainly I can remember the Depression days. Route 66 was packed with people then. They would work for anything. You couldn't give them a room or you'd be snowed under," she said. She is eighty-six and has short graying hair. "I guess I'm still in that business. The city gives the transients vouchers and so do the churches. They pay me for them at the end of each month."

She has the darndest penny candy selection I've seen in ages. Choices are packed inside huge glass jars. A kid would go bananas in here.

She has thirteen rooms, and you can still get a room for two for $20. Dona Bonner, who is maid, bouncer, and chauffeur, said the rooms are guaranteed.

"We guarantee clean sheets, towels, soap, and hot water," she said. "The rooms have a hardwood floor and a black and white TV that works."

The motel with its neon sign of a huge blue swallow still beckons to people. The old fishpond made from glass brick that once had colored lights splashing from it has been cut off. But still people stop. Maybe it is because Mrs. Redman has been in *Playboy*.

Make that Japanese *Playboy*. She showed us a magazine with a half nude woman on the cover and started flipping through it.

"No, I didn't make the center fold," she said. "But here I am."

She pointed to a story about her motel. It does not bother her to be in a magazine with all of those "nekid women."

"Any publicity is good publicity," she said.

She directed us to the old depot where she said many laid over while following Route 66 to California. We find the old adobe building with a red tile roof. Some of the old glamour is still inside behind the peeling paint and cracked wood.

Murray Saul, a conductor for a train crew, said he thought the building was built by Rock Island about 1903. He invited us inside to what used to be a huge dining room but now is full of communication equipment. Another employee said that the building is only one of two of this type architecture remaining in the nation. He doesn't know what type it is. I don't either but it is obvious it once was majestic.

We said our goodbyes and headed on west. We stopped in Montoya, a ghost town full of old vacant, stucco buildings. We walked inside a cemetery. The gate is a huge, wooden cross with wheels on the end of a center board. Nailed into the corner of the cross is leather padding, indicating they still use it.

Our next stop is Clines Corner, which has become a garish tourist stop. The parking lot was packed with people from everywhere, looking at the specials like a combination tomahawk-peace pipe and stuffed lizards. A sign said Clines Corner was started in the 1930s by Roy Clines, who kept having to move it because the roads kept changing.

I waited for my two friends outside. A skinny, emaciated-looking man with jeans hanging loose like an empty cotton sack drooped over a saw horse made from two by fours came out. He reached into his shirt pocket and removed a super king-sized cigarette. He cupped his hands, struck a huge kitchen match, and lit the cigarette. He sucked deeply until a wracking cough that sounded like a flat tire running on the rim in gravel erupted from his mouth. His face became red. Finally he gained control and wiped his nose and his watering eyes.

He looked into the distance at the Sangre de Christo Mountains. Then he looked at me.

"Goddamn, this mountain air sure is good for your lungs, ain't it," he rasped.

He sucked the cigarette again. John and Doc joined me. We crawled into our van and headed back for Texas. As the song goes, "We got our kicks on Route 66."

# Chapter 4
# Day Trips

A regular request I still get from readers familiar with my columns is for me to tell them an interesting place they can go to and visit and return home in one day.

There are bunches of those out there. I still go back to many places that I discovered during my times at the *Star-Telegram*. Most are easily found on a Texas highway map, so I have not included directions beyond telling in what county the sites are.

If you live in the Dallas-Fort Worth area, all of these can be made easily in one day. I call them day trips. Have fun.

## Indian Creek

We are driving to this tiny almost ghost town eight miles south of Brownwood off U.S. 337 in Brown County.

Past rolling hills and mesquite flats and grain fields with huge tractors breaking the land for another planting. It is indeed, said Charlotte Laughlin and Tessica Martin, an unusual place to find the grave of someone such as Katherine Anne Porter.

She was an actress, teacher, reporter, and author of the well-known book *Ship of Fools*. And in 1965 she won both the Pulitzer Prize and the National Book Award with *The Collected Stories of Katherine Anne Porter.*

So as Laughlin's auto air conditioner works overtime, they talk of that time in 1976 when Porter returned to Brownwood for a symposium honoring her at Howard Payne University.

"She had been saying for several years that she wanted to be buried at Indian Creek," said Martin, a retired English professor at

Howard Payne. "She identified with her mother. I think it was a romantic identification."

During that symposium, Porter was taken to Indian Creek Cemetery where her mother and grandmother are buried.

"We had a picnic for her," said Laughlin. "She really enjoyed it."

Laughlin stopped beside the road at a historical marker recently erected in memory of Porter. It tells of her being born in Indian Creek on May 15, 1890, and leaving there in 1892 after her mother's death.

"We thought about erecting it at the cemetery," said Laughlin, a member of the Brown County Historical Society. "But we thought more people would see it here."

Huge mesquite trees standing near the marker, their limbs full of beans, lick at the lettering.

"Well, let's go to Indian Creek," said Martin.

We drive past more mesquites and fields of feather bluestem, wind scattering their tender seed heads. The women talk of that symposium again. How Porter was scheduled to speak. But the local newspaper ran an unflattering photograph of her.

"She said it was cruel for someone to run a picture like that and she was not going to give her speech," said Laughlin.

They took her to the auditorium anyway. Several hundred people waited.

"She saw them and began these dramatic gestures," said Martin. "She said, 'They have come to see me. Of course, I must speak.'"

Later Laughlin visited Porter in her Baltimore home.

"She had ordered her own casket. A wooden one from a mail-order catalog," she said. "She had seen one like it in Mexico with wildflowers painted on it. She had the flowers painted. Then she showed it to us."

It was inside a hall closet full of umbrellas and shoes.

"She showed us that casket like I would show someone pictures of my children," said Laughlin. She stopped the car. "Well, here's the cemetery."

We walked to Porter's grave. Huge mesquites and other trees dot the grounds. Dust from a tractor plowing smelled heavy.

The marker is simple with one sentence that reads, "In the end is my beginning."

Laughlin and Martin shook their heads.

"She wanted a spire like her mother's," said Laughlin. "She wanted a poem she had written in the 1930s when she visited her mother's grave written on it."

But a distant relative chose the simpler marker. And nobody was told that Porter's ashes had been buried until months later.

Grasshoppers shouted their crazy chant, which carried to nearby Indian Creek, now just a few houses and vacant buildings. Who would dream that such a famous person's grave lay nearby in the cemetery near a field where the ground was being plowed for a new planting.

# Ranger

Practically anyone in this town in Eastland County west of Fort Worth can give you directions to the Merriman Community.

"Oh, you mean the place that wouldn't sell its cemetery to the oil drillers," they will say.

Well, that is true. The folks in the Merriman community do respect their dead as evidenced by their actions when the oil boom in this area was going on. Prospective oil well drilling companies tried to lease the Merriman Cemetery.

Estimates are that from $100,000 to $1 million was offered for that privilege during the boom when oil was so abundant that it was splashed around like water.

Derricks surrounded the cemetery, which was created in 1873. Elzie Pruett remembers those wooden structures and the "pow, pow" made by the pump jacks powered by old single-cylinder gasoline engines.

"Those pumps go up and down and their explosions totally fascinated me as they sucked the oil from the ground," he said.

His parents and others turned down the oil companies' offers to drill on the cemetery land. The figures have not been documented, but some say they are as high as $1 million, Pruett said.

"The story I remember is that they came and wanted to talk to the owners of this land," he said. "So the church [Merriman Baptist] members pointed out here and said, 'There they are. Talk to them.' They were pointing at the tombstones," he said. "Money didn't mean as much to them as honoring their dead."

So we stood there looking at the markers with the smells of fall strong in the mesquite and cedar trees. Every so often a wild dash of fall color appeared like a giant firecracker had exploded and splashed yellow and red paint around.

Elzie's wife, Jeane, stood with us. She's a sturdy woman with long, brown hair. Talk Texas history and she blooms in enthusiasm.

We walked to the old church tabernacle, its tin roof hammered by time and wind. Here people once sat during summer meetings as the oil well pumps made that pow pow sound.

Elzie told about being born here and his father operating a water company during the oil boom. He sold water for $5 a barrel. Oil was selling for a nickel a barrel.

Jeane Pruett, a Virginia native, told of repeatedly moving when she was younger. Then she met and married Elzie and learned about Ranger and its history.

"It's the only place I ever got homesick for," she said.

And she loves this area's history.

"The frontier just really took me over. It is exciting," she said.

It's been so exciting for her that she and Elzie have logged countless hours on the creation of the nearby Ruth Terry Denny Library-Research Center in Ranger.

And naturally, her research led her to this cemetery. She led us around the grounds, pointing out tombstones of early residents. She stopped and pointed at the remaining foundations of old oilfield rigs ringing the fence.

Rusting steel bolts that look like the gnarled fingers of a mechanic pierce the concrete. The wooden derricks were bolted to these.

Then we looked at the historical marker.

"I'm so proud of that. That was the first one that I researched and got erected," she said.

She beamed as wind eased through the mesquites, bringing warnings of the first freeze.

# Strawn

When customers visit Mary's Café, they can get their fill of some of the best chicken-fried steak or tastiest Mexican food in the country.

They can also get a good idea of what problems the locals are facing in this town about seventy miles west of Fort Worth off Interstate 20.

Like during this visit, the diners were talking about the lack of rain. Said one hefty rancher-looking patron, "Mary, if I don't get a rain soon, I'm gonna have to load my old truck and move back to Oklahoma. Meantime, gimme one of them large chicken-fried steaks."

One thing about the order. It might well rain before he finished eating the large chicken-fried, which weighs three-fourths of a pound.

A longtime friend, Doug Clarke, told me about Mary's, owned by Mary Tretter, right after she bought this place eight years ago. In between her cooking and answering the phone, she laughed about that beginning.

"Actually, I have been on this one block for twenty-one years," she said. "I got started washing dishes and being assistant cook when I was still in high school."

I asked her about the story I had heard of her skipping the senior class trip so she could work.

"Yeah, that is true," she said. "But I was making sixty-three bucks a week, and that was a lot of money back then."

She answered the phone. Somebody asked about today's lunch special, which was fried chicken. She said, "We also have plenty of vegetables that will match your diet."

She's an attractive woman with a splash of dark hair and dark eyes. She is thirty-eight and she is loaded with energy.

"You know what I wanted to be when I was just a girl," she said. "I wanted to be an airline hostess. I thought that would be fun."

But she loves the restaurant business.

"I love the people," she said.

She knows most of her customers by their first names. And most of them call her Mary. One man wearing boots and overalls came in and pronounced that he had just sold seventy-three cows.

"Mary, if we had gotten some rain, I would never have sold them," he said. "But I did and they brought a pretty good price. Hey, let me have some fried chicken, French fries, and a glass of beer. Okay?"

Mary went to the back. She returned in a few minutes, wiping flour from her forearm. She explained her success.

"We have some people who come in here from fast-food places and complain about the time it takes to get their orders. They say, 'Hey, did you have to kill that chicken?'" she said. "We tell them that we cook everything from the ground up. We don't have it ready until you order it."

She said she is frequently amused at the image new customers have in their minds about her.

"I think they are expecting to see an old woman. Maybe a fat old woman with a long dress or with gray hair or something," she said.

Regardless, she is strict on her help about how they treat customers.

"That customer is who we are working for," she said. "I don't care what race they are or what kind of vehicle they drive. When they come in here, it doesn't make any difference. If it weren't for them, we wouldn't be here."

My order of the medium chicken-fried steak (half a pound) arrived with a baked potato. There was also a salad made of lettuce, freshly sliced onions, and tomatoes.

The meat, with Mary's special batter flavored with garlic, milk, and eggs, was so tender. As I ate, Mary came out and looked out the window at some pieces of black clouds gathering in the west. Maybe my steak would last until the rains came.

# De Leon

Strangers to this city in Comanche County sometimes stop at a downtown intersection to wave at a group of men standing on a sidewalk beside piles of watermelons.

Some have even rolled down their car windows to ask for directions.

They leave with neither directions nor acknowledgment from the men. And probably they are a little red faced and laughing at themselves.

They've just been fooled by the Wall of Recall, a 100-foot mural of old advertising logos and realistic-looking characters. It is impressive.

The wall is the result of a year's work by Elton Brownlee and Charles Chupp, two men who were reared here, moved away, and later returned.

Brownlee showed me the mural. He's a strong-looking man, laughs easily and quickly, and on this day wore overalls and a gray denim shirt and straw hat. He has painted signs for years.

"Yeah, I've painted everything from a hog [for a hog farm] to a poodle [for a couple who wanted their pet poodle emblazoned on the side of their RV]," he said.

But none of his work has drawn as much attention as the wall. As we walked down the wall of the 100-year-old building, he told how the idea started.

"I was restoring an old Coca-Cola sign put on the wall in the 1940s," he said. "Chuck [Chupp] and I got to talking and thought why not find sponsors and paint the logos of the 1940s here."

They found logos in old copies of the *Saturday Evening Post, Ladies Home Journal,* and *Colliers*. Then Brownlee began his painting. He stopped at an old green Lucky Strike cigarette logo.

"We found sponsors for everything but that. Nobody wanted to sponsor a tobacco or cigarette logo," he said.

We looked at a picture of a youngster standing beside a tire. The words read, "Time to retire. Get Fisk."

"I was responsible for all of the logos and Chuck did the figures and we both painted them," he said.

He pointed to the Bright and Early Coffee logo with a yellow background and a crowing white rooster.

"Morris Nance in Desdemona did that," he said.

There is a "Kilroy was here" cartoon made famous during World War II by Bill Mauldin in his Willie and Joe cartoons. There's the Smith Bros. cough drops. And naturally, there is a logo for Burma Shave, which once sponsored short advertising poems on roadside signs. Brownlee wrote the words for the sign that reads "Peaches we love. Melons we crave. Much better than a Burma shave."

That message and piles of watermelons underscore the two major cash crops grown here.

One sign is an eye teaser. Look at it straight on and it's a pretty woman. Turn your head slightly and she becomes a witch.

Certainly the mural brings back memories to those reared here. It stretches its way down what once was called Market Street, where farmers brought their produce to sell. And just down the street is a building that Brownlee called the turkey picking place. He worked there briefly as a youngster.

"They killed turkeys and you made eight cents for picking feathers from toms and six cents for hens," he said.

We looked at a painting of an old man standing beside a pile of watermelons and rolling a cigarette. Nearby are two men talking. One is sitting on a bench.

"Those are the ones that people wave at when they stop at the stop sign," said Brownlee.

In the future, there may be still another traffic stopper. Brownlee pointed at a blank window across the street.

"Chuck and I want to paint a cattle drive on that," he said. "Check with us in a couple of years and see how many cattle we've got up there."

There should be quite a herd because the window stretches for 110 feet. I can just hear comments now from city visitors as they pass by:

"Hey, Susan, look at those cattle. We'd better drive really careful past them."

# Roaring Springs

Words about the famous natural springs here carried both promises and warnings.

"I grew up in that pool," said Jeff Tacker, a native. "The water stays at 65 degrees. It's refreshing but it will take your breath away."

I had been hearing the same thing since my friend Tom Dodge and I had left earlier on a five-day trip for interviews in this area. Dodge had bathed in the noted springs several times. But to do this, you have to get an invitation because it is at the private Roaring Springs Ranch Club.

Dodge knew the manager, so during our drive here with temperatures scorching past 100, he kept reminding me of how important he is.

"See I can get you into places that you are going to love if you have the guts to jump into them," he said.

We had reached the entrance to the 746 acres of land south of this town ninety miles east of Lubbock in Motley County. The gate attendant said, yes, indeed, this was the place of the famous springs.

"Please make sure you say this is private property," she said. "We have had articles that didn't mention that, and we have lots of people come out here and are disappointed because they can't just walk in."

But memberships are available, as noted in information she gave us. That information also said the springs flow from 400 to 600 gallons per minute.

"I can't wait to get you there," Dodge said, "to see if you are man enough to dive into them."

The gate attendant kind of giggled. "You are in for a surprise," she said.

We continued toward the promised delight, following the curls of the South Pease River. We passed beautiful red, green, and orange rocks. A roadrunner darted in front of us, making moves like a miniature cutting horse.

I read how the springs had long been a favorite campground of the Comanches.

We passed huge mesquites with twisting limbs. I remember as a youngster growing up in West Texas and riding through mesquites that bloodied my legs with their thorns.

Then we were at the famed springs. Clouds swelled in the sky. Thunder began rumbling.

People already in the Olympic-size swimming pool came out. We all stood and watched and hoped for a rain. Big drops fell for about five minutes and then stopped.

We listened to the roar of the springs, almost as loud as the thunder. The water came crashing down a hillside and made a small fall.

"Well, are you ready for this part of nirvana? Or are you going to be a chicken?" Dodge asked.

He leaped into the water. I did, too. My weight carried me to the bottom, past the outside 100 degrees into this blanket of 65 degrees. I thought, Jane, come and get your crazy husband.

I pushed to the top, gasping for air. I realized everyone had been right. These suckers do take your breath away.

I said what the hail. I took another huge breath and plunged under the water again.

I thanked somebody...I couldn't remember whom...for introducing me to Tom Dodge who introduced me to these springs that proved I am not beyond having my breath taken away.

# Eliasville

Commit any destructive deed to the old mill in this community, and you'll face the wrath of the "grumpy old gray-haired lady."

That self-imposed label belongs to Jo Ann Stroud, who with her husband C.B. has owned and protected the mill for the past decade.

"Anybody bothers the old mill and they have to answer to me," she said.

Stroud led me to the mill built in 1876 and operated until 1946 in this town twenty miles south of Graham in Young County. The mill sits on the banks of the Clear Fork of the Brazos River. Some of the old cogs and gears that once turned the massive grinding stones and massive hand-hewn rafters are still in place.

The Strouds have put bars over the front doors and have tried to cover the windows. But people try to rip out wood and get a piece of the mill.

"When we first acquired it, it was full of trash. It was dirty nasty," Jo Ann said.

The massive rock used in the walls was cut from a nearby hill. Each rock has holes in its center to which huge tongues were clamped to lift the stones into place during the mill's construction.

I walked down a steel stairway to look at the water easing over the rock dam. It looked like melted chocolate.

I gazed at the massive walls. I heard the river making soft moans. I thought of the calls I had received from several readers after reading my first column about the mill.

"I was born in our family home in Eliasville on December 29, 1926," Harry Jarret of Granbury said. "I have fond memories of that place."

So does Gene Hicks of Fort Worth who fished here with his father.

"My uncle James Gibbs would call us when the river was flooding and we'd go there and camp out. I've seen them catch yellow cat that weighed from 30 to 50 pounds," Hicks said.

He said the men would tie wire around their shoes in order to stand on the dam without slipping. Some would tie a huge weight to a folding chair and toss the weight into the river to hold the chair in place while they fished.

"Once, I saw Raymond Gibbs washed off the dam. We thought he had drowned, but he came up and swam to safety," he said.

The Strouds still allow people to fish and camp on the property.

I looked at the rusting cogs and thought of the men who once worked there, coming out with white coats of flour clinging to their clothes like white paint, then going home to cook cornbread from fresh-ground meal.

I thought of what I had read in *The Story of Eliasville* by the late Tom Cunningham and how the first bridge across the Brazos was built here in 1893.

"That ended the hazards of the old crossings which involved steep plunges into the river, wagon brakes screaming....[teams]

lunging forward until horse flesh and muscle were strained to the limit in the mighty struggle upward to high ground again."

I looked up the river. Heard locusts singing and saw a monstrous alligator gar with a mouth like a saw blade easing along the bank, looking for a meal.

I'm glad the grumpy old gray-haired lady is protecting this place and wish she had protected another place just down the river that burned a few years ago, sending a priceless piece of history up in flames.

That place was called Stovall Hot Wells and for years attracted hundreds to the tiny town of South Bend. They came to bathe in the mineral waters that gushed from the middle of a farming field. Cures of everything from athlete's foot to impotence were promised after taking baths in the springs.

I had been there when it was still operating. A sign had read, "Boil out the poison. Bathe your way to better health."

That's what folks had been doing since 1929 when the hot springs were discovered by a drilling crew searching for oil. They had a main lodge and bathing room plus several cabins that people rented to spend days soaking in the milky looking sulfur water that registered 103 degrees.

But in 1994 the famous health spa burned to the ground. Smoke could be seen from ten miles away as fire consumed the facility.

Visitors today can still see the sight of piles of burned timbers, broken glass, and ceramic tile. I walked inside what remains of one of the old buildings. A wheelchair with its wheels rusted stuck sat in the hallway. I thought of what one bather had told me the day I had actually bathed in the wells.

"These springs will cure everything but bad breath," he had said. "My granddad came here all crippled up and bathed a week. He came home walking like a young man, but his breath still stunk like a hog."

Aw, the stories that this place gave birth to.

# Brady

For years Brady declared itself the geographical center of Texas.

That point fell on the ranch owned by John G. Jones and his sons, William and John W. Jones. But along comes the Texas Society of Professional Surveyors in 1989 with a bunch of fancy electronic equipment. They made measurements and declared that this site was not the center of Texas.

No sir, the true center is in Eden, some thirty-two miles west.

So did that make John G. Jones mad? Not at all.

"These boys got all of those high-powered measurement things and got to figuring," he said. "Hell, they even used Shreveport in their calculation and it isn't even in Texas. But anyway, they turned on their devices and said the center was in Eden."

He shook his head and swore.

"I'll bet they aren't within fifty miles of being accurate. But it doesn't bother me. Eden needs all of the help they can get. All they got over there is one of those POW camps [a holding center for undocumented aliens] and one café. So if it will help, then let them have being the center of Texas."

He spoke from the Brady Chamber of Commerce office. He looks like a rancher. He has huge scarred hands and forearms and a full head of gray hair. He called himself a smoothmouth, a term used to denote aging livestock whose teeth are worn smooth.

Before he talked about the center of Texas, he commented on the weather and a recent rain.

"We needed it," he said. "Folks talked about how dry it was. But, we've seen it a damn sight drier."

Then he told how the original geographical center was determined in the 1920s. W.N. White, who then owned the ranch in McCulloch County, met with the Texas land commissioner to make the determination.

"They cut out a map of Texas and balanced it on the end of a pencil," said Jones. "And they said that this fell where our ranch was."

And so it stayed for nearly seventy years. The state even placed a bronze marker at a roadside park north of here on Highway 377 declaring this fact. A marker on the courthouse lawn in Brady proclaims the town the Heart of Texas.

Then came the Texas Society of Professional Surveyors. And then came their announcement in 1989 that the site was wrong.

And then came a TV person to John G. Jones for comments.

"I spent a day carrying him around the country. He asked me if it bothered me, this new announcement, and I said, "Hell, no, it hasn't made me any money yet being in the center of Texas.""

What is more important to Jones is the fact that his 10,000 acres is a good outfit. They run cows and sheep on the land. The mention of the sheep brought another blast at the government and its regulations about how ranchers cannot use poison to take care of coyotes that kill sheep.

"The guy who did that lives in Dallas. He never has been to this country so how can he tell us how to take care of our coyote problem," he said.

He stood up, stretched, and said once again as he left, "Being in the center of Texas is nothing to brag about. Having a good ranch is something to brag about. And that's what we got."

So we drove to the park some twenty miles north of here that once was declared the center of Texas. We climbed a steel tower erected for viewing.

The land is covered with mesquites and cedars with limbs heavy with bunches of blue berries.

The smell of rain was heavy from a thick bank of clouds that looked like one of those huge quilts that youngsters fought over for cover as they slept three to a bed during the winter.

The pasture needed rain. That was evidenced by bare spots that look like raw places on the feet of a person who has worn shoes with no socks.

As I looked at the land, I agreed with Jones. It doesn't matter where the center of the state is. This is beautiful ranching country anyway.

# Clairemont

Clairemont may live only in memories, but evidence of the tiny town's jail bites vividly into those thoughts.

The once-thriving but now ghost town lies about 70 miles southwest of Lubbock in Kent County at the edge of fields with winter grain just punching tiny green leaves through the earth's skin.

There's the smell of West Texas oil in the town's gut section at the intersection of Texas 208 and U.S. 380. Three deserted stores line the street, their fronts camouflaged by dying tumbleweeds. Nearby, the old jail arches dominantly among wilting sunflowers and careless weeds.

Gosh, what a place to be jailed.

The walls are monstrous red sandstone. Tiny iron stars are embedded near the structure's top. Inside are massive steel cells with messages of irony written on them. One reads, "The Devil comes in here nightly."

It's easy to imagine the devil in here. And it's easy to imagine those who were jailed here, praying long and loudly to Jesus to get them out. David Bickley of Dallas, who had traveled with me on this trip, put it succinctly.

"This jail was a long time before William Wayne Justice's ruling," he said. Justice, a U.S. District judge, ruled in 1980 that the state prison system was so crowded it violated the constitutional rights of an inmate.

We looked at another hand-painted message. It said Bill and Joe were here. Another reads, "Ross Hill wuz here."

The security system is still in place. Bickley pulled one of those massive iron handles, and heavy bolts of steel slid the doors from one of the two cells.

We walked inside. Overhead was more steel. And many feet above that was the ceiling with mortar that looked like the tongue of a thirsty horse.

Nearby was graffiti that read, "I slept here once and not very good at that."

"Billy Bob was here," reads a nearby sign.

In a side room, the wind howled through that window like coyotes with a three-day hunger gnawing at their guts.

We walked outside.

"Gosh, almighty," Bickley said. "If you had been locked up here, you would be praying that somebody quickly found out about it and would come to make your bond. Particularly if it were spring or summer or winter or fall."

Or anytime.

We walked down Clairemont's main street. Inside the window of one of the empty stores was a sign that read, "We are currently in need of large quantities of live poisonous snakes for venom research."

The door's hinges creaked loudly as I walked inside. There was an empty mustard jar and piles of plastic toys. One toy resembled an old dungeon, and when a chain was pulled, a tiny red bird jumped up and down in an upstairs cell. Maybe it was a jailbird.

We walked outside and looked at the jail in the late afternoon sun. A buzzard flew over, making squeaking noises as it soared on the thermal currents high above the old jail.

I pulled up a tumbleweed. Its web of limbs rustled with dryness. I pitched it into the air and it spun away to escape from here and the Clairemont jail.

Still another old jail that was once as equally forbidding but today is being used sits on Highway 377 as it passes through Comanche, county seat of Comanche County. The old massive rock two-story building, which looms like a European castle, is Christopher S. Till's law office.

Till, a slender man, hears many jokes about his office. Lines like, "I saw you working this morning, and Chris, you look good behind bars."

He laughs at those and his unusual office, which he has tried to restore as closely as possible to its original condition. He moved to Comanche in 1990 after spending years in Houston.

"I had seen the old jail and knew it had closed in 1987 after being condemned," said Till. "But I had never really thought about buying it."

Then on a trip to Albany, Texas, he had seen that city's old jail, which has been converted to a museum, and thought of buying the old Comanche jail. But his wife, Elizabeth, was reluctant. After looking at photographs showing its condition, those feelings were understandable.

"Yeah, it was a mess," said Till. "There was conduit running everywhere. None of the windows worked. They had nailed paneling onto the walls, and the woodwork had layers and layers of paint on it. My son, Clay, and I stripped every piece of wood and the doors. My goal was to put it back as close as to the way it was when it was built and have air conditioning and heat added."

We walked up steel stairs to the second floor, which was once full of cells.

"I had to cut them out and remove them. They weighed over 100 tons and were putting a tremendous stress on the ceiling," he said.

We looked at an old shower for inmates and a steel trapdoor over a hole made for hangings.

"I don't know if they ever had a hanging in here or not," said Till.

Outside, I backed off and looked at the old jail. I appreciated what Till has done. I thought about one of the other persons who had made a bid for the structure. That person had said he would tear the structure down and cut the cells into scrap iron.

And another bit of Texas history would have been gone.

# Eastland

Bobbie Livingston and Linda Williams seldom miss work at their second jobs, even though they don't get paid.

They are two of about ninety volunteers at the Majestic Theatre in this town on I-20 west of Fort Worth. The volunteers come to the theater after putting in eight or ten hours at paying jobs. They don't complain because were it not for them, the Majestic, which opened in 1920, might have become a parking lot. Perish that thought.

"I'll do anything to keep it open," Livingston said.

She's been going to movies here for most of her life. She smiled at the mention of the midnight horror films in her childhood.

"Scared us to death," she said. "Remember *The Thing*? Gosh, what a movie."

As we talked, Ed Allcorn, the manager and the Majestic's only paid employee, started the popcorn machine. It's one of the old ones, full of yellow and red splashes of color.

Allcorn has loved theaters such as this one for most of his life. He came here after managing the Paramount, a restored theater in Abilene.

"One reason for this theater's importance is that it is one of the few places other than church where everybody can come," he said.

Moviegoers can rest assured that they won't see any hard R movies such as *Pulp Fiction*. Allcorn said they may show a soft R rated movie but not a hard one.

"We don't show anything but family movies during the summer. That way, parents know their kids can come here and not be exposed to...well, you know what," he said.

And the movies do draw. Allcorn said the Majestic's 825 seats are often packed for Disney films. The theater is open Friday through Monday nights.

"What else do you do in a town this size except maybe go to Wal-Mart?" Allcorn asked. "We have a group of adults who come every time the doors open. They sit in the same seats and they buy the same thing every time. It is a social event for them."

At one time the Majestic was called the largest and best theater west of Fort Worth. But in the 1980s the movie house was shuttered. So how did it survive?

After rumors started floating that the building was going to be torn down, the city bought it and then for $1 a year, rented it to the Eastland Fine Arts Association, which began an arduous restoration.

Allcorn gave one example of the Majestic's condition.

"A blanket had been stretched across the stairway leading from the balcony to prevent cold air from coming downstairs and straining the heating system," he said.

Visiting the theater today is delightful. It has murals depicting western scenes. And of course there is the smell of that fresh popcorn that sells for $1 a box.

Allcorn has short, graying hair and a moustache. He looks like the old-time movie manager who walked so smoothly in the theater darkness as the film was shown.

"The Majestic has to stay open," he said. "At one time, this town alone had six theaters, but now the Majestic is the only remaining theater in the whole county."

He stopped to empty the popcorn machine. Livingston watched.

"This is a landmark," she said. "It must not close."

Her words sounded like the title of a movie...The Majestic Will Not Go Down.

# Dodson Prairie

The steeple of Saint Boniface Church beckoned like white paint splashed on tar.

I followed Highway 16 north of Strawn into northern Palo Pinto County, watching the steeple for miles. I drove past cattle eating feed and sheep grazing on winter grain fields surrounded by mesquites stretching their twisted, leafless limbs into the air.

And finally there was the church with its green roof, white siding—so simple and beautiful.

Inside, Mrs. Lenora T. Boyd greeted me warmly as sunshine fell through ten stained-glass windows in beams of color. She lighted an open gas heater that cut through the cold from a norther, but we still kept on our coats.

She has a strong voice and short, graying brown hair. She smiled as she looked around the chapel with its wooden floors that made soft moans as a result of the cold.

"I was confirmed here and my late husband and I celebrated our fiftieth anniversary here," she said.

So naturally she feels a close kinship to this church that once had more than 200 members but now has only ten families and celebrates mass at 3 P.M. on Saturdays.

Her voice was caught in echoes from the towering ceilings as she told about her grandfather moving here in 1900. That was before there was a church building.

"We had mass in different people's homes," she said.

Those were happy days when families hosted other families. The women cooked while the men played dominoes and drank wine.

"Everyone had wine. We had vineyards and made our own," she said. "We were almost self-sufficient. We had our own molasses mill, grew our own cane and made molasses. That was a mainstay in the winter."

The church, built in 1912, has a bell that came from St. Michael's Church in Weimar, Germany. That church was destroyed in a storm in 1917. Her uncle, Louis Kainer, who had attended that church as a youngster and heard the bell, rang it here after it was installed.

"When someone died, they tolled the bell for as many times as the person was old," said Mrs. Boyd. "We'd walk to the cemetery, and during the procession somebody rang the bell."

She also recalled a huge chandelier with a myriad of candles. The chandelier was donated by the Joseph Nowak family.

"My uncle [Louis] also was the candle lighter," she said. "When we were children, we loved to watch the twinkle of those small candles during benediction."

Her father, the late Charles A. Teichmann, was church organist for fifty years.

"He attended St. Edward's University and studied music for two years," she said. "When he came home, he taught others in the community and formed a band called the Dodson Prairie Band. They played for years around here."

I watched the beautiful colors spill through the windows as Mrs. Boyd told why the church is still open in this sparsely settled area.

"I really feel like it is by God's grace," she said.

When I left, I stopped several miles away and looked back at the white steeple. I hoped God continued that grace for other travelers like me.

# Regency

One of the last old suspension bridges in Texas still spans majestically across the Colorado River near this tiny breath of a town.

Many people, probably mostly locals from Brownwood, which lies 28 miles to the north, wait for a full moon to come and look at the old bridge.

Gosh what an experience.

"It's, well, almost spiritual," said Mark Abbey of nearby Comanche.

He came here during his days at Howard Payne University in Brownwood. Groups of twenty and thirty would come and sit on the towering banks of the Colorado and play a guitar and sing. And, well, just listen and appreciate.

And on this day Bryan Healer, a Brownwood attorney who had told me about the bridge in Mills County, was bringing me to see it.

We drove south on Farm Road 45 past fields of bluestem standing beautifully in its blue colors in the hot sunshine along with thickets of post oak and mesquite. Healer told about the original bridge.

"I think this happened in 1922," he said. "They were moving a herd of cattle across the bridge and the river was up. The cattle spooked and started crashing against the bridge."

The bridge gave way.

"Cattle and riders fell to the river and one rider was killed," said Healer. "I think they rebuilt the bridge in 1923. I have also heard that it is the only one of its kind in Texas that is still being used."

We drove through the tiny settlement of Ebony down a narrow twisting road and into Regency. There's an old, vacant general store leaning in age and crusted by weather. A birdhouse sits on top of it.

Healer laughed as he looked at the store. He told how some friends first found the bridge back in the early 1960s. They were in a motor home and decided not to cross it.

"So they came back on motorcycles and stopped here. An old man yelled at them to leave. He said, 'We don't need no hippies out here,'" said Healer.

About a mile south is the bridge. A sign says, "Weight limit, 8,000 pounds." We drove slowly across. The bridge began to undulate gently. Abbey stood on the other side taking pictures.

"My girlfriend, Michele Cole, first showed me the bridge," said Abbey, an insurance salesman. "It was a tradition for students to come out here and play a guitar and look at the stars."

He smiled.

"You could see billions of stars because the sky was so clear," he said.

Healer pointed at some holes in massive rocks near the end of the bridge.

"These were grinding holes used by Indians," he said. "There used to be some pictographs here."

We looked down the ledge made of layers of limestone with soft colors of whites and browns to the Colorado. The concrete pillars from the original bridge still were there. The river was a large ribbon of green. Huge turtles stuck their heads out of the surface.

We walked across the bridge, the driveway made from two-by-fours set on edge. The wind whined through the massive cables. On one was a spider web, caught by the sun in a dazzling gold color. It looked like a gold chain caught in slow motion in a haphazard pitch to a jewelry box.

Far down the river, film from trees lining the banks lay on the water. Every so often a fish ripped through the film to snap at an insect.

The sun dipped lower. In the east a half moon—a dirty, dusty silver—began its climb.

This would be a good night to bring a guitar here and sing some of the old cowboy ballads and listen to them bounce off the thick bloodweeds. This would be a good night to lay back and think of that day so long ago when those cattle broke through the bridge and fell bawling to the river below.

I'll bet you'd swear you could hear those echoes this night.

# Glen Rose

Richard M. "Dick" Moore does get your attention when he roars at you from a distance. Such was the case as I strolled around Granbury and Moore, a tall, lanky man with a mustache, yelled at me:

"You've been sick, I heard [I had heart surgery]. Well, I'm glad you are out and about. And while you are at it, you need to come back and visit the gallery. When? Hell, anytime."

Several people gawked at Moore as he grabbed me by the shoulders as if he were going to hit me. He roared more profanity at me. I roared some back. But it was all in fun, and a few weeks later I did come here to revisit the Barnard's Mill Art Museum. It is inside what was once this city's old hospital and sits not far from the courthouse square, a picturesque setting full of antique stores and other shops.

The museum is made of beautiful native stone and is connected to Barnard's Mill, built on the banks of the Paluxy River in 1860. Moore lives in the old mill. And if you are lucky, you can talk him into a tour and a look at his vast and exquisite collection of antiques.

But today I concentrated on the museum. Moore, an attorney, gave the hospital building to the museum, owned and operated by the Jewell Miears Fielder Foundation, and truly one of the least discovered treats around. Moore acknowledged that in a burst of words.

"Only problem we have is we don't have enough people. I've had people come from as far away as India, but people two doors away don't even know we are here," he said.

His eyes snapped. "Why? Aw hell, it is like when I lived in Fort Worth. The only time I went to some of the great museums there was when I had visitors. It's the same way here. But we do have some pretty good art."

They do indeed. In the twelve rooms are original works by Robert Summers, Jack Bryant, R. Kleinfelder, Morris Henry Hobbs, and Amy Miears Jackson. Moore freely recited information on each piece as we walked through.

"Here is one of Jackson's works. She was a close friend of Georgia O'Keefe," he said.

Two of her paintings, "Poppies" and "Water Lilies," have the vivid burst of colors so typical of O'Keefe's works.

Moore stopped at a beautiful hand-tooled western saddle.

"I bought that. Why? Hell, I don't know. I don't even have a horse. But I think it is a work of art," he said.

We walked into a room that has ornate panels of gold thread embroidered on silk that once decorated robes of Chinese royalty. They are done in what is called blind stitch.

"Only young children could see how to do this. And it was so demanding, they went blind doing it," Moore said.

The work is stunning. And nearby are trade plates that old clipper sailing ships used for ballast when they were bringing goods from China.

Moore then showed me the western room and an 1861 map of Texas. The West Texas area is marked, "Destitute of wood and water."

So why has Moore done this?

"I feel like as you pass along this way, you ought to leave something behind for others to enjoy," he said.

Folks can do that from 10 A.M. to 5 P.M. Saturdays and from 1 to 5 P.M. on Sundays.

# Gainesville

The popularity of the fried pies served at the Fried Pie Co. continues to rise like baking dough in this town, which is the county seat of Cooke County.

Recently a rather large man marched into the café that once was a service station. He sniffed the cooking food, savoring the delightful aroma of fried pies sizzling in skillets of shortening.

"I'd like to sample your pies," he said.

"How many?" Diane Osborne, a waitress, remembered asking him.

"Oh, just a good sampling," he replied.

So she brought him four kinds of fried pies. He ate all of them in fewer than six bites.

"Those are good fried pies. I'll take 150 of them," he said.

That's close to $200 worth of fried pies, even with the discount of a dozen for $15. But since Jo Clark, the owner of the popular Fried Pie Co. began making the fried pies some fifteen years ago, there have been many huge orders.

We came here because one of Tom Dodge's late friends, who had been reared here, had told him that if he ever came here, to be sure and try the fried pies.

We had no trouble finding the Fried Pie Co. The first person we asked, a woman standing near the courthouse, smiled, rubbed her stomach and pointed the way.

Even at 1:30 P.M. the place was full of the noise of customers and the smell of lunches cooking. Dodge looked at the list of fried pies. Since they had already sold out of several kinds, he ordered Dutch apple.

Osborne soon brought the pie, covered with powdered sugar. Dodge, a sweet freak, eyed the pie for a moment and then consumed it in two bites. He reminded me of the character drinking moonshine in the George Jones song "White Lightning." The lyrics go, "He took one look and drank it right down. And his eyes turned red and his face turned blue."

"That is ecstasy," Dodge said of the pie.

So he ordered another. John Tushim, another friend who swore he never eats between sunup and sundown, eyed this pie. He asked for a bite.

Osborne laughed.

"Thought you never ate during the day," she said.

"This is an exception," he said.

Then Vickie McKnight, cook and manager, came to our table. She said Clark was out of town. But it is the store owner's secret recipe for crust that makes the pies so delicious.

"And that is in her head, and she says she will never share it," said McKnight.

She said the pies are cooked in vegetable oil shortening. And yes, they are loaded with calories.

"But I've got the solution for that," she said. "Just take small bites."

They sell as many as 800 fried pies on Saturdays.

"We have one woman and all she does is stand there and box up the pies that people are ordering," said McKnight.

Doyce and Marilyn Phillips of Mount Pleasant came in and ordered a dozen fried pies.

"I discovered them when I worked this territory for Nabisco," he said. "We are coming back from Denver and it is out of the way, but we had to come by and get some fried pies."

He apparently feels about the pies as Dodge does, who calls them, "the Sammy Sosa of fried pies."

That's a great compliment from a guy who calls himself a former Pillsbury Dough Boy.

# Ballinger

People can see Jim and Doris Studer's thanks to God for their success from ten miles away.

My friend John Tushim and I verified that as we drove to this town, 65 miles west of Brownwood on Texas 67. We had topped a hill, and there in the distance on a ragged hill blanketed with mesquite trees and other brush stood a silver-looking structure.

"My gosh, what is that?" asked Tushim.

"The cross," I said.

The cross was impressive as its 100 feet cut into the sky, giving entirely different impressions almost by the minute as the sun hit it. On this day it looked like a stroke of bright silver washed by the sun in early afternoon.

We drove on to Buddy's Plant Plus, a Miracle Gro Plant owned by the Studers, to ask why anyone would build a cross of this magnitude in this region. Studer greeted us warmly. He is a strong-looking man with huge hands. He's easygoing and speaks in a low, solid voice.

"The cross was a thanks to God for all he's helped us with," he said.

That has been a lot, as noted when he talked about his life. Not only has God been good to them financially, but God has saved his life several times from almost certain death in accidents, he said.

One of those times came when he was taking flying lessons in Florida. During the lesson, the flight instructor lost control of the plane and it zoomed down toward a large forest.

"Normally, trees would be your undoing. But they turned out to be our savior," Studer said.

The trees did rip off the plane's wing and tail. But when the plane finally stopped, it was hanging upside-down above the ground in the limbs of the trees. Seat belts held Studer and the instructor.

"It was so quiet that I thought I had been killed," he said. "When I realized otherwise, I unbuckled my seat belt and fell to the ground and got a cut on my face."

That was his only injury. The pilot was equally lucky.

From that and several other close brushes with death, Studer decided he had a guardian angel. He named him Buddy, the name used in his plant, which the Studers opened after moving here in June 1988.

Hard work saw their business thrive. So in 1992 when they considered buying a 1,300-acre ranch, Doris Studer said, "If we come up with the down payment for this, then we should build a cross for the help God has given us."

They made the down payment and began building the cross. Originally they had planned a cross only forty feet tall. But something happened that changed their minds.

That event unfolded in Florida as Studer helped trim trees for his mother-in-law. As he held his steel saw upward, he accidentally touched an electric power line.

"The electricity went 'ssssct. ssssct.' Well, you know how it sounds," Studer said. "I never felt anything. I was not hurt."

Apparently, the electrical surge had grounded only inches from him.

"That is when I said, 'God, we owe you another sixty feet.' So we extended the cross up to 100 feet high."

They built the cross on the 1,300 acres of land they own southwest of this city. The cross is particularly impressive during the Christmas time of year with three 1,000-watt bulbs bathing it in light and making it appear almost saintly.

"We built the cross because God had been good to us," he said. "Come on, let's go look at it."

As we drove to the site, he told of spending $70,000 to build the cross. Steve Jansa of Jansa Construction in Rowena was hired for the job.

"He said he had never built a cross but said he would like to give it a try," Studer said.

It was a commanding task. The cross section is 70 feet wide and 60 feet off the ground and weighs 50 tons.

"When we got ready to erect it, I paid $280 an hour for a 1,150 foot-high crane to be driven here from Dallas to put it up," Studer said. "Every morning when Doris and I get up, we can see the cross from our house. I look at it and say, 'Good morning, Lord.'"

But, he emphasized, the cross is not theirs.

"I don't want my name on it. It is not my cross. It belongs to everybody," he said.

We turned onto the gravel road leading to the cross. It's amazing how many different images the cross presents as it is viewed from different times and locations.

We parked. I got out of the vehicle and had to back off and tilt my head to see its top.

A stiff wind tore at my notebook and chilled my hands. But it did not chill the warmth this man has for God.

"I really believe we are instruments for the good Lord. He wanted a cross built and he brought us here. And now he has a cross," Studer said.

The wind ripped through the rough country. The sun was falling rapidly as I walked down a pathway, turned, and looked again at the cross.

Shadows had chased away earlier images. The sun brought a burst of light, causing golden spirals to bounce off its side.

It was indeed an impressive sight.

# Gordon

There are two rather unusual sites in the country outside this town in Palo Pinto County. One is a mausoleum. The other is, well, they are still looking for answers as to what it is.

But first the mausoleum. Local resident John Wilson's dreams are still filled with images of the country where he spent two years of his childhood and where the mausoleum made from native limestone is located. The structure, which looks like a miniature castle, looms out from a mesquite flat on what is known as the Johnson

League Ranch north of Gordon, which is about sixty miles west of Fort Worth.

Inside the structure are the bodies of W.W. Johnson, his wife, Anna, and their daughter and son.

The mausoleum has always interested me. So have the Johnsons, who did not believe in burials.

When their daughter died at age three, they kept her body in a tiny casket in a room in their house in nearby Strawn. They did the same thing with their son who died in 1894 at age seven.

Johnson, who came here in 1890 to mine coal in the then rich coal fields, bought this land about 1900.

"We moved here in 1944," said Wilson. "That was twenty-two years after the bodies had been placed here."

Wilson had returned to the ranch along with others to rekindle his memories at the invitation of Don Crawford, who owns the land with his brother. We had driven across roads with ruts cutting into clay that looked like it had been soaked in blood. The need for rain was obvious as pockets of dust exploded from bottoms of brown grass.

Wilson's late uncle, Sim Wilson, worked for Johnson.

"He said Johnson had some peculiar ways," Wilson said.

That statement is buttressed by the mausoleum. Wilson, who is built strong and solid, touched the rock walls with his rough hands.

"Look at this good. This is true history," he said in a rasping voice. "My dad [the late Buster Wilson] was here when they sealed this in 1923. Come on, let's go look at the house we lived in."

So we drove to that old house.

"Before we moved in, my dad said, 'I'm not sure I want to live here. They used to keep dead people in that room,'" Wilson said.

We walked to the room, which has walls nearly two feet thick.

"This is where the bodies were kept before the rock mausoleum was built. We used it as a smokehouse," Wilson said.

We walked inside the house, its floors covered with hay that softened our footsteps. We heard the wind outside chasing through huge live oaks, causing their branches to send echoes to nearby Palo Pinto Creek, a tiny shoestring of green.

I kind of understood Wilson's emotions. I have only visited here a few times. But I often dream of the place.

The other site is equally mysterious. It is a tremendous hole and lies in the rugged ranching country north of here. It has puzzled residents for more than 100 years.

The mystery lies on the side of a mountain that is heavy with green from mesquites, cedars, and other vegetation common to this area. Except in one spot. That spot is barren, looking like a bald-headed man sitting in a convention of long-hairs.

John Nelson and Charlie Brown, longtime residents of the area, had taken me to the site. We had stopped about a mile before to look at the mountain before hiking up to the site.

"See that. Can you tell me why no grass is growing there. Why it looks like dirt dug up by a bulldozer? Well, there's never been a bulldozer up there. But, enough of this. Let's hike on up to it and let you form your own opinion," Wilson said.

So we began our walk up the slope of what is called Whitt Mountain. We walked through mesquite trees just leafing out in sheets of pale green. We walked past many beautiful but dangerous devil's pincushion cactus, perfectly round with just the beginning of striking red flowers covered with a thick mat of thorns so strong and sharp they can penetrate shoe leather.

We stopped at a huge rock that weighed several tons. It, like several others in the area, is precariously balanced on a sliver of mud. Then we reached the bare spot that looks like a huge dam somebody has made. It's hard to realize that it has been here all of these men's lives and all of their fathers' lives and still little is growing on it.

Wind cracked through the brush in loud echoes. But certainly it didn't compare to that day when whatever it was hit this mountain.

"Okay, here's my theory," said Wilson. "I think it was a meteor that hit here. It barely missed the top of the mountain. I think it hit and boiled the ground up. It was like when you were a kid and threw rocks into mud and the mud erupted on the other side."

We walked across the earth. Brown showed me a thin piece of rock with multiple formations of mussels, clams, and ferns. One of the formations came from a plant that once grew deep in waters that covered this area. It had a head that looked like an opened hand. Woe be unto fish that settled in the hand, which snapped shut, trapping the fish for a meal.

"The old-timers call them pop rocks," said Wilson "You can throw them into a campfire and they will go off like a shell."

Brown also showed me pieces of what he called isinglass, a thin sparkling plate that does look like glass.

"I've scouted all over this country, and this is the only place I can find this glass," he said. "And you know what makes glass…heat and sand."

Like heat from an exploding meteor? Wilson smiled at the question.

"I can't tell anybody that is what caused this," he said. "But, it sure looks like it."

"Yeah, and stuff is growing all over this country except on this," said Brown.

We began our return.

"You know the reason this has never been answered is because it is so hard to get to," said Wilson. "If it had crashed down near the road, we'd already know what caused it."

And probably somebody would have built a mausoleum to cover it that would have dwarfed even the Johnson Mausoleum. And they'd probably be charging admission.

# Baird

Gene Swinson still wonders if the pistols are inside that old cistern on this city's downtown streets.

He and some buddies once crawled down into the rock-walled water storage facility where this town once got much of its drinking water. They found nothing. But he still thinks the six shooters could be there.

The pistols were involved in a rather sad story that took place when this community in Callahan County was a wild ranching and railroad town. Several cowboys in a moment of grief tossed their pistols into the cistern.

Swinson absorbed that story and many more while sitting in the barbershop that his late father once owned and operated in Baird. Swinson recalled some of those tales for me as he sat in what once was the Texas & Pacific Railroad Depot, built in 1880. At the time he was seventy and gray hair spilled from his baseball cap.

Swinson not only heard many of the old stories. He also talked to many of the participants. Such is the story of the cowboys, the pistols, and the cistern.

He said it happened in 1908. As was the custom, cowboys came to town about once a month, generally on a Saturday. They often spent the night in one of the many hotels that then lined Baird's streets.

This group of cowboys really was no different from any of the others. They came from a big ranch and generally did their partying together, said Swinson.

This party began in a bar. The cowboys began drinking huge mugs of beer. The more they drank, the more wild ideas entered their heads about ways of having more fun.

"Hey, let's shoot some of these mugs off of each other's heads," shouted one of the cowboys.

So began a rather dangerous game of placing beer mugs on top of their heads to make targets for their buddies.

They decided they needed more room. So they went to a hotel. They continued drinking. They continued shooting the mugs off one another's heads.

"Then one of them accidentally missed the mug and shot his friend," said Swinson. "Killed him."

The cowboys gathered around the victim. They removed their hats. They began crying. Then they wrapped their buddy in a blanket to take his body back to the ranch for burial. But before they left they did an unusual thing.

"They went to the cistern and threw their guns in there," said Swinson. "Naturally, that cistern became a drawing card for youngsters. Oh, yeah. We let ourselves down into the cistern by rope. But we never found the guns."

That brought up a story about a train engineer who probably owed his life to the fact that the cowboys quit packing pistols. Swinson actually witnessed this incident, which happened because of Baird's location in ranching country. Ranchers brought their cattle here to be shipped to major markets.

"They were bringing in about 3,000 head one day," said Swinson. "The cowboys had them all lined out as they neared the railroad tracks."

A new engineer sat in the locomotive. He heard the cowboys popping their whips and yelling. He didn't know what that meant. So he pulled on the train whistle to answer them. He shouldn't have.

"Those cattle scattered everywhere," said Swinson. "They ran through chicken houses. Tore up gardens. My brother and I could see them coming our way. So we crawled up a mesquite tree to a limb that was just barely over their backs. Man, what a mess."

It took the cowboys three days to round up all the scattered cattle. All the while, they were cursing that train engineer.

He probably was not cursing. He was probably thanking God that the cowboys had quit carrying their pistols to town some years earlier.

# Chapter 5
# Cemeteries

Cemeteries are vast deposits of our history.

Many cemeteries are all that is left of what once may have been a thriving town.

I have always loved visiting these facilities for the deceased. Often a page of deep tragedy from the past flashes at you as you walk among the graves.

Such is the case when you find rows of tombstones made in the late teens of the 1900s during the terrible influenza epidemic. So many of these graves from these years mark the burial site of infants and youngsters.

I always try to visit cemeteries near sunup or sundown. Those times seem to sharpen the atmosphere, and one can almost hear soft whispers in the wind as they walk among the graves.

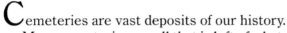

## Victor

Birds sang their throats raw sitting in the bare limbs of winter trees around the Victor Cemetery.

The naked smell of peanut fields with strings of hay left from harvesting caught us as we walked through the gates.

We had come looking for the grave of O.H. Moore. Or rather the grave of Moore's hand and arm. Information sent to me from the *Dublin Citizen* said that Moore lost that hand and arm in a shooting accident in 1896. (I didn't find the grave, but as result of this story, I heard about several more arm burials.)

According to records, some residents put Moore's hand and arm in a container of formaldehyde to display in a drugstore. People rode for miles to see it.

Moore pitched a fit about that. So his grandfather buried the arm and hand here in this cemetery about ten miles northwest of Dublin in Erath County.

Acorns crunched under our feet as we looked and walked past graves. My friend Doc Keen waved at me. He'd found a huge gray marker near an old tabernacle. Winston Lee Moore, professionally known as Slim Willet, a popular country and western singer, is buried there. He wrote "Don't Let the Stars Get in Your Eyes."

In his picture on the marker, he is wearing a cowboy hat and playing a guitar. He is making one of those bar chords that when I tried to make in my younger guitar-playing days sounded like a chicken about to get its head chopped off.

Ah, but I did remember Willet's song. I learned to two-step to it in high school. I hummed the words.

"Love blooms at night. At daylight it dies. Don't let the stars get in your eyes. Don't let the moon break your heart. For someday I will return and you know you are the only one I'll ever love."

We continued looking for Moore's headstone. I felt funny when I saw John Matthews' marker. He was born July 28, 1837. I was born July 27, 1937. We were both named John, only my Jon is misspelled.

I looked to the west. The sun looked like it was dipping to a bucket of blood. I saw a horse with a white flag in his forehead. A farm truck roared down the road making ragged echoes with its gutted muffler.

We found Joe B. Smith's grave. He was born September 19, 1839, and died October 8, 1908. "He carried an Indian spike in his body for 25 years," an inscription reads.

He is buried beside Texas Smith and Jerome Bonapart Smith. Nearby a sign says that the Victor Cemetery Association annual meeting is the last Saturday in May. I'll bet you could get some fine fried chicken, fresh cantaloupe, and sliced home grown tomatoes at that.

We didn't find where Moore's hand and arm were buried. So we left and drove across Flat Creek and stopped to talk to Johnnie and

Debbie Tunnell. They didn't know where Moore's arm and hand were buried. But they did know about Slim Willet.

"My husband [W.O.] knew Slim. Only he wasn't slim. He was stocky. He was raised right over there," Johnnie said.

She pointed through live oaks at another peanut field.

I thought of Willet's song again and how I had danced to it after learning the two-step. And how sometimes I'd stumble and my partner would fall against me and I'd feel a stirring in my emotions like I'd just seen the grave of somebody's arm being buried.

# Lingleville

I really wasn't surprised when I heard the story this time.

"What would you think if somebody told that they knew a person who had lost an arm? Not unusual, huh," they had said.

No, I had replied.

"Well, what if the person's arm was buried in a cemetery...still not unusual. But what if the arm had a tombstone...is that unusual?" they had said.

That had sounded unusual after I had written about the arm buried in the Victor Cemetery west of here. Then I heard about the arm that belonged to Sam Chisum, the late uncle of Dr. Dannah Proctor, school superintendent in this community in Erath County west of Stephenville.

She was about five when her uncle lost his arm, she said. And no, she didn't think it unusual that they buried it.

"They brought it to the house and cleaned it, put it in a box, and buried it," she said. "But what do you do with an arm? You don't feed it to the hogs."

She invited us to go look at the arm's grave. As we walked to our car, we met Jerry Brock, school principal. His father also lost an arm.

"What did they do with your father's arm?" Proctor asked.

"Well, I imagine old Dr. Terrell threw it into the trash," Brock said.

Then we drove west. We passed houses that had huge stacks of wood standing beside chimneys with smoke curling from them like ragged pieces of string.

We stopped at Lowell Cemetery, immaculately cared for in a country setting. Proctor led us to a tombstone. It reads, "Sam's arm."

Nearby is the grave of Chisum, the man to whom the arm belonged.

"He was my mother's brother. Let's go talk to her," Proctor said.

We drove to Delilah and Blake Morrison's house, still feeling a little surprised at seeing that tombstone. They invited us in and we stood around a space heater that sent out spirals of heat and felt so good.

"I don't remember the exact year he lost his arm. But it had to be in the summer because we were canning corn," Delilah Morrison said.

"He was combining. Wheat, I think," Blake Morrison said. "The combine had clogged up and he stopped to unclog it without shutting it off. As he walked to the back, he stepped into a hole, stumbled, and the combine grabbed him. If he hadn't been so big and strong, it would have dragged his whole body into the combine."

As it was, it torn off only part of his left arm. They took him to the hospital. And later Delilah Morrison's brother went to the combine and retrieved the arm.

"My aunt washed and cleaned all of the straw off of it and put it into a box. Then they took it over there and buried it," she said.

No, she didn't think it was unusual at the time.

"What do you do with an arm...throw it away?" she asked.

She said the family recently put a new tombstone over the arm. "We were afraid it would get lost if we didn't," she said.

And that is the story of the arm that got buried. Except for one other thing.

"I still have his artificial arm," Delilah Morrison said. "I don't know what to do with it."

Well, how about...aw, forget it

# Granbury

When I first saw a grave for an arm in a cemetery sixty miles west of here, I thought I had really seen something.

Then Eva Elliott told me to come to the city cemetery in Granbury and look for an arm marker.

So I did, on one of those scorching days that curls the leaves of plants.

I felt kind of stupid walking around in the cemetery with a notebook. I mean, what was I going to say if someone asked me what I was doing? Here I was wearing shorts, jogging shoes, and a big western straw hat. How would someone react if I told them what I was doing?

Well Monroe Davis, a city employee who cares for the cemetery, showed no concern when I told him I was looking for the arm grave.

"Come on and I'll show you where it is," he said.

He's a big man with a drawl and is a native of Hood County. He led me up a hill to some old graves. He stopped at some massive markers with hand-carved messages.

"Here it is," he said.

There are three gravesites covered with huge concrete blocks. He said the middle one was for the arm. Age had blotted out the inscription.

"I can solve that," Davis said. "I'll get some water from my jug."

He did.

"I discovered this one day when I was working up here and it began to rain and I noticed how much easier it was to read the old markers with some water on them," he said. "OK, watch."

He rubbed water onto the marker, which age had fractured in the center. The lettering came out. It read, "The arm of W.H. Holland. Amputated Nov. 10, 1875."

"It's amazing what a little water will do," Davis said.

Beside the arm are two graves of Holland infants. In front are three more larger concrete markers of the Holland family. So, do people ask about the grave of the arm?

"Oh, yeah. But my feeling is, it was a part of a man and it needed to be buried," he said. "The thing that impressed me even more is that a person could survive such a serious wound back then. Those people were tough."

Things like the arm grave makes Davis enjoy his work. He also loves the outdoors and has all of his life.

"I made a living catching fish on the Brazos River for several years," he said. "I'd set out three trotlines with fifty hooks each and catch enough fish to make a living. Sold them in Fort Worth on the north side."

But a stint in the Army ended that work.

"Well, actually, it was the lake [Lake Granbury] that killed it. They had built the lake when I got out of the Army. I spent about $3,000 on a boat and other stuff, and I didn't catch a fish. That's when I decided I'd better go back to working for a living."

He's been caring for the cemetery for two and a half years.

"Right over here is General Granbury's grave," he said.

He pointed to a freshly cleaned stone for Gen. Hiram B. Granbury, for whom the town is named. He was killed in a Civil War battle.

"I think these other stones should be cleaned that way. I think they are the real history in here," he said.

Well, at least they are an arm of that history.

# Trickham

Two stories I had written about arms that had been amputated and then buried eventually led me to this tiny community in Coleman County.

Lem Robbins of Granbury had read those stories and had called.

"I was intrigued by the stories of the arms buried in cemeteries. I would like to tell you of another," he said.

So I visited with him. He's a red-faced, gray-haired, self-effacing person. He remembered his late father telling the story of his uncle Joe Flores when Robbins was a youngster.

His father was born and reared in this community in the ranching country of Coleman County. Flores was also raised here.

According to his father, part of Flores' right arm was amputated after an accident involving a shotgun.

The arm was buried in the Trickham cemetery. But Flores kept complaining that the arm was hurting. The pain must have been devastating because Robbins remembers that it was said that Flores and his girlfriend, Naomi Mae, postponed their marriage for a year.

"Finally, his [Flores'] father went to the cemetery, dug it up, straightened the arm and then reburied it," Robbins said.

And the pain stopped.

After the reburial of the arm, Flores and Naomi Mae had a fruitful life. He became a mail carrier from Santa Anna to Trickham. He drove a Model-T Ford during good weather and used a horse and buggy when roads turned muddy.

Actually, Robbins discovered these facts while doing genealogy work at the Fort Worth Public Library. He found this information in the book *Historical Families of Coleman County.*

"The story had fascinated me as a kid, but as I grew older, I kind of forgot it and never dwelled on it. Then I began the research," he said.

He learned that the Flores family settled near Trickham in 1897. And while looking at the cemetery records of the Trickham Cemetery, he found the record of Joe B. Flores' arm.

So one day while driving in that area, he decided to find the grave of Uncle Joe's arm.

"I found many markers of my ancestors from both my grandfather's and grandmother's line," Robbins said.

He kept looking.

"And sure enough, right there between the marker for his [Flores'] mother and his father was a marker engraved 'Joe B. Flores' Arm.'"

Robbins had found in other research that his uncle had become quite successful after the accident. He was elected to the county office of public weigher. That made him in charge of weighing wagons and trailers of grain and weighing and sampling baled cotton for buyers and shippers.

Flores died in 1949. He was not buried beside the arm. Instead, he was buried in the Santa Anna Cemetery, several miles away.

"Perhaps you can now see why I found the other arm stories so interesting," Robbins said. "I hope this doesn't bore you."

I told him no. I like to be "armed" with plenty of stories.

# Lake Palo Pinto

John Wilson never dreamed that a man whose body he helped move from a tiny island cemetery in Lake Palo Pinto would become so famous.

The body was that of One-Armed Billy Wilson, who earned his nickname after losing an arm in an accident. Despite the loss, he still became an expert with cattle and horses.

One-Armed Billy, who was not related to John Wilson, was the basis for a character in *Lonesome Dove*, the novel that became a popular TV miniseries. Or at least Wilson thinks so.

"He was that character who went for help when he and Robert Duvall got pinned down by the Indians in the movie," Wilson said. "That all actually happened to One-Armed Billy Wilson. So his life sure sounded like that of that character called Pea Eye."

One-Armed Billy's feats were detailed in a 1968 article in *Frontier Times*. The write-up was accompanied by a photograph of One-Armed Billy and his wife.

"My dad had the article and he said, 'Do you remember being the pallbearer in that woman's funeral?' Well, I didn't. And then he told me and I did remember," Wilson said.

Wilson had helped dig up One-Armed Billy and his family and moved the bodies to a Mineral Wells cemetery. Wilson, who owns a ranch near Gordon, a town about an hour's drive west of Fort Worth, drove us to where the graves had once been. He recalled playing around a small gravel knoll in the area before Lake Palo Pinto was built.

"Wilson Holler is right over there. That was named after Billy Wilson," he said. "Me and a buddy used to come up here and explore and hunt all of the time."

He told about the little gravel knoll that contained five graves.

"All right, they come along and built this lake and it filled up and surrounded this little knoll," Wilson said. "And when the lake got up, it would get over those graves. My dad said that wasn't right."

So his father, the late Buster Wilson, contacted Thelma Doss, a writer in Mineral Wells. She wrote several articles, and the decision was made to move the graves.

"A funeral home guy and his helper came out here one day when the lake was down and we could get in there," Wilson said. "They brought out a backhoe to dig with. We also used shovels and screwdrivers."

They found the bodies of a young person and of One-Armed Billy's wife. Then they found One-Armed Billy.

"His grave had a pane of glass over it. It was completely shattered and lying right on top of his bones," Wilson said. "The funeral home guy said he couldn't find but one arm. My dad, who had known of Wilson said, 'That's because he only had one arm.'"

They put the bones into separate pine boxes, nailed lids on them, and carried them to a station wagon.

"They had been there since 1878. Let's see, we must have moved them in 1968," Wilson said.

We had reached a pasture beside the lake. Wilson stopped and we began walking. The thick, tall bloodweeds smelled sweet as we plowed through them. Beggar lice, a weed seed, popped onto our pants' legs and hung there.

Wilson parted some tall weeds and grass and pointed to the lake.

"Well, there it is," he said.

We looked. About a quarter of a mile away a tiny knoll with clots of willows and ragged grass jutted out of the water. Hog Mountain and Kettle Holler stretched in the background.

"We just drove out there, dug them up, loaded them into a station wagon, and away they went," Wilson said.

They never dreamed that one day one of those bodies would become a character in such a popular novel and miniseries.

"And you know something kind of funny? I never have finished watching that movie," Wilson said.

Far away some bobwhites began their songs. Their cries sounded so lonesome as they echoed in this raw, ranching country.

# Bluff Dale

Norma Wright's contagious enthusiasm filled the van as we headed down U.S. 377 toward this town in Erath County west of Granbury.

Norma's the kind that if I had a rusting boxcar I wanted to sell, I'm sure she could persuade somebody to buy it as a possible motor home.

"This is the greatest thing, Jon. David [her husband] and I were going to Jim's [Roberts] to look at a truck, and we pulled into his driveway and there in his front yard is this grave and this really old tombstone and well, Jim, you tell him," she said.

Roberts, a kind of quiet man, smiled and continued the story. We had turned south and driven past grazing cattle, their black and red colors a beautiful contrast to the grain fields turned a blast of green by recent rains.

"I've owned the property [67 acres] for four years," he said. "When I first looked at it, it was kind of grown up, and I didn't even know the grave was there. But we had to have it surveyed three times because of the grave in order to keep access to it."

When he found the grave and cleaned the tombstone, he found the name Caroline Orum on it. He began checking and a nearby neighbor, Francis Bramlet, told him this story.

Orum's young daughter disappeared one day and was never found. Orum grieved herself to death and asked that she be buried beneath a huge live oak tree.

"The story goes that that was the last place she had seen her daughter, and she wanted to be there in case the girl came back so she could find her mother," said Roberts.

We drove across railroad tracks and into the driveway. And there was the grave and the tombstone, gray with age and green with mold.

The inscription reads: "Rest mother. Rest in sleep. While friends in sorrow, o'er thee weep."

She died in 1880.

Thick clumps of clover soon to burst into purple blooms hugged the grave. A mourning dove's lonely voice faded into the wind.

"I used to come out here and hunt and stay in a one-room house," Roberts said. "No, I never heard anything mysterious at night."

He laughed.

"But I never left the house until daybreak," he said.

Nearby are two old barns made from one by twelves hauled here from Thurber. Both are leaning with age, like old men who spent their lives mining.

Roberts showed us a monstrous concrete cover over what was once an artesian well. Then Norma and I walked to a nearby smoke-house made from native limestone. The rocks each fit into the wall like huge pieces from a puzzle.

"And imagine, that was done by hand," she said.

We walked back to Roberts.

"I've heard the woman has relatives in Johnson County," he said. "It's kind of peculiar because we've had visitors to the grave, but so far no relative has visited."

Other birds began singing with the mourning doves. The symphony was broken by the screeching crack of a piece of sheet iron on a barn as wind twisted it.

They were lonely echoes for a woman still waiting for her daughter to come home.

# Thurber

O.B. "Buttercup" Bridier's emotions were jolted like somebody had tied a high-voltage electrical wire to them here in a historical cemetery.

He found a piece of a toy train that had once marked his grandmother's grave in the Thurber Cemetery. The grave had no other marker. And Bridier of nearby Parker County had not seen the little iron train since 1934.

"The odds of me finding this..." he said, his voice trailing off.

The odds were certainly not in favor of the discovery. We talked of those odds as we stood with Bridier and his wife, Fay, in this cemetery of this almost ghost town about sixty-five miles west of Fort Worth. At one time several thousand people lived here. They came from Poland, Italy, and other countries to work in the coal mines here. Bridier's family came from France.

The cemetery flashes evidence of those immigrants. Names like Giovanni and Beneventi are on tombstones. Mesquite trees are abundant around the nine acres. They have a light green shade on their limbs, reminding somebody of a young girl's playful application of makeup.

Bridier remembers coming to the cemetery as a youngster and looking at his grandmother's grave. He showed a picture of her. She was a strong-looking woman with short black hair and wore a formal black dress.

"She died of a heart attack and was buried here August 11, 1916," he said. "I can remember seeing her grave and that little train and telling my dad how much I wanted it. But he always said no."

Bridier moved away in 1943. He never returned until he read a column I had written about Leo S. Bielinski, who was also reared here and who was cleaning up the cemetery.

"Leo and I were friends as kids," said Bridier. "I hadn't heard from him in all of these years. But I called and asked if I could come out with him with my metal detector and look for my grandmother's grave."

Evidence of what the cemetery looked like before Bielinski and others began working on it is still here. There are piles of prickly pear that they have cut and stacked. There are many old wooden crosses that stayed in the ground so long they have rotted. Bielinski and the others have repositioned them.

Bridier, a large, strong man, gestured with his huge hands.

"I found a lot of things with my detector," he said. "Pieces of hinges, springs, light bulb bases, and other junk."

But he did not find the train.

"After coming here, I realized the chances of finding that little train were very remote," he said.

But he kept looking. And one day the metal detector began that high, accelerated whine that indicates something metallic. Bridier knew he was in the general vicinity of his grandmother's grave.

So he began to dig. One inch. Two inches. Three inches. At four inches, his fingers felt something. He pulled it out. He felt his heart race.

"I yelled at Leo," he said. "I told him he was not going to believe what I had found. He came over and he nearly fainted. He couldn't believe it. I couldn't either."

It was the coal tender part of the small train. It is made of cast iron and is about two inches in length.

"Can you imagine? Finding this?" he said.

The sun had hidden behind rolls of clouds the color of a worn-out typewriter ribbon. The wind flashed from the north in cold bites.

I thought of all the people who had walked over this ground. Of the storms and rains that had battered the cemetery. And yet that little train had remained and Bridier had found it. I felt warm as I thought of his discovery and thought of a similar experience that Gino Sartore had experienced when he saw for the first time the grave of his uncle, Giovanni Sartore.

His uncle had come to this country in the late 1800s to work in the Thurber coal mines, which closed in 1921 after a massive strike. Thousands of immigrants who came here had left behind families they would never see again except in fading photographs.

"My father had two wishes before he died," said Gino Sartore, who had come here from Pittsburgh. "He wanted to see the grave of his brother, and he wanted to see what the country around here looked like. Unfortunately, he died before that happened."

The fact that any of the Sartore family would be able to see the grave can be attributed to the meticulous work by people like Bielinski and the Thurber Cemetery Association.

"There were over 1,000 people buried up here," said Bielinski.

The grave of Sartore's uncle was one of the first 300 that were identified. Sartore said his uncle was the oldest in a family of four boys and three girls.

"My father [Lorenzo] was only seven when he [Giovanni] came to America. But as far as we can tell, my uncle worked in the coal mines near Pittsburgh before coming here about 1897," he said.

Apparently, soon after his arrival he joined the company band, called the Hunter's Band. He played the trombone. Bielinski, who has done tons of research on the area, showed a copy of a picture of Giovanni. He was dressed in a fancy band uniform and had a lock of dark hair falling across his forehead.

Sartore said he heard his father talk about his uncle most of his life. So when Sartore was attending a Dallas convention about fourteen years ago, he rented a car and drove here for the first time. He tried unsuccessfully to find his uncle's grave.

"The cemetery was so overgrown," he said.

But he told Les Mullins of Hereford about his efforts. One day Mullins stopped and made a two-hour unsuccessful search of the cemetery. He left his card at the nearby Mingus City Hall. Somebody gave it to Bielinski.

"My hair stood up on my neck," Bielinski said. "We had just dug up a broken tombstone and were putting it back together. It apparently belonged to Gino's uncle."

After confirmation, Sartore returned last week to look at his uncle's marker. We had followed him to the cemetery. He stopped at the Sartore marker, engraved in Italian.

Sartore translated the words.

"Born June 20, 1875; died March 29, 1901," he said. "And on top of that is a 'Star of Italy.' We think that must have been some lodge."

Lettering on the bottom is broken. But Sartore knelt, felt it, and finally said, "I've got that. It's 'Pray for his soul.'"

He stood up. Tony Sico, his associate, took his photograph. The wind caught his hair, dashing it onto his forehead. It looked just like that lock of hair falling onto his uncle's face in the photograph with one difference. Gino's hair was white.

# Indian Gap

I'll use any excuse I have in my cache to come to this tiny settlement on Farm Road 218 west of Hamilton in Hamilton County.

Its name came from the fact that Comanches used the gap between two mountains on their raids through this area.

I had offered to show my friend John Tushim a very unusual grave marker here as we ate lunch in nearby Priddy at the Hohertz Grocery Deli and Beer and General Store. I had one of their whopping delicious turkey sandwiches. As we ate sitting on folding chairs near bays of pipe fittings, I suggested the trip. He agreed. So we headed east.

The grave marker on top of the mountain can be seen from miles away. It looked like a gray Popsicle stick standing out from a blast of leaves fired red by fall's coming.

The Indian Gap cemetery lies at the bottom of the mountain. Across the road is the old Indian Gap brick school building with two stories of memories stretching back to 1923, the year it was built.

We drove to the home of Willard Partin, a man I had talked to years ago about his tremendous collection of antiques and junk that surrounds his house like a herd of buffalo.

An employee, Zen Hall, greeted us.

"Want to see the grave of the old man who started this town, huh? Well, when you get through looking at that, his house is down yonder on this side of the road. It's also worth looking at," Hall said.

So I hiked up the mountain. Gray clouds that looked like they'd been dusted with chalk floated overhead. I reached the top. The twenty-foot-high monument peeked out from sumac ablaze with fall colors.

Lettering on the monument says it marks the graves of several people, including Hawley Gerrells, a native of Bridgeport, Conn., who came here in 1857. Other lettering is for his wife, Ester Ladd, born December 18, 1815, in Herkimer, N.Y.

There's a great view from here. I saw a herd of goats in the distance that looked like dark ink spots on parchment paper.

I walked back to the car. Tushim and I drove to the deserted Gerrells house. The walls are still standing strong. The ground around the house was plowed for winter grain.

I later read about Gerrells in a book on Hamilton County written by the County Historical Commission.

It said Gerrells bought land here for 50 cents an acre. He cut the rock from the mountain to build his two-story house in 1879. The house also served as post office, church, social center, store, and school.

He donated the land for the local cemetery with stipulations that plots were never to be sold but reserved, a measure still in effect.

I backed off and looked at the old house and the string of mountains. I heard the crazy cry of guinea chickens from a nearby farm. Cows grazing nearby looked at me for a moment.

I felt right with the world for a while. And that is why I use any excuse I can to come to places like Indian Gap.

# Chapter 6
# Ghosts

I was repeatedly asked during my writing career if I believed in ghosts.

After years of listening and writing ghost stories, I can truthfully say, "I don't know."

But regardless of my beliefs, there are many people who do believe in ghosts or spirits or something existing out there in the shadows beyond our abilities to define or explain.

I once thought that people's fascination with ghosts was tied to their fear of death. By believing in ghosts, they were endorsing a life hereafter. I do not want to get into religious beliefs about death and heaven and hell. I respect those beliefs. But there are lots of people whose beliefs in heaven are strengthened by believing there are ghosts.

Another fairly common ingredient of ghost stories is buried treasure. I have been amazed at how much dirt has been moved in this state by people looking for buried treasure. Many of these supposed caches are protected by some kind of ghost or spirit.

So back to my beliefs...is there something like ghosts out there? Do they particularly abide in areas where some great treasure is buried? Again I say, I don't know. But I have had some experiences that made my heart go into high acceleration much like the hearts of some of the people I have interviewed on this subject.

# Bridgeport

The story that Edgar Cowling told should be told around a campfire when the moon is hidden by filmy clouds and thunder from a coming storm explodes in the shadows.

But then you wouldn't get to meet his charming wife, Jane, or get a look at some of her beautiful quilts with stunning designs and colors. They remind you of the subject her husband of fifty years tells about...treasure, buried treasure.

Cowling is a slender man with a soft rasp to his voice. He made it clear from the beginning that he has no proof of the story.

"Absolutely none. Nothing in writing. In fact, most people who have known about it are now dead," he said.

But this is the story he first heard when he was a youngster. He told it from his home in this town in Wise County.

"It happened as early as 1838 or later. There was a mule train of ten to twenty mules out of the state of Hidalgo in Mexico with 125 pounds of gold or silver. They were going to St. Louis. Why is pure speculation.

"But on their way through this country, a band of Indians chased them for three or four days. They finally caught them near here... where the old Mexican cemetery is. Killed them. But they had hidden the gold before that happened. The story tells it happened in an area of about two or three miles square."

That area is on land owned by Cowling's family. Beneath it are old tunnels where coal was once mined.

Cowling once saw some huge rocks with funny markings that had been turned over. Beneath them was what might have been a vault carved into the rock. The site was on the Cowling property. Two men came there in the 1930s with metal detectors. One of the rocks was smooth and long and pointed toward a specific spot.

"I went to the house for some post hole diggers," said Cowling. "They dug a hole about five feet deep. Nothing was there."

So the years passed. He was graduated from Texas A&M University, served in the Army during World War II, and came home. And then two brothers, Mugs and Benny, came to him one day and said they had information about where the treasure was buried.

He smiled.

"Mugs convinced me that he had something. I guess that I convinced myself. But one thing that did convince me is that they chose the hardest part of the area to dig in," he said.

They never found anything. At least they told Cowling that. And now both are dead. So does he think the treasure is still there? He answered in that soft rasp.

"I don't want to run the risk of being too sassy like us old-timers who sit around and talk about the old times. I'm guilty of that. I have my doubts...grave doubts. But every once in awhile I think of that area. I think of the three or four years ago that I bought a bulldozer to control some of the mesquite and I found a place that I may someday go back to and do some digging."

Again he smiled.

"I'll tell you where it is. The grass is kind of high. The brush is kind of thick. And the snakes are crawling," he said.

And the ghosts of yesterday are heavy in the area, he said.

So we declined to go. But my friend John Tushim and I sure did talk about it on our way home.

And we didn't even have a campfire.

# Walnut Springs

Kay Moore said most ghost stories have explanations.

As she talked in the nearly 100-year-old building that she owns and thinks has ghosts, a rainstorm gathered outside. Suddenly, thunder crackled like a shotgun blast. The lights went off.

I jumped. She smiled. The lights came back on.

"Now that can be explained," she said. "But there are other stories that have happened here that I cannot explain."

The building, which was closed for remodeling when I recently went through this town on Highway 144 in Bosque County, housed her tearoom and antiques shop. It seemed the perfect place for ghost stories. It once was a funeral home and furniture store.

Jack Norton of Alvarado had told me about the building.

"My dad used to own that old building," he said. "He sold it because he didn't like the dead bodies lying all around and the things happening in there. We still have an old Victrola that came from there. It still plays, kind of screechy-like. But you go talk to Kay Moore. She can tell you some wild stories about that place."

Moore does have some wild stories including the one about how she and her husband found this community. They moved here from Las Vegas where she worked for Caesar's Palace.

"My mother was dying of cancer. She lived in Hillsboro. So we came back to take care of her," Moore said.

While driving around one day, they saw that this building, built in 1901, was for sale. So was a 100-year-old house. They bought both.

But when she first came, she did not believe in ghosts.

"After all, I am a Baptist," she said.

She did find that the building had a history with all the ingredients for a good ghost story...like being a funeral home.

"And under the layers of dust I found some old caskets and funeral shrouds," she said.

The old viewing room for bodies and the old embalming room are still there, but the embalming room has been boxed off. After Moore and her husband, John, acquired the building in this farming community, strange things began happening. One night she and her daughter were working close to the embalming room.

"My daughter suddenly stopped and said, 'What is that smell? It smells like flowers...bunches of flowers.'"

Later Kay smelled the flowers. So have other people. But there have been no flowers of any kind inside the building more than five years.

Then there was the fog.

"I was working late and walked down the hallway past the viewing rooms. There was this thin film like fog on a highway. And it was cold as ice," she said.

That is when she made an agreement with the ghosts.

"I told them they were not going to run me off. But if they would leave me alone in the daytime, I would not bother them at night," she said.

Rain drenched the windows as she talked.

"I'm really not afraid of them anymore," she said. "But if I step out of line, they let me know."

That happened last year during this town's annual rattlesnake hunt. Moore and one of the snake handlers were inside talking after dark. Suddenly, a huge candle sitting squarely on a table rolled onto the floor.

"The snake handler said 'I'm out of here,'" said Moore.

She led my friend John Tushim and me down a dim hallway. We passed the old examining and embalming room. Suddenly, I smelled a sweet odor of wilted flowers. I looked everywhere. There were no flowers.

The old wooden floors creaked like somebody moaning. Tushim stopped.

"What is that? It smells like a bouquet," he said.

I looked into the ceilings with their thin ribbon-like wood boards. They are so tall that the shadows killed the light's illumination. There were no flowers.

"You are standing beside where the embalming room was," Moore said.

I jumped.

"About a year ago, a man came in here and told me, 'You have several ghosts in here. I can sense them,'" Moore said.

We walked to the front, past a door that had handles made from casket pulls.

Thunder crackled again. The smell of the fresh rain was strong and good like the smells of the terrific homemade pies Moore sold in her tearoom.

She does have one thing about her life that suggests ghosts. That's her birthday. She was born on Halloween night 1942.

# Stephenville

Mary J. Clendenin has written a book about a ghost that has tantalized area residents for more than a century.

She probably knows as much about this ghost as anyone. Her father, Joe Fitzgerald, had written numerous articles about the ghost of a woman he said he had known.

"For all of my life, I can remember hearing stories about the ghost at the McDow Hole," Clendenin said.

The ghost supposedly is the spirit of Jenny Papworth. She and her baby mysteriously disappeared in 1880 from the cabin she and her husband, Charles, had built south of Dublin on Green's Creek. Another son found crying inside the cabin could never offer any clue to what had happened.

At the time, Charles Papworth had gone out of state to secure an inheritance. But his missing wife wasn't the only nightmare he faced when he returned.

He was charged with horse theft. A vigilante group hanged him and six others. Among the vigilantes was the man who eventually confessed to killing Jenny.

And the topper was that Charles Papworth's life was saved when his son, Temple, who had been locked in the cabin during the hanging, cut his father down before he died. They fled to Oklahoma shortly afterwards.

All of that makes for fine ingredients for a ghost story in this Erath County country.

"My dad was reared near the McDow Hole," Clendenin said. "He was living when they hanged Papworth, and he never thought Charlie was guilty."

Her father wrote many stories about the case including the ghost sightings, which became quite regular in the late 1800s.

"We used to go fishing there," Clendenin said. "It was such a pretty place."

We talked from Clendenin's home here. She was a strong-looking woman. Cold mist hung in sheets outside, making it a good day to talk about spirits.

Her latest book, *The Ghost of Jenny*, is the second Clendenin has written about Jenny Papworth. In this one she personifies the ghost and blends in her feelings and thoughts. Both books are based on stories she heard from her father. In one story, he told about writing a letter to the local newspaper.

"He said that the killer was still alive," Clendenin said. "He signed it 'Jenny Papworth.'"

Shortly after that a man named Brownlow confessed on his deathbed that he had killed Jenny and her baby and hidden their bodies in a well.

Since then, periodic reports of Jenny's ghost have been made. Clendenin's husband, Ray, laughed about some of those.

"I've seen the ghost," he said. "But it was only old Bill Jones who had rigged up a pulley and a stuffed dummy that he would pull back and forth across the water hole."

His wife smiled. She recalled as a youngster camping at the McDow Hole.

"We were scared several times," she said. "I'm sure there was a rational explanation. But we didn't want the explanation. We wanted to be scared."

The location is a place where it's easy to become anxious, particularly as night is filled with the creek's hollow echoes and cries from nocturnal birds.

In her first book, Clendenin talked about those things. She wrote, "Perhaps our bodies are only the houses we live in, created to be discarded when they can no longer serve their purpose here on earth—perhaps then we merely step out of them as disembodied spirits free to traverse the earth for eternity."

So maybe that is what has happened at the McDow Hole. I've been there at night. I can accept that. Clendenin has strongly captured this possibility in her new book.

# Cleburne

Ken and Donna Davidson have devised one tremendous haunted house for Halloween.

It's called the Death Express and is on the second floor of the 1920 Wright building at 1 James Street here in the downtown. The building has been beautifully restored by the Davidsons in this city, which is the county seat of Johnson County.

On this particular Halloween, the Davidsons along with Halloween specialists had created some truly breathtaking creations from stories about a character who traveled across the Southwest with a specially equipped funeral train.

They should fit in nicely. For upstairs where the spider webs and plastic bodies and parts were being placed, workers began feeling the presence of spirits. Six psychics were summoned, and on separate occasions all reported conversing with spirits. Could it be just a publicity stunt finding these things before the opening of the haunted house?

"It makes no difference to me if people think we invented this just before opening our haunted house. That will ride on its own with or without the ghost. But I am convinced the phenomenon is there," said Donna Davidson.

She had a serious look as she told the story of the psychics going upstairs. And without previous knowledge of what the others had said, all told essentially the same story of talking with a woman with red hair who said she came here in 1882, worked in a hotel, and apparently died of a broken neck after she fell or was pushed from an upstairs window. The psychics picked up the name of Lilly or Joy.

"I think there is something up there. But I am not afraid of it nor do I think it means to do any harm," Donna said.

We went upstairs in an elevator that smelled of age. She told about discovering that a hotel built in 1874 occupied part of the space where the Wright building now stands.

"As for the date of 1882, which is when the psychics said the spirit told them she arrived, that was the year that the first train arrived in Cleburne," she said.

We had stopped in a shadowy corner.

"I can feel something right here...Can you?" she asked.

Well, I did. It felt like fingernails lightly touching the tops of my ears.

Donna stopped at the spot of the old hotel window from where Lilly said she fell. I felt my heart accelerate. The hairs on my arms stood up. But hotshot reporter that I am, I dismissed it.

So we walked on past other exhibits of coffins and the crematorium coach. I got repeated ear tinglings. Finally we walked down the creaking wooden stairway.

Suddenly at the landing, the name "Ruby Thompson" flashed into my mind. I don't know anyone by that name. Then a scene of an old cemetery near Cleburne that I had once written about came into focus. I saw an overturned small tombstone covered by grass.

I did feel strange. Maybe a tad scared just like I am certain the crowds to the Death Express exhibit felt that year in the old Wright building.

# Fort Worth

The story had come from a friend who had read about psychic experiences in a newspaper. He had said the story concerned an elderly widow who claimed that her husband's spirit still lived in their house.

She said that one night a burglar had broken into her home. He was a huge man. He had attempted to rape her. Her husband's spirit had clubbed the man over the head with a lamp and then had knocked him unconscious with another furniture piece, the woman said.

Such chronicles are fascinating. Have they really happened? I don't know. But I've heard enough of them to make me wonder. And certainly they are interesting stimuli for conversations.

So on this day when I was making a long out-of-town business trip with a friend and the conversation had lulled after several hours of driving, I mentioned the story of the widow. I asked the friend if she believed in such things.

Really, I was anticipating a skeptical response. For this is a person who has a pragmatic approach to life. Tell her that the sunset was a blood red a few days ago and if she hadn't seen it, she will respond, "Show me a picture."

With this knowledge in mind, I had prepared myself for a friendly argument. You can call me one of the believers in these things. I assumed she wasn't. Was I surprised.

"The story is probably true. I can believe it," she said. "I don't know whether I would have believed it a few years ago, but I believe it now. Let me tell you why."

She told me about her mother. She said she is a very strong person emotionally. Her love for her family goes particularly deep. Such were her feelings for her husband.

"He and Mother were married thirty-five years before he died some years ago," she said. "He had a rough life. He had a successful business but lost it during the Depression. He and Mother married and had several children, and he had to work extremely hard. He had many years of having to scrape to just get by, and I guess you could call them unhappy years."

Her mother had known him at both times...during his successful years and during the rough years. And after his death, she thought about both times, hoping that he was now happy.

"One day she was at home alone. She was in a very relaxed state. She said she looked up and there my father stood. He was dressed in the clothes he had worn when they were on their honeymoon. And he was smiling. He was happy and he was holding out his hand for her," said my friend. "My mother was not frightened. She knew it was all right. So she said, 'I'll come, but I'm not ready yet.'"

My friend stopped talking. The car air conditioner's humming was the only noise. Then she continued.

"That's happened twice. And neither time has scared Mother. She knows Dad is now happy, and she calls him her friendly ghost," she said.

We drove on. We were in ranching country now. The sun curled its way through the car's tinted windows, making hot patches on my arms.

"And then there was my experience with Betty," said my friend. "I guess that is when I really began thinking about these things."

Betty was her cousin, some twenty-nine years younger than my friend. She had a birth defect that made her life painful and difficult.

"But she was so alive with emotions. She was such a fighter, such a beautiful child, and I loved her so much," she said. "I felt about her like I would a daughter."

When Betty died at the age of ten, my friend felt the loss deeply.

"One day I was at home recovering from surgery. I was thinking about how I could have died and other things. I became very relaxed and almost asleep, and I thought of Betty and all of the pain she had gone through," she said. "Then I heard her laugh, and I felt her touch my arm. It was a warm, loving touch. And suddenly I knew that Betty was in a place where she no longer was hurting and that she was happy."

A large bale of white clouds floated over the sun, making shadows inside the car.

"I've always been skeptical whether there is any life after death. I was brought up to believe it, but there never was any evidence of it for me," said my friend. "But now, well, I know that life after death exists for Betty. I know it. And yes, I think that woman's husband's spirit is inside her house."

We continued our drive toward the west. Suddenly I knew something. I certainly would not go into the house of that first woman without an invitation.

# West Texas

The following story is one of the weirdest ghost stories in which I was personally involved.

So there we were heading into West Texas on this bright, hot day, on perhaps one of the strangest trips I'd ever made. It involved Kit (not his real name), a nice-looking middle-aged man.

He is tall and well built. There's a resemblance to Robert Redford in a certain way he sets his chin and holds his eyes. He's a nice guy and certainly not a nut. Though he says many people would probably think otherwise when they hear about his dream—make that nightmare—and how it has affected him since 1978 (this was written in 1983). The dream kept coming back and back. And each time, Kit was left terrorized. So he had gone to a psychiatrist.

The doctor had helped some. At least Kit had been able to control the dream to some extent. Then on a Monday he had the dream again.

In it he is a monk or some kind of religious person. He is walking up a hill or a mountain. He sees figures chained. They are blaming him for betraying them. He hears voices speaking Spanish. Then he is led into a cave, and he sees piles of gold. And that is when they kill him and a voice says, "They may have your body, but I will always have your soul."

He did not go back to sleep that night. He never can after the dream. He heard the morning newspaper as it clunked against his door. He opened it and began to read. One of the first stories is about buried treasure in West Texas. A rancher has been looking for it for years. He claims the treasure came from Franciscan monks who had taken it from Indians, and, well, it matches Kit's dream perfectly.

So he had called the writer—me.

"I've got to go to that place," he said. "I feel like it may help solve this thing. And I have to solve it. I have got to."

I called the rancher who asked not to be identified. Let's call him Bill. He agreed to let us come to his ranch. So here we were headed to far West Texas to end a nightmare.

Kit watched the country slip by. He repeated several times that he had never been in this part of the country. Then he talked of his nightmare.

"You know, I think that something violent may happen to me if this is the place I have dreamed of," said Kit when we were about fifty miles away. "I don't know what...but something bad. I just have that feeling, and yet, I must go and check it out."

Then we arrived and headed to the ranch in Bill's pickup. He told about looking for the gold for the last ten years and leaving an abundance of craters scattered over the ranch.

"I actually bought dozers and diggers to help me in my search," he said. "I've spent about $150,000 looking for the gold."

Kit asked him if the name Dave had anything to do with the treasure.

"That name has been in my dream," said Kit as the truck bounced down a caliche road, leaving spirals of white dust biting at the windows.

"Let's see now," said Bill. "Yeah, it does. There was a guy from Jamaica came in here and did some looking for the treasure by that name. Tall SOB. Must have stood seven feet tall."

I felt a little funny as Kit looked at me. His face was tight, like wet rawhide left in the sun for half a day.

Then we drove onto the ranch. There were cattle there. Also mesquites with branches heavy with beans. Dust was thick. It was hot.

"I think I have been here. But I really don't know how I feel. It's funny," said Kit. He pointed at a hill about a half-mile in the distance. "I've been there. I know I have. Can we go there?"

Bill drove the truck through some plowed ground. He pointed to a dead tree and said a recovery was made there.

I looked at Kit. Tears streamed from his eyes. He shook with sobs. Suddenly he said, "That hill, I've got to go there...now."

So Bill drove toward the hill. An oil well rig sat on top of it. It was pumping.

We reached the bottom. Suddenly Kit asked Bill to stop. He got out of the truck before it stopped. He started up the hill, which is rough. There were mesquites and dwarf cedars. Huge rocks that looked like whale backs lay on the ground. But Kit was going so fast. It was like...

"By gawd, I think he's been up there before. Look how he found that trail," said Bill.

I asked him if there was a cave on the hill.

"Hell, yeah, right up there where those rocks are. Used to be a cave there but now it's a snake den," said Bill. He spit out a cigarette and hollered, "Watch for them snakes!"

We drove to the top. The sound of a windmill was going, "thunka, thunka, thunk." There were animal trails and dead tree limbs thick with dust and flies. Finally Kit made it to the top. He was sweating. Dust covered his boots.

"It is just like my dream. The trail, the big rocks," he said. His voice was cracking. "I definitely felt like I had made that walk before. I think that is where they killed me."

Bill left. Kit and I stayed. We walked around where some of the diggings had been made. There were sunflowers and the smell of a drying creek. We walked over orange and red dirt.

"Look at my hands," said Kit suddenly. They were white like the blood had left them.

Finally we said our goodbyes and headed back for Fort Worth. Kit said he had ambivalent feelings about the experience.

"To know that I came here and nothing happened, yes, that makes me feel better," he said. "But it doesn't make me feel better that this place looks like my dreams. And as I told you, I have never, never been in this part of the country before."

We continued driving. Kit's face seemed more relaxed, and his conversation was loose and easy.

"I want to come back and do some more poking around," he said. He laughed. "And it won't be looking for the gold."

Behind us, the sun blotted out a huge chunk of sky. It looked like a burning gold nugget. Or a monster's angry eye.

# Chapter 7
# Fiction

I seldom resorted to fiction with my columns. I always felt there were enough true stories and characters around that I did not need to use fiction.

However, occasionally, particularly on holidays, I did use fiction. I never tried to hide the fact. I always wanted the reader to know they were reading a piece of fiction.

But even in those stories, I always based them on a true story I had heard or a real person I had known or heard about.

The reaction to these stories from readers always surprised me. Even though I insisted they were fiction, readers would swear they knew about whom I was writing.

That was particularly true on the July 4th column I wrote in which I mentioned the meanest man in Somervell County. I still have people today stop me and say, "You don't have to tell me who that was. I know."

So far all of the answers have been the names of different people. That indicates to me that either there were a large number of tough people in my home county or fiction is truer than truth.

Regardless, all of the stories in this chapter are mostly fiction.

Old Earl never ate turkey. And finally, one night as we crowded around a campfire on the Brazos, I found out why.

Maybe it was the stiff north wind that made us hug our clothes close. Or maybe it was the few shots of whiskey we took to ease the cold's bite. Or maybe it was the campfire, its coals winking at us like lighted diamonds as we huddled around it.

Things like that free a feller's tongue. Anyway, this is Earl's story and why he always says "no" to turkey.

He was reared on one of those old cedar brake places that turned hard as pig iron during the drought of the early fifties. We were too young to remember the Depression. But, boy, the fifties taught us a lesson in hard times.

Folks did anything to make money. Things they'd ordinarily never consider, like me cleaning toilets at that all-night filling station.

Earl's family raised turkeys. Every Thanksgiving, people came out to buy their turkeys. Stood around looking at them and nudging each other and talking about how fat this one was or that one was, and how good they were going to taste with cornbread stuffed in them and cooked all night.

Earl didn't care until the year he was twelve when he made a pet out of one of the toms. Called him Junior. Trained that turkey so he could lead him with a piece of string. Saved back food from the table and fed him extra.

Junior took to Earl. He would see Earl coming and know he was going to get a handful of biscuits. He would put his wings down to the ground, start strutting, and making that sound that toms make.

Oh, they were a pair.

Then came Thanksgiving. People started showing up to buy their turkeys. Looking at those big birds, smiling at each other and saying, "Boy, he's going to be good all stuffed and cooked."

Soon there were just two turkeys left. Junior was one of them.

Earl knew what was going to happen. So that night he put his string harness on Junior and headed south.

His dad, a large man with a huge gut, found them the next morning cowering in the brush at Salt Flat.

"Earl, what in the hell are you doing?" he demanded.

"I'm running away. Me and Junior," Earl said. "I can't stand somebody buying him and chopping his head off and stuffing him full of cornbread and eating him."

His dad looked at his son holding that turkey. He looped his fingers in his pockets and said, "Well, Earl, I'll just swear."

He stared into the rising sun for a while then turned back to Earl and said, "Take him home. He's yours."

So Earl did. And he and Junior were like a boy and a dog until one day Earl went to get a drink from the windmill and get some water for Junior. Junior was dead.

Earl stopped and kicked the coals in our campfire.

"I buried him somewhere out there on that old place. Had to use a pick to dig his grave, and I cried a little when I covered him up," he said.

He stared at the fire.

"He probably was the only turkey who died a natural death," he said.

And that's why Earl never eats turkey...anytime.

Paul and the rest of us had made our camp in this stand of timber two days earlier.

We'd arrived here about the same time, spilling from boxcars and heading for the trees. We'd been riding the rails for more than a week. But somehow we all headed here for Thanksgiving.

We'd come up with a turkey, a half sack of sweet potatoes, some big sweet onions, and a pot of beans.

So it looked like us men of the road were going to eat well. The turkey was cooking in a mud sack on a huge mound of coals, and the sweet 'taters sitting next to it smelled like something from a king's table.

"Looks like we're going to eat like skinny hogs in the morning," said Tom.

We waited for Paul to flash that smile and agree. We considered him our leader and whatever he said, we did.

Paul said nothing at first. And because I had a king-sized hunger, I didn't figure anything that Paul said would matter.

As the sun crawled up the next morning, I fished around the fire for a sweet 'tater. The smell from the turkey cooking was delightful.

Paul walked up with dew all over his shoes.

"Wake up the others," he said.

I began poking them, but men who had ridden boxcars for several days don't wake easily. Paul stood close to the fire and listened as they gasped and spat and cussed. Finally he said, "I got a plan for our great Thanksgiving dinner. I want to give it away."

"Give it away?" moaned Lender, a man so skinny it looked like his hips might cut through his pants.

"Yeah, I want to give it to somebody who has less than we do," said Paul. "I found them this morning when I was walking."

Well, we argued until the sun burned away the morning dew, and still nobody agreed with Paul.

"Okay, then I'm giving my share away. I'm going to cut up this turkey, take my part, and my part of the sweet 'taters, and give it away. Y'all eat your part."

He started whittling off his portion. Somebody cursed and said, 'Aw, Paul, you are crazy. But don't cut up that turkey. You can have my part."

Slowly we all agreed that he could have our part. And now Paul was smiling.

"Well, let's go then," he said.

We put all of our goodies inside a couple of buckets and began walking. I was getting hungry and ate another sweet 'tater. We finally came to a tiny house in the middle of a meadow and heard noises from inside.

"That's the man, his wife, and their family. That's who we're giving this to," said Paul.

As we approached, we heard a woman's voice say, "I'm sorry, but we just don't have anything to eat but this cornbread."

Paul marched to the door and knocked with that huge hand that looked like a mallet.

A man opened the door. He had black hair and a fairly long beard dotted with gray.

"What you fellers want?" he asked. "But let me tell you. We ain't got no food if that is what you are after. Sorry."

"Don't want nothing," said Paul. "We brought you all something for Thanksgiving."

The man looked scared as Paul handed him the bucket with the turkey. At first he hesitated to take it. But he finally did, and when he looked and saw what it was, he yelled, "Sarah. Sarah. Come here."

A tiny wisp of a woman came to the door. She wore ragged but clean clothes.

The rest of us stepped forward and gave her the rest of the food.

"You sure you wanna do this. You men look like you could eat this," she said.

"Aw, naw, we got twice this much back at camp," said Paul. "We wanted to share. Ain't that right boys?"

We all kinda stammered and really said nothing as three children peeked around their mother's skirt at us. They were cute as fresh-born calves. They smiled but didn't say anything. We looked back at them and winked. Then we started to leave.

"Hey, what are you fellers called?" asked the man. "Bound to be from some kind of group to do something nice like this. Maybe from some church or something."

Paul looked at him and said, "Yeah, we are from a group. We are called the knights of the rail. We're a real select group."

We started walking back to our camp. I hoped maybe we had missed another sweet 'tater in the campfire. But I didn't care. I felt pretty good already.

There's no doubt youngsters can sow acid meanness with their tongues.

Thus it was with Three Fingers, a tall, gangling man who lived in our community.

He lived by himself and always wore overalls. He was a hard worker and most of the time had a grin on his face. Even when the youngsters called him Three Fingers, well, really, Three Fangers, he smiled and went about his business.

None of us knew how he had lost those two fingers. But all he had left on his right hand were the thumb, his little finger and the finger next to that. The rest of the hand was scar tissue that looked like flames when the sun caught it just right.

Since we didn't know how he had lost the fingers, we made up things.

We said he lived in a house with hogs and one of them had gotten so hungry it had bitten off his fingers. We also said it was so dirty in his house, you couldn't see out the windows because of the flies.

Old Three Fingers' appearance discredited those stories because he always wore clean overalls and his remaining fingernails were always clean. He must have bathed often because he certainly didn't smell as bad as some of our dads when they sat down to eat.

But I don't think we really cared how he lost his fingers because we never really tried to find out.

One year about two weeks before our July Fourth parade, we got a little carried away in talking to Three Fingers. We called him a bunch of other things that were pure mean.

That's the only time I saw Three Fingers lose that smile. When we made insults about his intelligence, he pulled out a handkerchief, wiped his eyes, and headed for home.

Right after he left, Bob Tankard, who worked cattle for a living, walked up. He was big and tough as a dried piece of hell.

"What's wrong with him?" he asked, nodding at Three Fingers.

"Aw, we kinda kidded him, and I guess we got carried away," somebody said. "We insulted his intelligence."

"If you can do that to old Three Fingers," snickered somebody.

We all laughed.

Bob's face got a hard look. I saw muscles ripple down both arms as he grabbed a fence post to calm himself and said, "I'm gonna tell you little sucking pups something, and I want you to listen."

Then he told about when he and Three Fingers were kids, they and some others were playing with large firecrackers. Somebody lit one and was about to throw it when he lost hold of it and it fell onto David Spivey's hair.

"Three Fingers never hesitated. He grabbed the firecracker. But he didn't have time to throw it," said Bob. "So he held the damned thing and it blew two of his fingers off. But he saved Spivey's face and eyes, just standing there, holding that firecracker. I'm telling you boys this, because there ain't anything wrong with his intelligence. Okay?"

Bob knew he had made his point two weeks later when the parade took place. And when the man we had long called Three Fingers marched by, we all hollered:

"Way to go...Mr. Curtis."

I hope youngsters learn the dangers of short and fast fuses on firecrackers without injury on July Fourth.

I learned. And it was not without injury.

I was living in the raw ranching country near Midland. One July Fourth I was practicing lighting firecrackers and seeing how far I could throw them before they exploded.

We had to purchase our firecrackers secretly because our father believed that any kind of fireworks ignited on our ranch would trigger a raging grass fire equaled only by Satan's roasting site for sinners.

He equated popping firecrackers to belching loudly or breaking wind during the Sunday preaching.

He would bellow blasts as loud as the firecrackers if he caught us with them. So guess what? Every July Fourth, we secretly bought firecrackers and practiced our throwing techniques.

One day I practiced by myself. When I lifted a lighted firecracker even with my head, it exploded. I felt a blast of pain. I knew my hand was gone, but I wouldn't look at it.

Instead, I ran to a barn where we kept a bin of cottonseed and buried my hand in those seed. I started thinking of how I could somehow always have a large glob of cottonseed around my hand so my father would not know that I had blown my hand off.

Finally I looked at my hand. Lo and behold, it was still there. I thanked God repeatedly, and I promised I would never sin again by doing such things as looking at Essie Mae with prurient thoughts.

I never looked at Essie Mae that way again. But I did resume throwing firecrackers.

Then we moved to Glen Rose. On one Fourth of July, my friends and I gathered on the town square. We were doing patriotic intelligent things like lighting firecrackers and trying to roll them under unsuspecting passersby.

I started one rolling toward a friend who stood with his back to me, but he moved. Backing into that spot was one the toughest and meanest men in Glen Rose.

As I watched that firecracker, my life and all the dumb things I had ever done flashed before my eyes.

When it exploded, that huge head and red face jerked violently around and he saw me. I immediately began thinking where I would like to be buried and to whom I would leave my old horse.

"Did you do this?" the meanest man in Glen Rose demanded as he grabbed my shoulder with huge tough hands.

"Yes, sir," I squeaked.

"On purpose?" he demanded.

"No, sir," I replied. "It was a pure mistake."

He glared at me and then a huge smile broke over the meanest man's face.

"Well, I can understand that. But you scared the $%*$#@%&* out of me. Ha. Ha. That's pretty $%&*+@# funny, now that I think about it," he said.

I stood there with this crazy look on my face. I didn't know whether to cry, beg forgiveness, or laugh.

He still had my shoulder in his grasp when he said, "I said, 'That's funny.' Why ain't you laughing?"

So I began laughing. I sounded like a chicken whose head had been given a twist or two before somebody changed his mind about wringing its neck.

"Go on and have some fun. But remember, be careful with those things," he said.

And that, folks, was the last time I tried to throw a lighted firecracker.

# Chapter 8
# Collectors

I have learned never to be surprised at what people will collect.

The list goes on and on from things that make sense like old plates to things that don't make a lot of sense, at least to me, like nails used to shoe horses.

I will admit after interviewing many of these collectors and looking at the particular item they are collecting, I admire them for becoming so fascinated with whatever it is they collect and the lengths to which they will go to add one of these things to their collection.

I have also discovered that some collectors become so consumed with their collections they are fearful if they share what they are collecting with the public, then they are bound to lose their priceless items to burglars or thieves.

This happened to me twice. I did not object to the collectors having these feelings. But what I did object to was they did not tell me not to write a column about their collections until after I had spent more than two hours looking at the objects and listening to the owners going on at length about why and how they had obtained these things.

However, the columns in this section are from people who willingly shared their collections. Maybe someday I will join them when I make my toothpick collection public.

# Fender Skirts—Whitney

Big Jim Tidwell has never seen a fender skirt he can do without.

"Since I got into this, I've bought every set of fender skirts I can find. I will go to a car show and I will buy every set there," Tidwell said. "I'll even buy singles because I know when I get them home I probably got one to match them. Like I will buy a left fender skirt knowing that I got the right one here."

Such an affinity for fender skirts has earned him the title of Fender Skirt King of Whitney. He smiled when asked about that.

"Yeah, I'm that," he said. "But I'm probably more than that. I'm the fender skirt king of the world."

The building in which we stood had fender skirts everywhere. They were piled high down a lane called Lincoln Lane. More were piled down another lane called T-Bird Territory. And more were piled near a sign that says, "If you don't see what you want, please ask. We have more than 6,000 skirts at home."

"I've got this building filled. I got a 72-foot trailer with a 16-by-40 addition to it and it's filled," he said. "And out back I got about 75 old junk cars and most of them are full of skirts. So, yeah, I'm in the skirt business."

His fender skirt place is on the southern edge of this town in Hill County and sits next to his barbecue stand and convenience store. A phone call interrupted the interview. He took the call inside his office, which is stacked with fender skirts.

"Yeah, this is Mr. Fender Skirt King," he said. He laughed. "Well, we got a few. Now what is it that you need?' A '57 Ford? Yeah, we got that. They're reproduction models. Cost you $89.95. Where you want 'em shipped? South Dakota. Okay. No problem. Let me get your address."

While he talked, I looked some more. A huge pile of fender skirts was stacked like a puzzle. Some were the singles he recently bought. Piles of fender skirts covered an original '56 Ford, a '57 Ford, and a '58 Ford.

Then Tidwell joined me again. He's a stoutly built man with graying hair and a gray beard.

"This deal wasn't planned, no way in the world," he said. "I just happened into it."

That happening came when he began looking for fender skirts for a 1955 Ford Fairlane that he was restoring. The car was particularly special to him because his grandfather, Ivy Gant, had bought it new. Gant, who lived past 100, reared Tidwell here in Whitney.

"Me and him put every mile on that car," Tidwell said. "When I got it, it didn't have any skirts. So I began looking for a pair for it."

That search lasted two years.

"I got to noticing how hard fender skirts were to find," Tidwell said. "So I started buying them. I bought 19 sets for $10 a pair. Then I really got into it. I bought 1,240 sets for $10 a pair in California. Cost me $640 to get them trucked here."

And about then is when Tidwell began buying every set of skirts he could find.

His fender-skirt business has grown so much, he would like to sell his barbecue stand and convenience store and only sell fender skirts.

"That's no small potatoes business either," he said. "I paid income tax on $960,000 gross on the store last year. But I'd like to just sell fender skirts...I've got more fender skirts than all of the rest of the fender-skirt dealers in the U.S."

His wife, Charla, drove up in an original black '56 T-Bird. The car is full of leather and chrome.

She crawled out and shook my hand. I looked at the back fenders of the T-Bird. You know what was there.

# Lightning Rods—Olney

Tony Kunkel doesn't know if the rather elaborate lightning rods on his house work or not.

But he says the rods, purchased by his late father in the early 1920s, have attracted something much worse than a lightning bolt. He told that story to me while a norther thrashed this area in northern Young County. He's a short, wiry man who chews tobacco. He wore two pairs of pants and never shivered as we stood outside in the norther.

"Yeah, them rods attract a lot of attention," he said. "Lots of folks want to look at them."

Then his narrative became rather profane as he told the lightning-rod story.

"I had changed my pants to hay my cattle. I left the pants with my billfold in them on my bed. These two men stopped and asked if they could look at my lightning rods," Kunkle said. "I said I didn't give a ---. So they did. When I came back to the house those two ------ were gone. So was my money and billfold. Those ---- had ripped me off. And, it was all because of them ---- lightning rods!"

The lightning rods are not the only thing on his ranch north of Olney to protect him from nature. He also has an old storm cellar, where people once spent hours sheltering themselves from tornadoes. He said he seldom uses his.

"But, we sure used it a lot when I was a kid," he said.

He raised the door, aided by the attachment of huge steel counterweights made from railroad track pieces. We walked down the stairway. The cellar smelled musty but offered protection from the screaming norther.

A friend, Howard Barton of Archer City, looked at the shelves. He recalled the cellar his family had in Comanche County.

"We kept our tomatoes and onions in it. Also had egg cartons down there that we filled and took to town to sell," he said.

We climbed the stairs. Kunkel then showed us his 1948 Chevrolet pickup that he bought new.

"I'm not going to sell it. It's got a sentimental attachment," he said.

He explained.

He came home after being discharged from the service in World War II, when cars were so scarce that people had to get on a waiting list.

"So in 1946, I got on waiting lists at the Ford, Chevrolet, and International dealers," he said. "Well, '46 went by and I heard nothing. So did '47. Then in May 1948 the Chevrolet man came out and said, 'I've got you a pickup if you want it.' So I bought it. It had only taken me two years and five months to get it."

So we looked at the truck. Kunkle at the time of the interview was seventy-four but did not look his age. I told him that.

"Ha. My secret is two cold Budweisers every day," he said.

I asked for his address. He laughed as he cited it and said, "Give it to all of those single women out there. Tell them to come see me. I'll show them my lightning rods."

What a line that would be.

## Cushman Scooters—Blum

Randolph Garner had his share of stress when serving as superintendent for the Blum School District in this town in northern Hill County.

But he had a rather unusual way of getting relief. He spent time with a buddy named Fred. And after driving the back country roads with Fred, things don't seem nearly so prickly.

Fred is a 1955 Cushman motor scooter. He'd been with Garner for thirty-two years when I interviewed him. And he seemed destined to stay as a visit to the house of Garner and his wife, Charlene, indicated.

Garner is a huge, solidly built man with thick fingers. On this day his fingers were grease-stained from working on Fred and other Cushmans, Vespas, and Mustang motor scooters.

Garner led the way into a building behind the house. There was a sign that read, "Garner's Classic Scooters."

"You have to understand, I got into scooters in 1962. Come on in and I'll show you my first one," he said.

Inside were shelves of parts for Cushmans, Vespas, and Mustangs. There was also a 1936 Dr Pepper soft drink box and old style bottles of soft drinks.

Garner walked past a line of restored Vespas and into a side room. There was Fred, painted bright red and completely restored.

"This is Fred; I paid $55 for him," Garner said rather proudly.

Garner was fifteen at the time and lived in Tatum, New Mexico. He had a paper route, and Fred replaced an Allstate scooter.

"Let's see if old Fred will start," Garner said. He pushed down the crank with his foot. Fred started on the second push. His engine made that old familiar "puca, puca, puca puca" sound.

"I like all kinds of scooters, but Fred hates the others," Garner said. "He has even written a book. Here, he'll give you one."

He handed me a book titled *Fred: The Story of a Cushman Scooter.* Another line simply reads, "By Fred."

"He'll autograph it for you," Garner said.

He pitched the book onto the floor and pushed Fred's front tire over the book, leaving his tire marks.

Beside Fred was the last Cushman Eagle motor scooter made by the Cushman plant in Lincoln, Nebraska, before it closed years ago.

We walked into another room that has among other things, an old milkshake machine that still works; an original Daisy Red Ryder BB gun; and an old, tall Dr Pepper ashtray.

Garner told how he became engrossed in restoring scooters.

"I had left Fred in New Mexico until about 1971 and brought him here. Then I started restoring him, and I bought another scooter. Other folks thought I was crazy, but about 1981, other people started joining me in restoring old scooters," he said.

As a result of the interest, Garner founded the Texas Cushman Club in 1983. Then he organized the Vespa Club of America.

He talked of why people are so fond of the old scooters.

"They were bulletproof bikes," he said. "They were made for dependability and long life and could be abused and still run."

The events that owners experienced on their Cushmans left solid memories. One man told Garner about the time he was so angry at his father, he climbed onto his Cushman and drove all the way from Houston to Fort Worth. And then there was the man who took all his dates with him on his Cushman.

Garner mentioned the pressures of being a school superintendent.

"Fred and I will get mad. So we will go out and burn the roads up at 25 or 30 miles an hour," Garner said.

And as the wind grabs his red beard and sometimes brings tears to his eyes, the pressures evaporate with Fred's exhaust fumes.

It takes about 30 minutes. Not a bad prescription.

# Antique Tractors—Meridian

Some people don't have to figure which antique tractor they will take to a show because they probably don't have that many antique tractors anyway.

Duncan Seawright is not in that category. When he goes to a show, like the Texas Early Day Tractor and Gas Engine Show held in Temple, he has a problem deciding which one of his tractors to take.

He has more than 100 of the antique farm behemoths.

"I don't know how many I've got," he said. "Probably about 110. But if you ask me about a particular brand or size, I can tell you if I have one or not."

Seawright is a strong-looking man. On this day he wore overalls and a white T-shirt, fitting attire for an antique tractor collector. He chewed on a cigar as we walked through his tractors, which resemble giant steel dragons and praying mantises.

"I have a policy not to buy anything until I have finished what I am working on," he said. He smiled. "But, I haven't exactly followed that. I'll find something and get excited about it and I'll buy it."

Although Seawright is a retired pharmacist and drugstore owner, a look at his huge, scarred hands makes one realize that he has worked in the fields and on his tractors.

"Oh, yeah, I do all of my own work," he said. "I've learned that if you have a hacksaw and a file, you can make or repair anything on these."

And, yes, he was reared on a farm in this county (Bosque) about fifty miles south of Fort Worth. And he has the first tractor he ever drove, a 1937 Avery that his father acquired for twelve mules. It's parked in the long rows of tractors patrolled by a pit bull dog.

Seawright is full of interesting history about each one. Like the huge 1910 steam engine tractor that came from a mine in Colorado. The massive size led to the downfall of the steam engine tractors.

"They were so large it took half their power just to pull the tractor's weight," he said.

He showed a one-cylinder International built in 1914. Then came a two-cylinder International followed by a four-cylinder model. Yet, they were sold by different dealers.

"That is why in the early days of tractors, more than 800 different tractors were sold," said Seawright.

He said the early tractors all had at least one major design flaw as we stopped to look at one of his rarest tractors.

"There's probably only six of these left," he said. "Look at the front end, which is their weak point. It weighed so much that when they hit a small hole or rock the front end would break."

The four-cylinder engine sits crossways on the frame, and the radiator is about three feet in front of that. A long fan belt that looks more like a conveyor belt turns the fan blade.

He showed another tractor that has the engine sitting to the left side. Its value came from the fact that farmers could pull their horse-drawn equipment with this model. Ah, but when they plowed on an incline, the tractor, because of the engine sitting to one side, tended to turn over.

"So the company sent a man through the country to talk to the farmers who had bought one of these," said Seawright. "He helped them pour concrete into the right wheel for balance."

Sure enough, the tractor's right rear wheel was filled with concrete.

Then we walked into his shop piled with parts and tools and filled with the smells of grease, oil, and gasoline. He pointed to an antique motorcycle.

"That is a 1914 Harley-Davidson," he said. "I'm rebuilding it."

When it is completed, he won't have any problem deciding which antique motorcycle to ride in parades. It's the only Harley he has.

# Buttons—Mansfield

Whenever Cynthia Boatman and her mother got separated from her father in some mammoth department store, he knew immediately where to go.

He went to the button counter.

"Mother and I always eventually would be there," Cynthia Boatman said.

Well, it still is a good place to look for her today as evidenced by her vast button collection. She has no idea of how many buttons she has. But she has buttons everywhere in her house in this town south of Fort Worth.

She showed a board of buttons made for her husband, Joe, who plays golf. Naturally, the buttons all have to do with golf.

As she retrieved other buttons from her collection, she laughed about her husband's reaction to her hobby.

"He doesn't mind the money I spend. He only insists that I keep good records so when he puts me away he will know what they are worth," she said.

Then she showed me another board of buttons. They are all heart shaped. Some are old. Some are new. Some are tiny. Some are large.

"Now look at these," she said. "They are genuine pearl, and I found these while I was on a bus trip to Amish country."

We kept walking past buttons made of horn, wood, and plastic.

"And under this glass case, and thank goodness the grandkids haven't figured out how to get inside, are more buttons made of pearl," she said.

They are of all shapes and sizes. We walked past a lamp made from a quart jar. Naturally, it is filled with buttons. Close by are buttons made in the eighteenth century in England. Some are exquisite, and as I looked at them, I couldn't help but wonder whose pants or blouse these buttons once held closed.

"Now, these are my very, very favorites," said Mrs. Boatman. "These are called enamels."

They are indeed pretty, with vividly colored flowers and designs.

"And, here is my collection called buckle buttons because each one has a buckle on it," she said. "And here's another group called pictorial because each button has a pictorial object like an anchor or stirrup."

So I asked her what was the big attraction for her for buttons?

"Well, gosh, they are just fascinating. They are just little works of art and they are all so different," she said.

The answer reminded me of my younger days when for entertainment on rainy days I would take down my mother's button jar and make formations and build castles with them.

And of course, anytime one member of our family lost a button from a shirt or coat, you could always find us at the button jar, looking for a replacement as well as having fun.

## Marbles—Desdemona

Don't say Garth Priddy has lost his marbles.

He hasn't. He had something like 25,810 marbles the last time he counted them. That took two days. And since then, he figures his marble count has grown considerably.

"I figure I have more than 30,000 marbles today," he said. He looked at me seriously. Then he flashed a huge smile that comes frequently. "I never met a marble I didn't like."

That certainly has been true for the past several years after Priddy was told by his wife, Nelda, to get a hobby.

"So one morning at 4 A.M., it came to me. I woke her up and said, 'I got it. I'm going to start collecting marbles,'" he said.

Nelda, a middle school principal, shook her head at the decision.

"He has gotten a little carried away," she said.

Priddy, an agricultural science teacher, does love his marbles. We shared some marble experiences from childhood during a visit to the couple's ranch near this town in Eastland County.

"Ever play keepers?" I asked.

"Does a pig like corn?" he replied.

"Ever win so many that your pockets bulged, and the teacher knew what you'd been doing and whipped you because keepers [a form of gambling] was forbidden?" I asked.

He nodded his head as he continued showing his collection.

We looked at marbles called Indian swirls and Jacob coats and onionskins. All have different colors and swirls that give them their names.

"There are something like 3,200 names of marbles," Priddy said. "They are made everywhere but Texas. There never has been a marble plant here."

He showed marbles that look like catsup and mustard. He showed Nelda's favorite, a Lutz, with green, white, and gold stripes.

Then he showed a marble that looked like it had an eye inside its red and white swirls.

"Nelda hates that one," he said.

That marble and others are valued by their condition, size, and eye appeal. They cost from $1 to $3,000, and a collector has to be careful about what he is buying because there are marble frauds.

"Here's one of those," he said. "This is called Mississippi Mud."

It is a pretty marble. When Priddy saw it in an antique store, he felt he had to have it.

"The story was that this marble was seen in the banks of the Mississippi while a family was going down the river in the late 1800s. They stopped and got it. Supposedly it was the only one like it," he said.

He paid $100 for the marble.

"That same day, Nelda and I went to Austin to a convention. While there, I went looking for marbles. I walked into a place selling marbles. There on the wall were twelve Mississippi Mud marbles for $3 each."

Even his grandfather wasn't beyond some shenanigans when it came to marbles. He had one that he told Priddy if he held it just right, he could see a blue rooster crowing.

"You won't believe the hours I spent holding that marble every which way trying to find that rooster," Priddy said.

There was no rooster inside the marble. When he found out the truth, Priddy did feel like he had lost some of his marbles.

# Caps—Stephenville

One thing is certain when T.C. "Tucker" Pemberton goes out each day. He won't have to worry about having a cap to wear.

Lined up six deep on shelves stretching from ceiling to floor in the den of the home are 4,811 caps.

When I interviewed Pemberton, he had caps from every state as well as from twelve foreign countries.

"I've only bought about 10 percent of them," said Pemberton. "The rest have been given to me."

Well, that's not exactly true. Pemberton has done some trading for the caps.

One of those times came while he and his wife, Joyce, were in Edinburgh, Scotland. Pemberton as usual had a shirt pocket stuffed with cigars as they walked the streets.

"We saw these men coming down the street with red caps on. The caps were from the sausage company the men worked for in Sweden," said Pemberton. "I stopped them and told them about my collection and that I certainly would like to have one of their caps. They saw my cigars and asked if I would trade some of them for a cap. I did."

We sat in the living room of the Pemberton home. He's a pleasant man and puffed on a cigar as he talked about his unusual collection. He said he actually started collecting caps while he was working in Fort Worth. He and Joyce had a relative who wanted a cap from the Caterpillar Co.

"She had tried unsuccessfully to get him one so I started trying to get him one," said Pemberton.

He was successful. And the morning he received the caps, he saw a man he knew who worked for Allis-Chalmers.

"So I asked him if they had any caps," said Pemberton. "He said they did and gave me one. That started my collection. Before that, I didn't even wear a cap."

Some famous people have added their caps to his collection. One is Red Adair, the famous oil-well firefighter.

"That cap is a hot item," said Pemberton. "It must be worth about $100 today."

Pemberton got that cap like he has gotten the rest. When he sees a cap he wants, he asks for it. Such was the case with Dan Devine, then coach of the Green Bay Packers professional football team.

"I saw a picture of him one day and he had on a cap," said Pemberton. "So I called his office and asked him if he would send me a cap. I had to ask him three times before he knew I was serious. Then he said, 'I've never had anyone ask me for a cap before.'"

But he sent Pemberton a cap along with an autographed picture.

Actually, Pemberton said he had only had one person who refused to sell or give him a cap.

"Then I met one of his sales representatives and he gave me a cap," said Pemberton.

One unusual event happened when he discovered a Midwest banker who sold caps to his customers.

"So I called him and told that I had a cap collection," said Pemberton. "He seemed pleased and sent me three caps. I have always thought that was funny. He charged his customers for caps but sent a complete stranger three of them free."

But things like that make him enjoy his cap collection.

"I enjoy stories like this as much as having the caps," said Pemberton. "A lot of times the chase is as much fun as getting them."

He also enjoys wearing the caps and has worn half of them at least one time.

"Right now, I'm trying to get a cap from every county in Texas," he said.

Then he led the way into the room where the caps are stored. Included are caps from Arm & Hammer, Black Diamond Oyster Bar, The Booze Box, and Rooster Run General Store.

So does he have a favorite?

"Well, that's hard to say. But I do like the caps I got from the cattle ranches owned by Leroy Jordan, Nolan Ryan, and Chuck Howley," said Pemberton.

But really he has never seen a cap that he didn't want to add to his collection.

# Penguins—Granbury

Anyone who visits Ruth Anne and J.R. Erwin, had better like penguins.

Visitors will see bunches of penguins from the moment they arrive at the couple's log home here in this city in Hood County.

There's a penguin flag flying from the porch.

Walk onto the porch. Delightful sounds come from wind chimes shaped like penguins.

"Come in," J.R. invited.

"What is this...a penguin floor mat?"

He laughed.

"You have to like penguins if you live here," he said.

He introduced Ruth Anne, his delightful wife of forty-three years. She has a story about each of the penguins in her house.

"I have over 1,000 different penguins," she said.

"It is easy to buy her a present. I just buy a penguin," said her husband. "That is if I can find one she doesn't have."

That is hard to do. She has a telephone shaped like a penguin. She has penguins embossed on umbrellas. She has cookie jars shaped like penguins and thirty-two penguin coffee cups.

So how in the world did this fascination with penguins happen?

By accident really, she explained.

"In 1981 I was looking for a present for a niece. I saw a penguin made out of burnished copper," she said. "I didn't buy it. But later I started thinking about how neat it was and went back to get it. It was gone."

That started the penguin collection. And guess what?

"That is the one kind of penguin that I've never found," she said.

She has plenty of other kinds, and she can talk for hours about real penguins as she shows off her collection.

For example, the emperor penguins are the largest. They stand up to four and a half feet tall and weigh 120 pounds.

"Here's a penguin made of Murano glass," she said. "I heard about this one from a San Angelo rancher. His son-in-law called me and said, 'I've got something you might want.' He did. I bought it."

She stopped at an umbrella with a penguin painted on it by her husband's sister-in-law, Jan Erwin.

"Yes, I use it," said Ruth Anne.

She picked up a large plate with seventeen kinds of penguins painted on it.

"This is a little blue fairy penguin. It is only eighteen inches tall and lives in Australia. It is the smallest of all penguins," she said.

She stopped in front of potholders with penguins. And over there was a bowling pen penguin. And an ice scraper shaped like a penguin. As I looked in awe, she cited another penguin fact.

"You see a lot of paintings with penguins standing with Eskimos," she said. Well, whoever painted those didn't know feathers about penguins.

"Penguins don't live on the North Pole where Eskimos do. Penguins live on the South Pole," she said.

And, speaking of feathers, penguins have seventy feathers per square inch.

So what kind of penguin does she not have? She does not have an egg timer penguin. Or a mailbox penguin. But she does have a horseshoe shaped like a penguin and a penguin made of dust off Mount St. Helen. And bathroom penguins holding brushes and paper.

"I can't even go to the bathroom without seeing a penguin," J.R. said.

# Old Cars—Valera

Three cows about ready to calve grazed in the front yard of Grady and Helen Laws' home.

"Your lawnmowers?" I asked moments after being greeted by a strong handshake from Grady Laws.

"Naw. That yard is my maternity ward," he said. "They get close to calving and I put them there. That way if they have trouble at night, I can just get out of bed and help them."

Helen laughed.

"Tell him about the winter you and the vet did that Caesarian right there on the front porch," she said.

"Yeah, we did. Had snow and ice on the ground. But we saved the calf," said Laws.

That's the kind of thing you expect from him after talking with him awhile. He's a genuine cut from the west. Stands six feet three inches, has huge, rough hands and a big nose and red face. Blue eyes that look like patches of indigo cloth. Their ranch is in this community in Coleman County.

Laws wears a big black hat that he never took off during five hours of conversation.

"I built this house," he said. "Hauled every rock up here from the pasture. Let's see. I spent $16 for some lumber. And that was it. Come on in, you want some coffee?"

We walked inside. The smell of coffee boiled over a wood stove spilled heavily into the room.

"That stove is over 100 years old. Helen loves cooking on it," said Laws.

Helen nodded.

"Not too bad once you get used it," she said.

They also heat the house with wood.

"Every winter I cut loads of wood. I bring it to the house and push the furniture back and stack it there," he said.

Helen poured coffee. She wore a long, blue print dress. She has graying hair and is pleasant. Grady pulled a can of Prince Albert and a wad of cotton from his shirt pocket. He moistened the cotton and stuck it in one end of the cigarette.

"That's my way of making my own filters," he said.

Then Laws told about some of the ways he saves money. Like freezing eggs.

"I was getting several dozen a day. All that the dogs wouldn't eat," he said. "So I decided I'd freeze them. Leave them out at night and by morning they are thawed. Then you can scramble them. They taste real good."

He was born on a ranch about seven miles from Valera.

"Quit school in the eight grade. There were a lot of horses to be rode and I could make a dollar a day doing it," he said. "You sure could buy a lot of chewing tobacco and soda pop with a dollar a day."

Helen smiled as he talked. They married in 1956. She was working in Washington for a congressman. She had met many interesting people.

"But, I never met a character like Grady," she said.

He laughed and led me outside. Near the front gate is a huge rock stuck in the ground. It stretches to eight feet in height.

"I call that my pet rock. Claim that I planted it and it just grew," he said. "Had some friends tell me that if it ever bloomed and made seeds they wanted some of them. So one day I picked up some pebbles and gave them to them. Said that rock had finally bloomed."

A huge Brahman bull stood near the front fence. Laws reached over and began to pet him. The bull had mud on his horns and flies on his back.

"This is Old Hump," Laws said.

I looked at him and asked about his hat.

"You ever take that off?" I asked.

"Not much," he said. "I feel half naked without my hat."

Then I looked at what amounted to the durndest collection I had ever seen. It was a long line of cars that surrounds Laws' barns and corrals. Somebody had said he still had every car he ever owned.

"Well, I've given a couple away. But I still got most of them," he said. "But it's no big deal. I'm not collecting them for antiques. It's just that when I get through with them, nobody will pay anything for them. So I just keep them."

Helen had joined us.

"Tell him about the VW, Grady," she said. "Goodness, you ought to see how he loads that thing down with goats."

Laws grinned and pointed to a VW sitting in the row of cars that curls around the place like a giant snake.

"That's one I wouldn't sell," he said. "When the nannies start kidding, I go out in the pasture and fill it up with the nannies and their kids and then bring them back to the house. You'd be surprised at how many goats you can get in that thing."

Helen agreed.

"He's hauled goats every way," she said. "But one day I looked up and here he came on his motorcycle. Had a nanny in the basket."

She laughed again.

"That's the reason he married me. He needed a car," she said.

"Well, my old Chevy's block had froze and busted. So I figured it was cheaper to marry her than buy another car."

Grady then gave me a tour of his corrals. Cattle milled around the pens in which several cars were parked. He gave a history on many of them.

"Here's the car that I came to this country in. That's an old '42 Chevy. Durned good car," he said.

We walked to another corral. He pointed at a 1956 Plymouth.

"That was a good car. But it had a push-button drive and I didn't trust it," he said. "So I parked it and when my boy got to be five, I told him, 'Son, here's you a car. You can do anything you want with it.' Well, he took that thing apart, piece by piece. He learned a lot doing that. Plus it kept him out of meanness."

We walked to the front porch of a three-story frame house built in 1914. Grady lived there before he married Helen. Inside are piles of ancient items, including old hats, boots, and antiques.

"This sidesaddle," he said, pointing to a saddle with leather cracked by age, "well, I traded a pocketknife for it. That bed over there belonged to my mama. I think I was born in that thang."

We walked back outside and he showed me a forge he had made from a vacuum cleaner.

"Gets metal so hot it will melt," he said. "Great for repairing axes."

Or straightening the fender on a car. Not that Grady worries too much about that.

(An ending to this story...I visited with Helen in 1998 after Grady had died. But she has left his cars winding around their ranch. "They were as much Grady as they were cars," she said. "I kinda like to look at them when I get up in the morning and think of him.")

# Windmills—Tolar

Finding Chuck Rickgauer's place is no problem once you make the right turn off Highway 377 east of this town in Hood County.

Just continue until you reach a road with windmill after windmill after windmill spiraling on each side all the way to the Rickgauer house.

On this day Rickgauer waited for me. He's a strong, big man with a moustache and a deep voice. He becomes almost hyper as he talks about his hobby, windmills. And get this, he is deathly afraid of heights.

"The only way I go up on one of those is if I have two safety belts on," he said. "And even then, I'm still afraid."

Then we went back to the start of the road, and he gave a history of each of his windmills.

"That is a Nebraska Stub," he said, pointing to a squat-looking windmill. "It was made in Nebraska where they had plenty of wind. By using this short tower, it was cheaper."

We stop at a Ward's windmill that cost $37 new. It is a simple machine with only two cogs and a spring to help make them turn.

"This is a Dust Bowl [Depression] mill. To save money, they only painted one side of the tail," he said.

We drive past windmills with oil-impregnated bearings and windmills without vanes or tails. We drive past a double-geared Sampson built in the early 1900s. We stop at a Model 702 Aeromotor.

"This was the one that started my collecting," said Rickgauer. "My wife [Ruby] listened to it when she was just a girl on the family farm in South Dakota. Her mother gave it to us, and we brought it here."

When Rickgauer reassembled the mill, he did it exactly as his wife's father had left it, including replacing an old pitchfork through the pumping mechanism.

We then drove to his workshop, full of parts of old mills.

"This is my bone pile. Most of these will probably never be anything but parts, and the attic is full of blades," he said.

He told about having a degree in electrical engineering, spending twenty years on nuclear submarines, and moving here to work for Texas Utilities at its Comanche Peak plant. Then windmills became his hobby. He loves it.

"Every one is unique and a challenge," he said. "I take them all the way down and do the whole thing rather than just fix a blade or a gear. And I try to do a different one rather than the same kind again and again."

He showed me some unusual jury-rigging in the old mills.

"These are ball bearings that somebody put in one," he said. "Notice that they are different sizes."

He has found mills everywhere. And actually he would rather find one lying abandoned in the weeds than standing up.

"That way, you don't have to do anything to get it down," he said.

Another thing he discovered about windmills came from L. Lindsay Baker's book *Blades in the Sky*. An old-timer told Baker that the West was not won by the six-gun.

"It was won by water and barbed wire," he said.

That's why Rickgauer loves collecting them and why he and Ruby named their place the Windmill Farm. Their love is not that unique. I have met many people in my travels who feel deep affections for windmills. And one who lives not far from Rickgauer and shares this love is Glendon Stokes of Granbury. He doesn't collect them. He photographs them and has more than 1,000 pictures of windmills from across Texas and the southwest.

He has captured windmills on film in all kinds of places. There are windmills with heaping mounds of prickly pear nearby with yellow flowers and gnarled mesquites. There are windmills near old falling-down corrals and weather-beaten ranch houses. There are windmills with cattle drinking from troughs of fresh water beside the windmill tower.

Stokes' love for windmills goes back to his childhood on a West Texas farm.

"We had two windmills. They were a necessity since we didn't have electricity and relied on the mills to pump water," he said.

They were such a necessity, if the windmills needed work, the family would quit plowing to work on them.

It wasn't until after he took a photography course to learn to take better pictures of grandchildren that he began photographing windmills. He was on the road then, making his living as a salesman, when he saw an old windmill sitting near some corrals.

The next week when he passed the windmill, a bulldozer was splintering its wooden tower.

"I think that is when I really started taking pictures of them," he said.

And today, well, his wife, Bobbie, said, "We never go anywhere that he doesn't find a windmill."

He said he has found others who enjoy windmills as much as he does.

"These people will let you hang around all day if you will talk windmills," he said.

Such was the case at a homemade windmill he discovered in West Texas. A man had built the entire thing himself.

"When I told him I would like to take a picture of it, he invited us out," said Stokes.

"And he started talking and we nearly spent the whole day there," said Bobbie.

Stokes said he thinks one reason people love windmills lies in their importance in developing the West. He made a statement much like the one attributed to the old-timer in Baker's book.

"I think they were one of the most important tools for conquering the West," he said. "People talk of the Winchester [rifle] conquering the West. But I think it was the windmill. If you had no creek or river, you had to have a windmill to survive."

And the music they furnished at night as the wind spun their blades was wonderful.

# Chapter 9
# Celebrations

Folks will throw huge celebrations in memory or honor of almost anything.

A person need look no further than in the sections in newspapers and magazines listing coming events for proof of this. As a writer, I attended my fair share of these occasions and even served as a judge in many of them. As far as I know, I never suffered any permanent damage from such participation though I have had afflicted upon me severe cases of sunburn and a few hangovers. The later came from having to fortify my courage to judge such things as stew and chili made from ostrich and emu meat.

But most of the celebrations are great places to find a day or weekend of fun and entertainment. And most of them, like Granbury's annual General Granbury celebration, are fine for the family.

The following are just a few special celebrations that I attended and which I felt were entertaining and somewhat unusual.

(Writer's note: My wife, Jane, is often asked if she participated in any of the things that I was invited to do. She did several times. But on a particular Veteran's Day celebration, I not only asked her to participate but to write about her experiences. Here's her story.)

## Anvil Shoot—Hamilton

Me, shoot an anvil?

How did I get myself into this, and what am I doing up at 4 A.M. on a Sunday?

Those thoughts bounced through my head as we drove to the American Legion Hall here in this town in Hamilton County. A rooster crowed at the darkness broken by bright stars and a quarter moon.

Just as we arrived at the building, a thundering explosion roared from behind the structure.

"You've just arrived at the anvil shoot," Jon said.

The smell of sausage cooking poured from the hall and mixed with the outside odor of wood fires. Many people wore gimme caps that said, "American Legion Post 222. Anvil Shoot. Hamilton, Texas."

I still didn't understand exactly what an anvil shoot was. I was soon to learn.

Post members James White, David Lee, and Charles Warsham prepared two anvils, the huge steel objects used in blacksmith shops. They poured black gunpowder into a small hole in the top of one and made a trail of powder to its edge. They placed a second anvil on top.

"Most people in the community know about the anvil shoot," said Warsham, event director. "But a lot of them don't know what it stands for."

As they made final preparations, Bill Snell, post commander, explained. He said when World War I ended, word reached Hamilton by telegraph about 4:30 A.M. The telegraph operator dashed to the cotton gin.

"In those days, sounding the gin's steam whistle alerted the community of big news," said Snell. "But that morning there wasn't any steam to sound the whistle."

The messenger ran across the street to Frank Homes' house. His son, Frank Jr., eighteen, had just received his draft notice.

"The telegraph operator yelled, 'Frank won't have to go. The war is over,'" Snell said. "The Holmeses were so happy that they shot an anvil to wake up the community to tell them the good news."

Lee nodded his head at the anvils.

"These are the same anvils the Holmeses used in 1918. Weigh about 180 pounds each," he said.

"They've been shot every year since 1918," said Warsham.

Roy Chumney took his turn. He picked up a fifteen-foot metal rod from the fire. It had been heated until its end glowed red. He pulled the rod across the black powder. Suddenly it exploded.

Afterward Chumney said the shoot was once held in the center of town.

"It woke everybody up," he said.

His mother, Celia, eighty-four, remembers those days.

"The whole Liberty school came over to the shoot in a wagon," she said. "I've always been able to hear it from our place until they moved it out here."

"Need another shooter," someone yelled.

Snell took my elbow and guided me toward the fire.

Warsham grinned and told me, "Just hold the handle and place the metal rod at the far end and drag it across the gunpowder."

I did as he instructed. Nothing happened on the first try. The rod was reheated. The same thing happened.

"We'll try it one more time," said Lee.

He handed me the rod. Its end glowed red like the lips of a young girl experimenting with her mother's lipstick.

"This has to be it. Third time's the charm," I said.

It seemed like I hardly touched the anvil the third time when the gunpowder exploded in a jarring "KABOOM." I closed my eyes.

"That was fun," I gasped. "That one was for you, Frank Holmes. And for all the others touched by World War I."

# Goat Cookoff—Brady

I'll bring home another trophy after this weekend.

The honor is given for rendering services in a contest. Many of my friends question my participation in such an event.

I eat goat meat.

It's not nearly as bad as some think it sounds. Barbecue goat, particularly as will be prepared at the Annual World Championship Barbecue Goat Cookoff held here on the Labor Day weekend, is really delicious.

Of course, this is goat territory. They raise them by the thousands in this ranching country in McCulloch County where a person can drive for miles without seeing much other than a goat or a sheep.

"They had to figure out something to do with all of those goats," said my good friend Eddie Sandoval of Fort Worth and head of the psychology department at Tarrant County College Northeast Campus, who was reared near here. "So they started cooking them."

Sandoval is responsible for my becoming a judge.

"Hey, I've got something that you will really enjoy," he told me before my first contest.

So I came here on his reference and at the invitation of Kathy Roddie, then executive vice president of the Brady Chamber of Commerce. It has become an event that I don't miss, though I did resign as a judge a few years ago. But it's still a blast to just come here and get your goat meat fix.

They have more than 100 cookers show up each year to participate for prize money, which really isn't that much.

"It's the idea of being named superbowl champion that motivates people to come here," said Jerry Baird of Snyder and former superbowl winner. "After all, how many people can say, 'I'm the superbowl champion goat cooker of Texas.'"

Because of people like Baird and their expertise in cooking, there is some superb goat cooked in the contest. Superbowl participants are made up of former first-place winners.

But judges aren't the only people who get to eat goat. Gilbert Currie, probably as good a goat cooker as anybody in this country, heads up a team that cooks goat meat for a giant Saturday luncheon at Richards Park when the event is staged. For a few bucks, a person can eat all the goat he or she wants.

There's also the usual contests found at country fairs. And there are some held here that you won't find at others.

Like the goat pill flip-off.

"Yes, they really use what you think they do in this contest," said Roddie. "And believe me, some of these people can really flip one of those things a long way."

I've forgotten the exact distance. But it is close to 100 feet when you get to the goat pill flipping championship.

There is also the tortilla toss in which kids try to toss a tortilla into a sombrero.

They also have reinstated, due to popular demand and the threat of a lawsuit, the women's tobacco spitting contest. Mickey Baird, wife of Jerry and a past winner in the contest, suggested the lawsuit after the contest was dropped.

"I love participating in this," she said. "Besides, it gives me something to do while Jerry is up there judging goat."

Spectators number in the thousands. And finding an available motel room is almost impossible because they are booked for months in advance.

"You might find a place in Brownwood," said an official "That's about fifty miles north of here."

Other activities include a Saturday night street dance on the town square and a giant arts and crafts fair.

Describing the contest results in some funny lines. One of the best I ever heard about the event came when Tracy Pitcox, popular local disc jockey, was interviewing an old-timer about the contest the night before it started. Pitcox asked the man how he felt that night.

"Well, Tracy," the man replied, "I'm sure glad I'm not a goat."

## Good Ole Boy Stew—Commerce

The afternoon is pregnant with humidity and the feeling of a coming rain.

We sense it as we head down a gravel road east of this town in Hunt County and find the bridge over twisting Smith Creek lined by a company of pecans, walnuts, and oaks with huge limbs rubbing against each other like humans elbowing each other at a dice game.

Down on the banks of the creek are three huge iron pots with spirals of smell and steam already leaping upward. Coals looking like foggy red traffic lights lick at the black bellies.

Yeah this is the place. This is the spot of the Lytle Stew. And over there on tables made from doors, men are waving away flies as they slice onions, celery, and tomatoes. And, hey, bring me another beer while I cut up this huge pepper, will you.

Dr. Jerry Lytle of East Texas State University here in Commerce and Joe Fred Cox stand there. They talk about the possibility of rain as they watch a low gray clot of clouds in the west, hanging there like timid boys on the edge of the social circle at a new school.

"I've been doing this for twenty years," says Lytle. "I started out doing it for my friends that I played football with and worked with at ET. But I can't draw a line on folks that raise cotton or anyone else. So everyone's invited. You tell him, Joe Fred."

Cox, who has taught history for twenty-five years at ET, smiled.

"Well, there are two traditions in Commerce," he says. "The Lytle Stew and the Cottonbelt Railroad."

He laughs.

"Let me tell you. There'll be junk dealers and millionaires out here. And they'll totally be level."

Level?

"Means equal in this country," he explains.

They leave for Dub's Liquor Store in town. That's where various people are leaving supplies for the event. Down at the table, Dr. Jack Bell, retired ET journalism department head, chats with Brodie Campbell.

Campbell is large with thick arms and a mass of graying hair. His eyes are stuck back in pockets, and he reminds you of one of the friendly pirates from Treasure Island. His voice booms as he recalls his football days.

"Remember, Dr. Bell, we used to play hard," he says.

"We had more fun than Ben Gum, the richest man in the world," roars Campbell.

"You mean Ben Gump," says Bell.

More people arrive. More stories bounce off the huge trees.

"Know how to pick the best puppy in a litter?" one man asks. No one does. "Take the puppies from the mama and then turn her loose. First one she goes to, that is the best puppy in the bunch."

Smells from those black pots grow stronger. One holds chicken. One beef. One, Lytle laughs, is road kill from nearby Highway 11.

More people arrive including Ben Bickham.

"No, I'm not a jock," he said. "Just a longtime friend of Jerry."

More stories. Fond remembrances of Lytle's father, Clarence, who made all the parties until his death.

"We'd sit him right in the middle, and we'd all talk to him," says Campbell. "He was a fine man."

His voice stops. He's crying.

Thunder booms.

"Lytle, I've always said that if you had any influence in this precinct, you'd talk to God and tell him not to rain on your stew," says someone.

Lytle smiles. He walks to a stew pot, sticks a spoon into the mixture, and draws it to his mouth for a taste. He smiles again.

"Stew's ready, boys," he says.

Men fill bowls they've brought with the thick, delicious concoction. They laugh, punch at each other, and return for refills.

"You talk about the flora and fauna of this area," says Cox. "This is it."

A gash of lightning licks at the ground. Suddenly, those clouds lose their timidity. Rain douses the area, hitting the fire in spurts and causing sizzling echoes.

What an ending for the annual Lytle Stew.

## Antique Village—Weatherford

The efforts that Mary Kemp and her family expend for their annual open-house tour of the family ranch are almost unbelievable.

They have created a frontier village that includes log cabins, an old school, a barbershop, and other facilities from the past.

Each year they seem to find something new and different to make the tour even more enjoyable than the past ones. Of course, the visitors to this free event are the ones who profit from this work. But for Mary Kemp, who has long studied and preserved the history of Parker County, just seeing smiles on faces of children and others is the only reward she expects.

"We have got to save our history and things that make us aware of that history. There should be no motivation for a person other than knowing that he or she has done or is trying to do this," she said as she gave me a preview to one of the tours generally held the second weekend in April. Times for the event are always posted in the local newspaper.

Mary had led me into a 100-year-old tin-roofed frame building.

"Okay, this is my school. It looks like the old Mount Nebo School that was south of here and where my daddy went in 1910," she said.

Actually, the building had been a barn on the Kemp ranch.

"It was covered with tin and I had decided to make a work shed out of it," she said. "But when we got the tin off and I saw those four windows, it reminded me immediately of the old Mount Nebo School. So I said, 'Boys, let's clean it up and move it down toward the cabin.'"

Mary, long an antique collector, has added old school desks and other things from the 1910 era.

"The teacher's desk and chair came from the Mount Nebo School," she said of the school that was closed in 1916.

Half of the building is an old church. She laughed.

"I call it Mount Nebo School and Church on Sundays," she said.

Next to the school is the combination grocery store, filling station, and post office.

An old hand-powered glass-topped gasoline pump sits in front. Inside the tiny building is a huge glass candy case that is filled with penny candy during the tour and given free to the children.

"Now, come next door and see the old barbershop," said Mary.

Inside this building that was once a railroad line shack are two 100-year-old barber chairs donated by Mack Martin of Weatherford, whose father barbered for years in that town.

"Look over here," said Mary.

There, behind a movable partition, were an adult's and a child's cowboy bathtub. A sign read, "Bath in first water, 10 cents. Second water, 5 cents. Foot wash free in third water."

"The numbers mean how many people have taken a bath in the water," said Mary.

We walked outside. She gestured at an 1895 log cabin and a house built in 1918 that was full of antiques and dolls.

"Of course they will be on the tour," she said.

Also on that tour were free buggy rides, gospel, country, and folk music, and historical reenactments.

"I want people who come here to leave with a little better understanding of how people lived back in those days," said Mary.

She has certainly accomplished that.

# Bob Wills Day—Turkey

Thousands arrive at this town every year on the last weekend in April to celebrate Bob Wills Day.

The celebration, which sees the streets in this small village packed with vehicles ranging from Cadillacs to Chevrolets to pickup trucks, is held in honor of the late Bob Wills, who was reared on a cotton farm in this country and learned early in life to play the fiddle. Wills later went on to create western swing when he added horns to his western band, called the Texas Playboys.

Wills and the Playboys roamed the countryside during the Depression years, drawing thousands to where they played. They also recorded many famous hit records, including "San Antonio Rose," still ranked today as one of the top selling songs of all time.

A highlight of the Bob Wills Day event is a Saturday afternoon concert, featuring the remaining members of the Texas Playboys. These sessions are always recorded and released for sale later. During the recording, security is tight around the stage. Nobody, and I mean nobody, is allowed up there except the musicians and the recording crew.

Well, nobody apparently told Loyd Cox that. As a result, Jane and I saw Cox do one of the durndest things I'd ever seen during this celebration that I have attended many times.

When the Playboys began playing, Cox just by gosh crawled up on the stage and turned on his tape recorder. He loved Wills music. And besides, his buddy Chock Criswell wanted him to get the band to play "Twinkle, Twinkle, Little Star." He badly needed a recording of that number.

It wasn't that Cox wasn't noticed by the several thousand at the concert. He was. He had on a pair of striped overalls. He had on a gray shirt, its pocket stuffed full of pencils. And he had on this striped railroad cap, its brim turned up. So it was hard not to notice him.

Cox stayed up there 45 minutes. He probably would have stayed longer but Criswell called him over and said, "Loyd, remember, 'Twinkle, Twinkle, Little Star.' Go ask them. Now. Loyd, I've gotta have it."

So Cox strolled over to the fiddle player and asked him to play the tune. That's when the officials making the album realized Cox was not supposed to be there. They asked him to get down.

"Well I got me 45 minutes of it, so I just deiced to get down. I didn't want to cause no trouble," said Cox.

So there he stood with this tape recorder stuffed inside a fancy leather case. It was the first time that Cox and Criswell had ever come to Bob Wills Day. They decided to get up early that morning and come here from their home in Sayre, Oklahoma. They look like men who enjoy Wills' music... working type men.

Cox has brown eyes that have been showered by the sand. Criswell was wearing gray jeans with a light-colored shirt, a black western hat, and black cowboy boots with paint splattered here and there.

Cox pulled a sack of Union Standard chewing tobacco from his pocket and loaded his jaw with it. He offered both Jane and me a chew. We declined so he worked on his chew, spit, and began talking.

"I write country and western songs," he said. "Yeah I do, and some of them are purty good."

Criswell shook his head in approval. He encouraged Cox to tell more about his songs.

"Well, one is about something that happened in Oklahoma. They had this crooked judge who applied for the job after another one quit. And they had a new attorney and marshal in this little town," he said. "One day this guy was coming through there and they arrested him on a traffic violation and throwed him in jail. When they let him out, he claimed they made him put up his false teeth for security for the bail."

He chewed his tobacco and spat. He said, "So I wrote me a song about that. I call it 'False Teeth Security.' Wanna hear it?"

We did. So he hummed a little and then recited some lines.

*When you are traveling through this city and you ain't got*
*long to stay.*
*Keep your teeth in your pocket and take a bypass way.*
*Cause the police in this city are the meanest guys around.*
*For when you run a red light, they will run you down.*

He laughed then. So did I. So did Chock. So did Jane. So did several other people standing with us. Cox told about another song he had written.

"It's about this hostess on a bus that is called the five-star. She used to come by and drink coffee with me. So I wrote a song about her. I called it 'Vickie on the Five-Star.' Yawl wanna hear it?"

We didn't have time. Then Criswell started talking. He said he played the fiddle and has written a few songs himself. Most are waltzes. He said that he is retired from the well-drilling business and he plays in fiddle contests. Last year he won a first. He played "Twinkle, Twinkle, Little Star" and "Liberty." Both are Wills' numbers.

"I got me a 26-inch trophy with a silver fiddle on top. I also got this nice camera here," he said. He pointed at a Polaroid camera hanging from his neck.

"The reason I asked old Loyd to get them to play that song is that I have never heard a tape of it, and I just figured if I could get it, well, it sure would be nice," he said.

Then Criswell and Cox said they had enough on their tapes so they were going home. As they walked away, Cox hummed another verse from "False Teeth Security." It went:

*And when the judge finds you in this city, and you ain't got*
*a dime*
*Put your false teeth up for security and travel on down the*
*line.*

Made sense to me. Sounded pretty good, too.

# Chapter 10
# History

Somebody accused me of using the term history rather loosely.

"A person of some renown can just spit on a tree, and you will make a big deal of it," one reader once accused me. "There is nothing historic about a bunch of people sitting around in sand trying to heal themselves."

She was making reference to the series of columns I did on the healing sands in the Newburg community. Maybe she was right. But I disagree in that I find things like that leave long lasting memories, and to me, that earns them a page in the history of our state.

Believe me, getting off the main roads and past the well-marked spots of history can lead one to many locations where something interesting or unusual happened. Take the cemetery in Peaster in Parker County. That is where Jack Fox is buried. So what is so special about Fox? Well, he was Buster Brown, who once traveled across the country promoting Buster Brown shoes.

I love writing about such people. Plus I love writing about what really can be classified as history like the New London school disaster in which 293 students and faculty members were killed in an explosion.

There is no doubt about the historical value of that tragedy.

## Sitting Sands—Newburg

There's not much, really, in this tiny community in Comanche County.

And as one drives through the countryside, it's hard to imagine that once these roads were lined with cars and people. There was even a landing strip where people flew in from as far away as South America.

They came for their health. They brought bodies wracked by arthritis and a variety of other debilitating diseases. Many left claiming they had been cured.

This cure had come from either sitting or lying in dirt dug from the countryside and poured into cattle troughs. The dirt earned a variety of names. They called it sitting sand and uranium dirt. It was bottled, packaged, and sold at counters in Texas airports.

Old pictures of signs that strung out along the road then show the imagination used to attract customers. One read, "Native Dirt. Gov. Tested. Sitting House. Welcome. It's air conditioned at U-Reign."

Another read, "For sale here. Original Comanche Chief Brand Uranium Dirt. Not warranted."

There was no medical evidence to back up the claims. But, gosh, that didn't matter. The people poured into this country for a period of years that began in the early 1950s.

James F. "Jim" Hallmark of nearby Comanche once delivered mail in this area where it all started. As he drove Doc Keen and me down a dirt road, mesquite tree limbs slapped the side of his pickup. He recalled what it once looked like when throngs of people came to the sitting sands.

"There were cars everywhere. They were lined up along this road all the way back to the highway. Airplanes were flying in. Oh, let me tell you, it was something," he said.

We arrived at the Jesse Reese Ranch where the late owner is given credit for first enticing the multitudes to come to the sitting sands.

Reese died August 10, 1957, in these pasturelands after drinking a poisonous concoction. Friends say his death was brought on by his owing a huge tax debt to the Internal Revenue Service.

His widow, Emma Mae Reese, was still alive and living on the ranch when Hallmark brought us here. She lived in the white-frame home sitting amid the mesquite flats. She had gray hair combed high, a good strong voice, and a quick recall of those days.

There was a touch of bitterness in her stories as she talked of the sitting sands and working eighteen years to pay that tax bill.

"I was born with a stick of honesty," she said. "I believe in paying your bills. So I paid that $15,000...all of it."

She said there were many stories about how the sitting sands started. One magazine article quoted her late husband as saying he suffered from phlebitis, an inflammation of veins in his legs. He said one day in 1952 he walked to his stock tank and felt his leg begin to tingle. He made regular visits to the area and eventually was cured.

Then in the fall of 1953 a man sat in a ditch by the tank, said Reese. It cured him of a variety of aches. The story got out. People began to flock to the Reese ranch. The family began charging $2 each to let people sit in the sands.

Mrs. Reese shook her head over the magazine story.

"Jesse did make a dam down there. And I think he found the dirt and sat down in it and it made him feel better," she said. "I learned a lesson here. My husband is gone and this busted our lives. We were just fifty-five when he died. We were in our prime. I'm telling you, this was something back then."

A headline in the *Comanche Chief* about those days read, "Comanche farmer strikes pay dirt as ailing folk beat path to door."

For a while, the family did find a gold mine in the dirt on their 417-acre farm and ranch. Customers numbered in the thousands before Mrs. Reese finally closed the business in the late 1950s. Even then, she still had people come to sit in the sands.

"I let them. I decided long ago that if it would help someone, I would just give it to them," she said. "I'm not saying it will help or hurt. I've got a woman from Baytown who comes every year and stays. She says it helps her eyes and knees."

So has it ever helped her?

"I don't have time to sit around in dirt," she retorted.

But she did show us where thousands once camped out.

"We had eight trailer houses, a landing strip, a hamburger stand, and a café. There were lights everywhere. It looked like a city at night," she said.

We walked into what once had been a dairy barn. The old wooden troughs are still filled with dirt.

"I hauled that in myself in a number-three washtub and then carried it in here in a wheelbarrow," she said.

A musty, earthy smell mixed with the odor of small animals was heavy.

"We had 1,500 one Sunday. Charged them $2 each. But I want to tell you something. I took a tenth out of what I got. I put it into a jar and then I would take it to the Lord on Sunday," she said.

We walked outside. The smells of winter were abundant in the oaks and mesquites. Mrs. Reese told of the closing.

"I just got tired. That's why. I paid the bills and I closed it down," she said.

Far off, a crow cawed out its message, a lonely echo ripping through the mesquites and oaks where once excited voices of thousands spoke of finding new health.

## Buster Brown—Peaster

As a result of missing the dedication of a monument for one of this city's famous residents, I met Mrs. Crystal McCarty.

After spending an hour with this commanding, forceful woman, I felt like I had been at the ceremonies on March 15 in this community in Parker County.

They included the dedication of a state historical marker for the Peaster Cemetery and a monument for Jack Fox.

Fox, who attended school here in the late 1800s, was Buster Brown, a character who traveled thousands of miles promoting children's shoes for many years before and after the Depression.

Getting those markers was the result of strong work from several in this town. One was Mrs. McCarty, president of the Peaster Cemetery Association and a long-time resident here.

She greeted me at her ranch house with a fierce handshake and a sudden spate of words. Her cattle grazed nearby.

"Oh, I love my cattle," she said, grabbing my hand and more or less ordering me to follow her inside to look at photographs of the ceremonies.

She has short hair, is seventy-eight and a retired schoolteacher, as evidenced by many of her ex-students being at the dedication.

"Here are the photographs. We had over seventy people there. Look, here is Raymond Hardin Jr. I taught him at Annetta. He sang 'Amazing Grace' and 'When the Roll Is Called Up Yonder'," she said. "My, he has a pretty voice."

Then she gave some history of Jack Fox, who became Buster Brown. He came here about 1885 and only stood four feet tall when he was grown.

"Some people with handicaps sit down and let the government feed them. But he didn't. He made the most of his life," she said.

Further information about Fox, who died in 1961 in Fort Worth, came from his sister-in-law, Mrs. Doris Dodson, who spent two years getting facts about him and the cemetery.

Mrs. Dodson said Fox was working as a railroad timekeeper when he was offered the job as Buster Brown because of his size.

"He was reluctant. He had never done any acting. But he took it," she said.

It was a good choice as he delighted thousands of youngsters for years as he and his dog Tige traveled around representing the Brown Shoe Co. of St. Louis. They'd perform tricks, including one in which Brown would ask Tige to pick the best shoe out of a line of shoes.

Of course, he'd go to the Brown shoe and pick it up with his teeth. As a result, Fox won wide respect.

"Although only 4 feet tall, Mr. Fox will stand forever tall by those whose lives he touched," read the words on his gravestone etched and donated by Ron Gaskill of Weatherford.

Near his grave is the historical marker for the cemetery, named after Henry H. Peaster, who settled here in the 1880s.

The cemetery sits off a road in a clearing. Cattle soaking up sunshine watched me as I walked across a loose carpet of acorns that made crunching echoes. An armadillo picked its way out of the nearby brush and dug for grubs and bugs.

His antics were delightful. Maybe it was because he was only half-grown. But somehow he gave me a better appreciation of Buster Brown.

# Frank Buck—Gainesville

We chased the dreams about a jungle pith helmet here.

John Tushim, a long-time friend, had as a youngster like so many of our generation been fascinated by the famous jungle explorer Frank Buck. Buck was known for capturing animals and bringing them back to this country.

So one day Tushim's father bought him a pith helmet with the words, "Frank Buck. Bring 'em back alive," written on it.

"I wore that thing until the letters faded off. I played like I was Frank Buck's assistant and going on those wild trips with him to the jungles," he said.

So when our friend Tom Dodge told us Buck was born here in 1883 and that Dodge was doing research for a magazine article on him, we joined him for a trip to Gainesville.

Dodge related the history of Buck as we drove. There had been a book written about his adventures, *On Jungle Trails*, that had been used as a textbook for Texas school children.

We arrived at the Morton Museum of Cooke County, a small, neat museum in the downtown area. Curator Shana Powell met us and fetched an oil painting of the famed Buck.

He looks like Clark Gable in the painting. He holds a cigarette, and a monkey clings to his right shoulder.

"We don't know who painted this," said Powell.

But, she said, there are many who know that Frank Buck was born here. She showed a book with that information.

Besides Buck, another famous person was born in the area—Gene Autry.

So do many people inquire about the famous Frank Buck?

"Oh, yes," she said. "Just last week I got a call from a man in New York who was trying to find some of Buck's relatives. He wants to start a restaurant with a Frank Buck theme."

Then she made a confession.

"I didn't know he was born here until I came here for my job," she said.

We thanked her and visited several antique stores, asking about possible Frank Buck items.

"No such thing," said one owner. "The locals suck 'em up before we can get them on the shelf."

We headed for the Frank Buck Zoo. The erudite Dodge told about reading *On Jungle Trails.*

"It had photographs in it. One showed this huge snake. It had crawled into a pen that had some pigs. It had eaten one of the pigs and had become so engorged it couldn't get outside," said Dodge. "I had nightmares about that snake."

I told about seeing a Clyde Beatty-Frank Buck circus when I was a youngster in Midland, Texas. But I didn't buy a pith helmet. Other ranch boys considered them sissy headgear.

We had reached the zoo at Leonard Park. A brochure said it is the only small, free admission zoo within 200 miles. It is open year round and has an elephant, monkeys, bush cows, and Texas longhorns.

I asked a youngster standing there if he knew who Frank Buck was.

"Yes, I do," he said. "He's the guy who shot Billy the Kid with a machine gun."

Well, okay. So did he know what a pith helmet is?

"Yes, I do," he said. "That's the kind of helmet Nate Newton [Dallas Cowboy lineman] wears."

With that, we put on our pith helmets and went home.

# School Disaster—New London

The man's face showed little emotion until he described the sound he heard on March 19, 1937.

"I had served in World War I, and when I heard that sound like a dozen of those big cannons going off at once, I immediately knew something bad had happened...something terribly bad," he said.

The shattering explosion apparently came as a result of gas coming from a leaking valve on a boiler in the basement of the New London School. A spark from the school wood shop triggered the explosion.

I don't remember the man's name. I interviewed him on the anniversary of the tragedy. After my story appeared, the late John Butner of Cleburne, long-time newsman, funeral home director, and friend, contacted me.

"I was there after the explosion. Here, read this someday."

He gave me a copy of his memories of that event in which 293 students and faculty members were killed. A plaque near the school site lists the toll at 311.

Butner was a funeral home director in Cleburne at the time and, like many others, had been summoned for help.

"News reports were sketchy," he wrote. "We left before daylight on that morning, and the magnitude of the disaster began to be realized when we stopped at a funeral home in Corsicana and some of the bodies had already been carried there...many miles from the scene."

Butner had gone to the Crim Funeral Home in nearby Overton. He had passed the demolished school.

"It closely resembled what is left now when a building is imploded or blown down. What seemed to be hundreds of volunteers were removing the stones by hand, being careful not to cause further injury to possible survivors," he said.

The Crim Funeral Home converted a twelve-car garage into a morgue.

"Prior to this time, disasters of this magnitude had resulted in mass burials or cremation. But it had been decided that each body would be prepared and individual funerals would be held," Butner said.

A fire hall was converted into a warehouse for caskets that had been shipped from all over the state. Butner was asked to take a victim, a young girl, to Pleasant Hill Cemetery and conduct a funeral service.

"When we arrived at the cemetery, we found scores of oil field employees opening graves. The extent to which the tragedy had affected the lives of the community was realized when we asked six men to be pallbearers and four declined because they had deaths in their own families," said Butner.

He recalled the silence of survivors as they identified victims.

"The shock was so great there were no outcries, just a seeming numbness as they nodded their heads to indicate their loved ones," he said.

Butner's memories triggered many others from people like James C. "Buddy" Cooper who lived in the area at that time. He felt like he had been at the scene when he heard the explosion. He wasn't. He was standing in his backyard about four miles away.

"I was in kindergarten but I was at home that day," he said. "I was in the backyard playing. I heard a tremendous explosion and then saw something that looked like a giant cloud rising."

His young mind strained with apprehension. He knew his sister Helen was at the school.

"But she had just gone out of the band hall and was standing outside," he said.

Legrand Buddy Knight then lived in Tyler. But he and his mother were probably among the first to get word about the explosion.

"My father was a civil engineer for the Cotton Belt Railroad. In those days, breaking news came via the telegraph. As a result, the railroad telegrapher received the news and spread the word," he said.

His father called his mother and told her about the disaster and to stay off the highway. They did not. They drove to New London.

"It looked like a war zone," Knight said.

He and his mother leaned against a school bus as they watched rescue efforts. Officials said they were going to move the bus but wanted to check inside it first.

"At the rear of the bus, they found the body of a fifteen-year-old girl clutching her books. Somehow she had made her way out of the rubble to her bus," he said.

One good thing did come as a result of the explosion. State officials ordered the addition of ethyl mercaptan to natural gas, which is odorless, to give it an odor.

"This is, according to some sources, the most powerful smell in the world," said Thomas Ryugo who has extensively studied the results of the tragedy.

# Coal Mining—Thurber

Follow Don Woodard around in this once thriving coal mining town and you'll swear he was born here.

Balding and bespectacled, Woodard looks like a college professor who would eat a student's lunch if the assignment is not completed. He can spout reels of information about this town seventy-five miles west of Fort Worth in Erath County. Things like there once were 10,000 people of some twenty nationalities living here, making it the largest city between Fort Worth and El Paso.

But Woodard never lived here. He learned those facts during six years of research for his book *Black Diamonds! Black Gold!*, published by Texas Tech University Press.

"I started writing this story of the Texas Pacific Coal and Oil Co. while recuperating from back surgery," said Woodard who lives in Fort Worth.

This is an interesting area to visit, as Woodard learned. The nearby towns of Strawn and Mingus both are prominent in coal mining history. Mingus, today a tiny, quiet village, was once known for its abundance of nightclubs and saloons where customers could not only find booze but someone to fight if they desired.

These facts flow from Woodard like oil gushing from wells in nearby Ranger, which eventually led to the demise of coal mining here.

We looked at a mountain of shale that looked scalped.

"Brick came from that. Brick that was sent to building the sea wall at Galveston. Brick that was used in Camp Bowie at Fort Worth and on Congress Avenue in Austin came from here," Woodard said.

W.K. Gordon, long-time superintendent of Texas Pacific Coal and Oil, whom the miners from Italy and Poland called the "Bigga Boss," discovered the clay.

"He was like a Midas. He had some mud on his boots analyzed and discovered it was good for clay. That led to brick making," Woodard said.

Actually, Texas Pacific was organized in 1888 in the old Mansion Hotel in Fort Worth. That came after Col. Robert Dickey Hunter made a deal with W.W. Johnson, who owned area coal mines.

"Jay Gould [early wealthy railroad baron] came here. And do you know why Gordon is not in the union pictures? He hated the unions," Woodard said.

The unions came after a meeting in 1903 in Fort Worth with John L. Lewis, union scion.

"Some people think Lewis came here. But he never did," Woodard said.

But it was a strike by the union in 1917 that eventually closed the coal mines. That came after oil was discovered in nearby Ranger and replaced coal as fuel for many uses.

So while we strolled around and Woodard gave his travelogue, Leona Roberts stopped us.

When she asked who he was, Woodard boomed out an answer.

"Well, my uncle was bookkeeper for the company and I was born just a short distance from here," she said. "I can remember going to the movie here and you know in those pictures of that old saloon..."

She hesitated.

"You mean The Snake?" Woodard asked, referring to a Thurber saloon known for its mirrors.

"Yes, that's the one. Well, I have those mirrors in my house. One of my relatives died, and my late husband discovered them packed in a box under a pile of junk. And that big old rolltop desk that belonged to W.K. Gordon...my cousin has that and it is in Stephenville. Say, I bet your book has all of this in it. I think I'll buy one of them."

As she and Woodard talked, from somewhere out there in the hills once laced with mines came the screech of a hawk, sounding like the whistle echoing the end of a miner's day.

# Dr Pepper—Dublin

Milly Walker's decision to change careers from medical technologist to collections manager of the local Dr Pepper museum might have seemed drastic.

But it's really not. Whereas her medical knowledge helped save lives for forty years, she is now saving Dr Pepper artifacts.

She loves her new job at the Dr Pepper Bottling Co.'s museum in this city west of Stephenville in Erath County.

As far as history goes, this plant is the oldest Dr Pepper bottling plant. The soft drink has been produced here since 1891, when the late S.H. Prim opened the doors to the Dublin Bottling Works.

Walker and I talked from inside the Old Doc's Soda Shop in the bottling plant. It has beautifully restored soda fountains from which comes the original Dr Pepper made with pure cane sugar.

Walker told how she came here after working in medical technology in the Waco and Austin area.

"I decided that I wanted to do something different," she said.

Different meant taking classes in museum study at Baylor University. That led to a six-month internship at the Dr Pepper corporate headquarters in Dallas.

That led her to be named curator of the Dr Pepper Museum in Waco.

During her work there, she frequently visited with the late Bill Kloster, long-time owner of the Dr Pepper plant in Dublin and a long-time collector of Dr Pepper items.

"His collections were truly amazing," Walker said.

After Kloster's death, his grandson Mark Kloster took over plant management and contacted Walker.

"He said he wanted to preserve the story of the local plant as well as the memory of his grandfather and to appropriately display the collection that his grandfather had spent most of his life putting together," Walker said.

That collection is indeed a full one. There are rooms stuffed with Dr Pepper artifacts.

As a result of his collecting, Kloster's knowledge of Dr Pepper items was legend. Walker told of a person calling her after he had found an old Dr Pepper vending machine. He thought it might not be authentic because it was painted a light brown, a color not normally associated with Dr Pepper.

"I called Bill, and he immediately said, 'Oh, that is the Queen Ann model. They didn't make many of those. Give me the man's address and I will send him some information,'" Walker said.

She offered other information about people who had been on Dr Pepper posters, all of which Kloster had collected.

Those poster people included the wife of Dean Martin; Barbara Hale, the actress who played Perry Mason's secretary; Ronald Reagan; and Jane Wyman.

"He had stuff in every cubbyhole," said Liz Albrecht, Kloster's niece and museum director. "We are still finding things."

The collection has a wide appeal, as shown by last year's 20,000 visitors. And you have to stand in line to get in the museum during the once-a-year Dr Pepper week here. That's also when they change the name of the town to Dr Pepper.

## Hilton Hotel—Cisco

Few people know that this city is where hotel magnate Conrad Hilton had his first hotel or that nearby Eastland is the home of Old Rip, a horned toad that survived thirty years entombed in a cornerstone.

But first the story about Hilton. Had it not been for a bank owner's greed kindled by an oil boom, Hilton probably never would have gone into the hotel business.

Those facts are here in a rather plain two-story red building with thick fingers of mortar. The structure is the Mobley Hotel, the first that Hilton acquired and one of the few that he did not rename after himself.

I had first visited the hotel years ago after an elderly man from Alaska bought it with the idea of turning it into a retirement home. After his death, the hotel closed. Homeless people often sneaked inside to sleep. Deterioration began.

"It was in awful shape," said Eris Ritchie, a local businessman.

That's when the Hilton Foundation in Houston quietly purchased the building. It gave the hotel to the University of Houston School of Hotel and Restaurant Management. The idea to refurbish the building and start a branch of the school here turned into a headache because of the distance.

"So they agreed to let us have it if we would restore it," said Ritchie.

"Us" is the local Conrad Inn Memorial Park and Community Center Park, of which Ritchie is board president.

"Small towns like ours are hard pressed to find something unique about them to attract people," he said. "We felt that in the vein of American success stories, the fact that the story of Hilton hotels had their beginning right here is quite remarkable."

And that brings up the remarkable fact that Hilton ever bought a hotel in Cisco, with a population today of 4,120.

Ritchie told some of that history, which is given in an excellent video about Hilton inside the hotel open for viewing seven days a week.

Hilton, a New Mexico native, came to Texas in May 1919 to buy a bank. The oil boom had struck and few financial facilities were for sale.

When he reached Cisco, the town had gone crazy from the oil boom in nearby Ranger. But there was a bank for sale.

"However, the owner was gone and by the time he got back, he elevated the price," Ritchie said. "Hilton withdrew his bid and came to the Mobley to spend the night."

Business was so good, people were slept in eight-hour shifts. So Hilton changed his mind about buying a bank. He bought the Mobley. He guaranteed spotless accommodations and good meals in its forty rooms.

From that beginning, he became owner of 270 hotels around the world by the time he died in 1979. He never forgot Cisco, as Ritchie discovered during an hour visit with Hilton in New York in 1971.

"He had fond memories of Cisco," said Ritchie. "He laughed about that bank deal. He said, 'You know, if that guy had not gone up on the price, I'd probably bought that bank. And if I had, I probably never would have gone into the hotel business. I'd probably be just a retired bookkeeper living in Cisco.'"

There's much history about Hilton in the Mobley, which has been rehabilitated with a $1.2 million grant. There are two rooms upstairs near a museum that are typical of those first rented by Hilton. The museum is small but packed with local history and photographs.

In nearby Eastland, which is the county seat of Eastland County, a person can find plenty of photographs of Old Rip. He was the horned toad that made this city famous in 1928 when workers opened a cornerstone on the courthouse and reportedly discovered Old Rip still alive after having been placed there thirty years earlier in dedication ceremonies.

If a person wants to find out something about this famed horned toad, then they should visit the Toad Lady.

The Toad Lady is Bette Armstrong, and she's crazy about the little lizards whose numbers have declined so much that they are now listed as protected.

During a visit, Armstrong beamed as if she had just found a treasure. She hadn't. She had found a horned toad near the town of Carbon.

"We took our grandson Forest John Waine to see this one," Armstrong said. "That was his first horned toad to see."

Just talking about horned toads makes Armstrong's blue eyes flash like neon signs. She loves the history of Old Rip, and she pays homage to the horned toad at home. She has a silver horned toad necklace, a horned toad toothpick holder, and a horned toad lamp.

A sign on her pickup says, "Caution, I brake for Horned Toads."

Armstrong is probably one of the few people, maybe the only one, who makes stuffed horned toads. She spends three hours on each one of these 18-inch-long models, which sell for $25.

But back to Old Rip, which some people claim was just a publicity stunt. That claim becomes downright blasphemous during the annual Old Ripfest, generally held here in September.

"We will have seven people here at this year's Old Ripfest who were here and actually witnessed the disentombment of Old Rip," said Armstrong.

So how did Armstrong become so wrapped up in horned toads?

It started when she was a youngster in Lubbock and found them everywhere, she replied.

"And I have loved bugs, snakes, and lizards all of my life," she said.

When Armstrong and her husband, Jim, moved here in October 1993, the local newspaper bemoaned the fact that no one had ever made a stuffed horned toad to honor Old Rip.

The Toad Lady went into action.

"Jim and I worked four months designing and building the first stuffed horned toad," she said. "And that is how I became known as the Toad Lady. I have made hundreds since then, and I have even made a costume that I wear to schools and in parades. Here it is."

She showed a photograph of her wearing the Toad Lady costume. Actually, she looked more like the creature from the black lagoon. But children see her, hug her legs, and say, "Oh, I love you, Horned Toad Lady."

That makes her about as happy as finding a horned toad. When she does find one, Armstrong said, she acts the way she did when she was five years old and found one.

"I am walking along, and then I see one on the ground, and I can't believe it, and I go kind of crazy," she said.

As if she's found a "disentombed" treasure.

# Old Bridge—Bluff Dale

They don't make bridges like they once did. And that is unfortunate. Those old suspension bridges with their cables and nuts and bolts brought emotions quickly.

Seeing them swaying across the rivers and creeks and hearing their aches and moans brought amazement of how anyone possibly could have built such a structure. They also brought a feeling of excitement as you wondered if the darn thing would hold as you walked or drove across it.

But you looked at those old steel contraptions with their huge bolts and nuts and you felt a pride in work that was much more evident then. Here was something that required some sweat, hard work, and busted fingers and profanity.

Such is the Bluff Dale Suspension Bridge in this community on Highway 377 in Erath County. The bridge, built in 1891, has been replaced by a new model. But a person can still come here and walk across the older bridge.

I frequently visit the old bridge that spans the Paluxy River. On one of these visits the stream was narrow and quiet, which is a paradox because after a thunder shower, it can suddenly become an angry body of water, tearing and ripping at trees and swallowing anything in its way.

Cathey Sims, who lives on a nearby ranch, has seen the result of the Paluxy and its anger many times.

"I've actually seen dead cattle and horses being swept down the river like they were just stuffed animals," she said.

But there was a peaceful air this morning. Fingers of mist hung in the air and moisture was thick on the ground. Patches of green lined the river's banks, growing evidence that spring was on the land.

And there was the bridge with its rusting pipes and thick cables, stretching across the river. Briars that tear into your body quickly and bring blood were twisted around its steel. Huge pecans and willows with broken limbs and dying branches, still black from winter, stretched into the air, looking like props for a horror movie.

We walked across the thick sheet metal flooring and touched the cables. Our footsteps made sounds like the props used on the old radio program *Inner Sanctum*. The sounds of the mourning doves and insects blended with our footsteps.

I remembered what Norman Bramlett, who lived in Fort Worth but was reared here, had said about the bridge.

"In the winter, kids would walk to school and we would come to the bridge and it would have a thin sheet of ice on its cables and pipes," he said. "That was always so inviting and kids would stop and stick their tongues onto the ice and the cold would grab their tongues and they would holler as they pulled them loose and ran on to school."

Bramlett also recalled the time his family was going home in a wagon pulled by horses. They reached the bridge about sundown. Suddenly the horses panicked.

"Now, these were good horses and well trained, and they never had done that before. Dad got down and then we saw what was causing the problem. A mountain lion was stretched across the top of the bridge on the far end," he said. "That was the only time I ever saw one of those cats in that country."

Such are the memories of the bridge. We walked on across to the end and read the historical marker.

For at least 20 years vehicles had to ford the Paluxy River to reach Bluff Dale and points west. Wagon traffic increased after the Fort Worth Rio Grande Railroad line reached the town in 1889. This iron bridge began to serve the public by spanning the Paluxy about 1891 on the main access road that became State Highway 10 and later U.S. 377. By 1933 arterial highway travel demanded a wider bridge. In 1934 authorities moved the swinging bridge 1.5 miles up stream to its present location.

Beneath the bridge are massive oak cross timbers. Time has eaten into them. There is the smell of wet dirt and new growth and signs of picnics evidenced by old mustard jars and soft drink and beer cans.

The remains of a campfire were near. You could bet somebody had built it while their dogs were chasing raccoons down the river. On a nearby sandbar there's an abundance of possum and raccoon tracks.

Letting one's mind wander, you could almost smell the smoke and see the tongues of fire as it cut into the darkness and highlighted the people's faces as they listened to their dogs and told stories.

Yeah, old bridges are caches of emotions.

## Rivers Beginning—Archer City

This country offers much more than those images fried into people's minds by the movie *The Last Picture Show*. We headed for one of those offerings about fourteen miles south of this town in Archer County.

"What we are going to see is a mound. And water drains into three major Texas river basins there," said Howard Barton. "It was used as a landmark by the early expeditions that came through here."

He is a tall, rangy man, friendly and full of information and history of this area. He came here in 1968 as an employee of the U.S. Natural Resource Conservation Service.

A haze stretched across the country, giving things a bluish-gray tinge like the scenes that an artist is just bringing into focus. We drove past pastures of mesquites, long a problem for the ranchers here.

"They coal oil them, spray them, chain them, and cut them by hand. They've tried everything, but they keep coming back," said Barton.

We drove past long-abandoned telephone lines, drooping like belts on old men's stomachs. We drove past wheat fields with vibrant greens like newly dyed carpet.

"Now this is going to be real subtle. You probably wouldn't know it unless somebody told you," said Barton.

We passed a pasture with many oilfield pumps with heads that looked like those on old skinny horses. Nearby were cows with new calves punching so hard at their mothers' udders that white foam covered their noses.

Barton eased the pickup to a stop. We climbed out.

"This is not as dramatic as the Continental Divide, but it is impressive when you consider the rivers that get water from here," he said.

I walked to a historical marker that read:

> The confluence of the Brazos, Trinity and Red River watersheds. The Trinity, a major Texas river, rises 250 yards west of this 1,250-foot-high mound. South of this site, water drains to the Brazos, north and west, to the Red. This high point has been important in Texas history.
>
> It guided Capt. Diego Parilla to battle Indians on the Red in 1759 and aided Capt. R.B. Marcy in mapping a California Trail in 1849.

We backed off and looked at the mound. A huge truck sped by, its tires awakening roaring echoes.

"This is so significant," said Doc Keen, a friend and world traveler. "The birth of a river...that's the seed that sets life in motion. And this is the site of three such things."

Some horses standing nearby watched us. The pasture was quilted by patches of blue thorn or chaparral and jumping-jack cactus. The horses suddenly whipped their heads around and began running north in a burst of speed, reminding me of the speed of a river's stream when it reaches flood stage.

## Mystery Grave—Grandview

After more than 100 years, the mystery of a young woman's identity still hangs in the wind and early morning mists.

The woman, called Annie, is buried in Grandview Cemetery.

During a visit to the site, a strong north wind caused aching noises in the trees near the grave, sounding a lonely symphony for this woman whose death has stirred imaginations.

One who has researched the mystery is Sandra Osborne, a member of the Johnson County Historical Commission and resident of Grandview, a town fifteen miles southeast of Cleburne in Johnson County.

She completed research for a historical marker for the whole cemetery, but now she thinks there should also be a marker for Annie.

"When Dub [her husband] and I were out here doing research, we were amazed at the number of people who would stop us and ask, 'Where is the mystery woman's grave?'" she said.

So she began searching for information. She found that the woman and a companion, well dressed and riding fine horses, appeared here late one evening on May 31, 1867.

A storm with thunder that sounded like cannon shots threatened the area. The couple declined the offer of lodging from a local resident and rode into the darkness.

The next morning, the woman's body was found. She had been shot in the head. There was no sign of the horses or her companion.

"The only identification was a handkerchief she held in one hand with the name 'Annie' embroidered on it," Osborne said.

Women in the town made the victim a burial dress. Nathan M. Hale, the owner of a sawmill, built a pine coffin.

"And they hung her red velvet riding habit in the branches of a tree near her grave with the hope that somebody might recognize them and reveal to whom they belonged," Osborne said.

That never happened. But the mystery grew when somebody placed cone-shaped stones at each end of the grave.

Little else is known. But Osborne did find that old Fort Graham was a day's hard ride from here. And during the time when the young woman was killed, the fort roared with life from gambling houses and houses of prostitution.

"There were women there who dressed elegantly like this woman," she said.

One person told Osborne about reading a newspaper article years ago about one of the women prostitutes disappearing from Fort Graham about the same time that Annie was killed.

"I have found the woman who wrote that article, but she has lost her copy of it and cannot remember when she wrote it," Osborne said.

So here we were at the cemetery. We looked at the grave. The two stones are still there. One is almost encased in a huge tree trunk.

"This place holds a particular fascination for young people," said Grandview mayor Louise Hudson. "But I don't know if we will ever know anything about Annie. I do think it would be an interesting twist to the story if we could find some history about Fort Graham and about the woman who had disappeared from there."

That will have to come from written material. The old fort, which was south of here, is covered today by Lake Whitney.

# Birth of 42—Garner

Bones rattle daily in this tiny mecca of domino playing.

Rattling those bones is another way of saying shuffle the dominoes, boys.

They've been shuffling dominoes for eons here at such places as the Back Acres RV Park and the Garner Store and Café.

My good friend T.J. Osborne of Fort Worth told me about the RV park in Garner on Farm Road 113 in Parker County.

"Go down there, Jon," he said. "Not only is the RV park a good place, but right there somewhere is where the game of 42 was invented."

Well, being a native Texan, I certainly wanted to check this out. When I was a youngster, knowing how to play 42 was as important as knowing how to change the spark plugs in your pickup.

So we met Ken and Carolyn Clary, owners of Back Acres.

He's a big friendly man. Their place looks like a domino heaven with plenty of tables covered with red-checkered tablecloths.

"I know a little about the game, but I don't play," Clary said. He laughed, "I'm not in the league with those who play here."

But Clary said that this is, indeed, the place where 42 was invented.

He gave me a brochure that explained how the game was devised in 1887 by William Albert Thomas.

Thomas was eleven and loved to play cards. But cards suggested gambling, which was sinning, making cards a no-no.

So Thomas and a friend, Walter Earle, developed 42. I won't try to explain the game other than to say it is fast and that most people pick it up quickly.

And they do love to play the game when the opportunity and place arises. Such a place is the Garner Store and Café here. During a visit, we watched as people ate piles of chicken-fried steak and bowls of gravy, two sure signs of 42 players.

Brent Butler, storeowner, realized his store had the proper setting. So he began holding 42 tournaments here. People who compete in them or any 42 tournament might do well to read Dennis Roberson's book *Winning 42*. The book gives strategy and rules for playing the game that Roberson of Fort Worth calls the national game of Texas.

"Forty-two is my game. It is my family's game. My father [Vaughan] grew up in Temple, and that is where he learned how to play," Roberson said.

He said his father had once considered writing a book about 42. That never happened.

So the younger Roberson, who has a degree in public relations and journalism from the University of Texas, decided he would write the book.

Roberson wanted a book for those who thought they might want to learn the game and for those who thought they really knew how to play the game.

"I didn't want the book to be only for all of us old crotchety 42 players," he said.

His wife, Charlene, read the manuscript.

"Since she didn't know how to play 42, she became my guinea pig," he said.

She liked the book so much that after reading it, she understood the game well enough to play.

Roberson's father also liked the book. But he did have one complaint: His son had given away all of the family secrets about the game.

He has shared some of those secrets that even an old crotchety player like me can appreciate. He recited some, sounding like a batting coach instructing a youngster.

"An average hand will have two doubles. That means that the odds are your partner will have two doubles," he said. "And if you are gambling that your partner will have a special domino, there are two-to-one odds against your partner having that domino."

Speaking of odds, several publishers turned down Roberson's manuscript, saying that it would not sell. Did they ever make a mistake. The book, published by Texas Tech University Press, is past its third printing and still going strong.

# Cynthia Ann Parker—Fosterville

Cynthia Ann Parker, trying to relive the white person's life after years of living with Comanche Indians, never made the adjustment.

She was kidnapped from Fort Parker near Groesbeck on May 19, 1836. She spent the next twenty-five years living with the Comanches and was the mother of the great Comanche chief Quanah Parker.

She was recaptured from the Indians in 1860 along with an infant daughter, Prairie Flower.

She eventually came to Anderson County to live with relatives. Prairie Flower died, and her mother, never happy, soon joined her. They were buried in a fitting place...a lonely cemetery in this near-ghost community in the towering pines in Anderson County.

This was the first of three burial places for Cynthia Ann, before finally being buried at Fort Sill, Oklahoma, beside Quanah.

Jane and I accidentally discovered the original grave several years ago while driving in the country north of Palestine.

A couple of years later we decided to try to find the grave again, although time had dulled our memories of its exact location. But after some help from the Granbury library, we found that Cynthia Ann had been buried near this community that at one time had several businesses, two doctors, and a school.

But by the 1930s the school was gone. By 1985 the county highway map did not name the community even though the *Handbook of Texas* said it was seventeen miles northeast of Palestine at the intersection of a county road and Farm Road 315.

I finally found the town on an Anderson County map sent to me by the Palestine Chamber of Commerce.

So we headed that way. As we drove, clouds thickened like plaque in an old man's veins. We passed a pasture with a beautiful paint horse grazing on winter wheat.

We saw a sign that said Foster Cemetery and pointed down a tiny two-lane blacktop road. Cattle stared at us.

The road twisted through the shades of the pines. We passed some old leaning houses and some small plots of rich-looking garden land.

Jane spotted the cemetery sign leading to a dirt road. We watched gathering rain clouds as we headed down it.

"I'd hate to get trapped in here," I said.

But there was the cemetery and its gate like a door between pine trees.

We again found Cynthia Ann's marker that had been made from native stone and at one time had lines of crystalline between them. Much of the bright stone had either fallen out or had been chipped away. A small marker read:

> First gravesite of Cynthia Ann Parker (1827-1864). Captured from Fort Parker by Indians in 1836. Recaptured by Texas Rangers in 1860. Mother of Quanah Parker, war chief of Comanches. First buried here. Reburied in Post Oak Cemetery in Oklahoma in 1910 and Fort Sill, Okla. Post Cemetery in 1954.

The pines' deep smell was strong.

I recalled reading the words of Maj. General Thomas C. DeShazo at Cynthia's last burial. He had said, "She is a shining example of motherhood in adversity everywhere."

Far off, a dog howled a greeting to us. His lonely echo seemed to match the last few years of Cynthia Ann's life.

# First United Methodist Church—Alvarado

Thank the Lord for those people who have a reverence for old buildings and their history.

That sort of reverence for the First United Methodist Church here in this town in Johnson County helped save this magnificent, gorgeous building a few years ago. Some members had suggested tearing it down because it had become an eyesore.

"I have been a member here since the 1940s. I love this old building," Lucille Mahanay said. "So did a lot of my friends. So a bunch of us old-timers, well, we threw a fit."

And praise the Lord for them and people like the Percifeld family, long-time residents here, the building still stands.

When we visited the 103-year-old structure, John Tushim, an expert on history, immediately recognized the uniqueness of the building while looking at the old steeple, which except for the city's water tower is the tallest structure in town.

"That is an imbrication steeple, the first one I've ever seen," he said.

That means that the edges of the steeple's tiles overlap in a regular arrangement.

Dr. Eric E. Smith, pastor, noted the work being done on the steeple. That, plus other work, represents an almost constant effort to preserve the building.

The work does bring changes. Some recent foundation work freed a front door that had been wedged shut for years.

"There's a funny story about that. Supposedly, years ago, a minister locked that door so members would have to pass him on their way out. But the foundation shifted and the door became stuck," he said.

As we walked into the main auditorium, Dr. Smith talked about people's reactions after coming inside.

"We do weddings for everybody," he said. "It seems like they walk in and they want to get married here."

That is understandable as one gazes at the cascades of soft colors falling from the towering stained-glass windows.

"You walk inside and it is real evident how unique and different this building is. It is not a fancy place, but it is a part of history," Smith said.

The smells of age are strong. I knelt at the mourners' bench and could imagine the stories that have been whispered from this position. Smith smiled at that.

"Yes, the whole span of life and the things in between have been seen here," he said.

Many of the early people who knelt at that bench carved their names in the massive timbers used in the roof. We climbed a steep flight of stairs to look at them.

Then we returned to the lobby. We stopped at a rope leading to a bell.

"We cleaned out the space around the bell. It was full of brush and straw that birds had carried in," he said. "When we rang the bell afterwards, many people could not get over how much louder it was."

He invited me to ring the bell. I pulled the rope. A beautiful pealing echoed. I thought of that old song about the church in the wild wood and the words that say, "No spot is so dear to my childhood."

Thank the Lord for Mahanay and her friends for pitching that fit.

# John St. Helen—Granbury

Jo Ann Miller and John Sims were both skeptical when first told the story of John St. Helen, a man who lived here from 1872 to 1878.

According to legend, St. Helen was really John Wilkes Booth, the man who assassinated President Lincoln in 1865.

Miller, producer and director of the Granbury Opera House, had been looking for a special show for the Texas Sesquicentennial. She wanted something strong. Something with history. Something that would grab the audience.

"Cynthia Brants told me that I had the finest story in the world right here in Granbury," Miller said. "She said it had everything I wanted."

Still skeptical, Miller began researching the story. Then she asked Sims, a local writer and actor, to help.

They spent nearly two years studying the legend and then wrote the play *The Myth and the Mummy*. It played to packed houses that year and the next.

The play contends that the man killed in a barn after the Lincoln assassination was not Booth, as history has recorded. According to the play, Booth escaped and lived in Granbury and other places before committing suicide by drinking arsenic in 1903. Then a carnival secured his mummified body and toured the Southwest, offering it for viewing.

It is an amazing story that leaves audiences questioning official versions of Lincoln's death. Sims said he had no idea the research would affect him that way when he began studying the story during a business trip to Memphis after Miller had told him to check the history of a character named Finis Bates.

"Bates had once been a lawyer here and claimed that St. Helen had confessed to him that he was Booth," Miller said. "I asked him to look up this character."

Sims did. And from there, Sims said, "The more we got into this, the wilder it became."

A last bit of wildness came in the mail to Miller. Dr. Arthur Ben Chitty of Sewannee, Tennessee, who has spent years researching the subject, told Miller that he and another man have asked for the exhumation of the body at Booth's grave in Baltimore. They are convinced, as is Miller, that forensic studies will show that the body is not Booth's.

So packed with facts like these, Sims and Miller had no trouble scripting a play that moves fast with strong dialogue.

"After we got into this, we were amazed at the material we had," said Sims. "All of the lines in the play come from sworn testimony."

One thing Sims and Miller found is a tintype made of St. Helen.

"We took this to Lee Angel, a professional photographer in Fort Worth," said Miller. "We asked him to blow up a picture of it and one of Booth and not to retouch either. Here are those negatives."

She laid them on a table. They matched almost perfectly.

Things like that erased the skepticism that Sims and Miller first felt about St. Helen, who owned two saloons in Granbury. The old rock walls of those still stand on the town square.

According to the legend, every April 14, the anniversary of the day Lincoln was shot in Ford's Theater, St. Helen got drunk and recited lines from Shakespeare.

As you walk down the alleys behind these old buildings, the squeaks and echoes cause your pulse to accelerate. Did Booth actually stand here and drink brandy by the quart?

"If St. Helen was not Booth," Sims said, "then why did he say he was? He had nothing to gain by that. By being Booth, he had to run his whole life."

One person who believed St. Helen was Booth was local resident Mary Duncan.

"Our grandfather used to tell us about Booth being here," said Duncan. "He said that Booth came here and lived with a cousin."

That cousin was Aunt Fannie Rhea.

"Granddad Rhea said that Booth figured neither she nor any of the family would tell anyone because they figured Booth had done the South a favor," said Duncan.

Author's note: Miller has since retired from her position with the Opera House but still lives in Granbury. Sims died a few years ago.

For more on the story, read W.C. Jameson's *Return of Assassin John Wilkes Booth*, published by Republic of Texas Press.

# Chapter 11
# Pets

Doug Clarke's knowledge about writing comes from more than forty years working in the profession.

He has worked for many Texas newspapers, including the *Fort Worth Star-Telegram* where he served in a number of positions, including city editor. He also has taught writing courses for years at several universities and colleges, including Texas Christian University.

That's a long way of saying I respect his opinions on subjects that make good stories. When we were once discussing this subject, he said, "Bunky [my nickname], there is no better subject to write about than pets. You write a story on a pet, whether it's an alligator or a snake, and you are going to get the majority of the readers."

I totally agreed with him. During my column writing, anytime I wrote about a pet, I knew my phone line would light up and my mailbox would be filled.

There is another reason that I liked writing about pets. I love them.

## Two Special Dogs—
## Stephenville, Granbury

The love people have for their pets causes many to bury the animal when it has gone on to the great beyond. Some go a step further than just burying the departed in the backyard. They bury them in a public cemetery.

Such was the case of a Granbury dog and a Stephenville dog.

The discovery of the grave of the dog from this town in Erath County actually solved a mystery in the old Valley Grove Cemetery.

For years many people thought that a grave with a tiny marker must have been that of an infant. Then a group, including Judy Lockhart, learned that the grave with a marker reading "Boots" is that of a dog.

Lockhart, a school counselor, told me the story as she drove to the old cemetery, one of the first in the area. For years getting to the cemetery meant carrying jugs of insect repellent to keep from being eaten by chiggers and ticks.

Then a local group decided to clean up the site. Lockhart had heard about the cemetery all of her life but had never visited the spot until she joined the cleanup.

During the activity, Lockhart's cousin Katy Lou Hancock asked about the old grave.

"It was little like a baby's grave. And it had a small tombstone," she said.

Ernest Boucher, who had lived here for years, stood up.

"Come on and I'll show you where it is," he said.

He led the group to some thick brush and vines, which he pulled back.

"There it is," he said.

That is where Lockhart had led me. The smell of freshly mown grass was powerful on that day. Thunder crackled in the background.

We walked past an aging rock fence falling apart like teeth on an old boxer. Lockhart stopped near some brush and pulled it aside.

There was the grave and tombstone about five feet away from the main cemetery. Irises surrounded it. The marker with lettering obviously done by hand reads, "Boots, 1937-1950."

"Mr. Boucher said the dog belonged to L.E. Edwards, the caretaker of the cemetery for many years. He said the little dog had been his constant companion, so when he died, he buried him here," she explained. "He also said that Mr. Edwards is buried here."

As we walked back to the car, Lockhart stopped.

"I feel like Ernest opened up a time capsule," she said. "It isn't really significant, but it is one of those little things that make life so meaningful."

We walked past bluestem grass with long blue blades. The thunder rippled again and brought the smell of rain. One could imagine little Boots hearing similar noises and scampering for his owner, who so dearly loved him.

That was the same kind of love that was felt for Rex, who is buried in a cemetery in Granbury.

"He was a big old white bird dog with black spots," said Mary Kate Durham, longtime Granbury resident and friend of his owners. "My son Randy used to play with him. He was a great, friendly dog."

Cal and Charlotte Stockton, who lived near Possum Kingdom Lake, said they had never heard of a dog like Rex, nor of the kind of love that his owners, Luther and Bertha Marie Jameson, whom they knew, had for him.

"That dog went everywhere with the old man," said Cal Stockton, who fished with Jameson for years. "The old man loved new cars, but he told me one time that he wouldn't trade Rex for two new Cadillacs."

Rex rode beside Jameson in his 1958 Chevrolet. He also slept at the foot of the couple's bed.

"He was one of the best trained dogs I've ever seen," said Stockton. "Luther could take a pound of fresh hamburger, open the package, set it on the floor in front of Rex and just say, 'No, Rex.' Then he would leave the room and come back in 30 minutes," he said. "Rex would be sitting there slobbering, but he would not have touched that hamburger."

When Rex died in 1959, Jameson had a man build the dog a redwood casket and brought him back to Granbury where the Jamesons had moved.

There are different versions of the story as to what happened next to Rex. But one thing is certain. Rex eventually was buried in a plot in the Granbury Cemetery. As Durham remembers it, that caused a bunch of people to howl.

"I thought the KKK was going to arrive," she said. "You can't believe how upset some people were."

But eventually feelings cooled and Rex was buried at the foot of a plot owned by Jameson.

"He's still there," said Stockton.

That he is, as a rather extended search revealed on a scorching day. My son Patrick had gone with me to the cemetery to hunt for Rex's grave. After more than an hour, he shouted, "Here's Rex's grave."

He stood at a stone marker with Rex's name. Above the marker are the markers of Bertha Marie and Luther Y. Jameson.

Rex died in 1959. Luther died in 1960.

"I'm convinced he grieved himself to death over that dog being gone," said Stockton. "It's really kinda touching."

As Patrick and I looked at the grave, a mockingbird erupted in a symphony from nearby. It was fitting music for a beloved dog.

# Old Fred—Midlothian

Want to hear a story about love and tenderness instead of the same old stuff of the wicked ways of people?

Well, listen to Fred the dog's story. I'll guarantee it will not leave you asking, "Where has humanity gone?"

Fred, a delightful part Airedale and wire-haired terrier, loves to be petted and to stick his nose into your face. He's delightful unless you get too close to his owner, Lindon Dodge. Then, shazam, Fred will be in your face.

Dodge has long, dark hair streaked with gray. He's a nice-looking man with strong arms built from obvious repetitions with the weight machines at his and Fred's house in this town in Ellis County.

He tells about getting Fred thirteen years ago after his original owner let the dog roam freely.

"The dog cops kept arresting Fred and taking him to the dog jail," said Dodge. "I kept making his bail until I finally said, 'Hey, this dog knows me better than his owner.' So I adopted him."

Fred had been licking my hand as his owner told the story. Then Gidget, a cute, petite dog, and her owner, Lanette Zack, arrived. Fred disappeared with Gidget.

When they finally returned, Dodge continued.

"About two years ago, Fred couldn't walk because he couldn't stand on his front legs," said Dodge.

But he still tried to follow his owner by dragging himself.

"It was torture for him," Dodge said.

So they took Fred to a veterinarian. He had bad news. Fred had bone spurs pinching nerves on his spine. Surgery was not hugely successful. The other alternative...put him to sleep.

"No way," said Dodge. "No way. I looked on it like the book *Of Mice and Men*. I wasn't going to kill my best friend."

And maybe he shared what Fred was feeling. Dodge has been in a wheelchair since 1982 when he injured himself in a diving accident.

They brought Fred home. Dodge's father, Tom Dodge, had heard about the chemical DMSO, which some athletes who had been paralyzed were using. He bought a bottle.

"It had become a family crisis," said the senior Dodge. "Other family members had thought of buying Fred a wagon or a set of wheels to put on his legs."

But Lindon Dodge preferred the DMSO. So he began rubbing Fred with the solution. He rubbed and rubbed that first night.

"The next morning, I got up and there was Fred...walking," he said.

He called his father.

"Guess who is walking," he said.

Tom Dodge and the family came quickly when they heard. When they saw Fred, there was an abundance of emotion.

"It was like he had been through the healing line," said the father.

"It was like he had been washed in the DMSO," said Lindon Dodge.

So what is Fred's future?

He's deaf. He has cataracts. He's skinny. But he's still the dog of the house. And if his owner gets his wish, Fred will be called to dog heaven after or during one of his visits with one of his girlfriends.

I told you this is a happy story.

# Dog Woman—Sadler

I thought I had a deep love for dogs until I met Martha Hovers.

This North Texas woman's love for dogs goes far deeper than words. It goes into her heart and has motivated her to live with and make homes for 250 dogs.

That is not just on the weekend. That is every day. Every night and around the clock. Living in a mobile home on the edge of 48 acres that are full of pens and kennels for her dogs.

She knows every dog by name. She knows their personalities. And she protects them at her facility, the Animal Refuge Foundation, or ARF. It is the third largest no-kill care-for-life canine sanctuary in the country.

I don't know what I was expecting when I went to visit Hovers. She had candidly said, "Well, I am known as the crazy dog woman."

Regardless, she is fifty-three, a slender, attractive woman with a soft voice and a smile that comes quickly like splashes of morning sunshine.

"Why did I do this? I don't know. But I can tell you, I love it and I don't regret it for a moment," she said.

She greeted us at ARF, which is west of Sherman in Grayson County. She revealed a bit of irony about herself. As a child, she was afraid of dogs and did not acquire her first dog until fifteen years ago.

Then twelve years ago her feelings for dogs definitely changed when she and her former husband moved to this 48 acres that has been in her family for three generations.

"We were going to retire," said Hovers, a former executive secretary.

That changed abruptly when somebody dumped four dogs at their gate. They began caring for them. Then came more. And more. And here she is today with 250 once-homeless dogs.

She finds homes for some, particularly the younger dogs. But the older ones, well, it is hard to find homes for them. Besides, they stay for a year or so, make friends, and feel like this is home.

"Euthanize one of them? Never. I cannot stand the thought of doing that," she said. "I have always said, 'Well, what is one more?'"

One more during our visit would have meant 251 dogs. And each one eats one pound of dog food every day. Then there are the veterinarian bills that amount to $1,500 a month, and that is at half price.

All of that must be squeezed from a $70,000-a-year budget. The money comes from donations to ARF, which is a nonprofit, tax-exempt organization.

Hovers struggles to make it. Volunteers like Julie Abbott of Weatherford make valuable contributions.

In a moment of reflection, Hovers said that she would like to find someone who would move to the facility with the thought of some-day assuming her role.

"It would have to be somebody who loves dogs," she said. "And they are not going to get rich."

But if they do love dogs, it doesn't get any better than this. That was shown when we walked outside, and here came Mouse, Andy, and Gilda. They greeted Hovers by licking her hand and looking at her like she was indeed the Big Dog around here.

## Greyhound Rescue—Hillsboro

I had a hard time coming away from Greyhound Rescue Society of Texas without a vanload of greyhounds.

Hope and Al Combest own and operate this organization dedi-cated to rescuing and finding homes for greyhounds retired from racing. As a result, they always have at least 100 of the lean, graceful dogs, which act like they've met a long-lost friend immediately after meeting someone for the first time.

We talked in the living room of the Combest home between Hillsboro and Itasca in Hill County. Five greyhounds relaxed around us.

"Greyhounds are considered 45 mph couch potatoes," Hope Combest said. One of the dogs had crawled onto the sofa and lay across her lap.

Then Lady, fourteen, their first greyhound, walked up to me, sniffed, and put her head on my lap. I petted her.

"She likes you," Al Combest said.

I'm not unusual. Greyhounds like everybody.

Their personality attracts many fans like Bonnie Fix, who is a foster parent for dogs being considered for adoption.

"I take them to our house and keep them until we are sure they are ready for adopting," she said.

That's how the Combests, who have the largest greyhound rescue group in Texas, got into the work. They lived in a historic home on Fifth Avenue in Fort Worth at the time. They had read about the need for foster families for greyhounds.

"We got Lady," Al Combest said. "After about four days, we said we did not want to be foster parents. We wanted to adopt her."

That eventually led Hope Combest to form the Greyhound Rescue Society.

The Combests had several funny experiences with the dogs in Fort Worth. One happened during a tour of historic homes that included their house. Al Combest had gone to the door to greet a woman on the tour. When he opened the door, Lady started out.

"I yelled, 'Lady, get away from that door.' The woman thought I was yelling at her. She got off the porch in two jumps," he said.

When their greyhounds exceeded city regulations, they moved to their 24-acre farm.

An amazing thing about their operation is that it is nonprofit and 100 percent volunteer.

That means a total commitment to the dogs by the Combests and requires an almost constant plea for donations.

"Our daily dog food requirement is 275 pounds," Al Combest said. "Our monthly veterinarian bill is about $2,200."

But the rewards of finding homes for the dogs pay for the sacrifices. Recently they acquired a white greyhound retired from racing. Nobody wanted the dog because he was deaf.

"A family from McKinney was immediately attracted to him," Al Combest said. "When I told them, 'He is deaf,' I knew they would not want him."

But the woman said that was fine. "I have a degree for teaching children with hearing impairments. I will teach this dog sign language," she said.

Naturally, the Combests are always looking for homes for the greyhounds. But even if you visit the facility and do not adopt a dog, be prepared to pet. A lot.

# Dog Goes to Butcher—Carlton

The intelligence of a dog that once lived in this Hamilton County town still is mentioned in storytelling sessions.

The dog's feats are frequently recalled by a group of retired Texas highway department employees who meet regularly for coffee in nearby Stephenville.

J.G. White, who retired from the highway department in 1987, is a member of the group. He wrote of the dog in a string of stories that he entitled *To Believe or Not to Believe: That's the Question.*

The story came from a highway department survey crew surveying the farm-to-market road from Dublin to the Erath County Line near Carlton.

One day they were near Carlton when noontime caught them. So they drove to Carlton to buy some additives for their lunches, White wrote.

While eating, they listened to a noon report on their radio. The announcer gave the weather forecast and then some local news.

Then he began telling about a Carlton dog that, when given a nickel, would trot to the local market and give it to the butcher.

"The butcher rewarded him with a piece of meat," the announcer said.

That triggered lots of laughter. But as the men finished their lunch, they noticed a large dog lying nearby. Could this be the meat market dog?

Maybe. So one of them pitched a nickel to the dog. The dog immediately picked it up and ran to the meat market where he was given a bone.

When the crew returned to Stephenville, the crew chief told the story. Nobody believed him. But apparently the story is true, because I have heard it from other old-timers in this town.

Another story that White told about bull nettles brought some more howls of disbelief.

Anyone reared in the country has knowledge of these plants, which though quite pretty, can really cause pain if somebody brushes up against them.

As Geyata Ajilvsgi explains in *Wildflowers of Texas*, "The hairs of this plant contain a caustic irritant which on contact produces a painful irritation and rash and can cause a severe reaction in some people."

I've had my confrontations with bull nettles and can certainly certify those facts. For this reason, few people ever think of eating bull nettle seeds.

But White and some buddies ate the seeds regularly.

"We would find a piece of baling wire...bend one end into the shape of a hook. We would then reach the wire inside the bush and pull the seed out, peel the thin crust off, and eat it. It is similar to a pinion pine seed," he said.

Many friends have said they either did or did not believe White. But very few have said they would attempt to eat a bull nettle seed.

Ajilvsgi said that even though the seeds are tasty, the plants have earned names like "Tread Softly" and *"Mala Mujer,"* which is Spanish for "bad woman."

So what does this have to do with the meat market dog? Well, if he was smart enough to carry a nickel to a meat market for a bone, he was smart enough to stay out of the bull nettles.

# Highway Dog—Dublin

Many readers learned about my love of dogs and dog stories.

So when I heard from John and Martha Ames about a dog I met years ago, I knew I had to come back to Dublin.

Martha had written me a letter. She wondered if I had forgotten about "Highway Dog."

She said she knew that I wrote about bunches of people and animals and maybe some of them get kind of hazy in my mind.

That's true but my memories of Highway Dog are sharp.

Highway Dog belongs to Latrelle Cain, a long-time animal lover. Cain had a business on U.S. 377 west of Dublin when she first met Highway Dog.

Somebody had dumped her on the highway. Her home became the space under a highway bridge.

People noticed her. They began pitching hamburgers and French fries to her. Some even threw her steak.

Cain took a special interest. She began giving her dog food, gradually coaxing her from under the bridge.

At first Highway Dog would duck her head between her legs and run from Cain. Her actions left little doubt that she had been beaten by previous owners.

But she finally got over that and moved to Cain's place. She had found herself a new home.

Then Cain moved east of Dublin on the road where the Ameses live.

"We love animals," Martha said, "and slowly but surely she became friends with us. She was timid at first, but as she got to know us she lost that. Now she seems like she is always glad to see us."

Then tragedy struck Highway Dog again. Shortly after moving there she became entangled in one of those steel-jawed animal traps that mangled a leg.

"Latrelle took her to the vet and he tried to save the leg," Martha said.

He was unsuccessful and the leg was amputated. But the absence of her left hind leg did not slow down Highway Dog.

"It doesn't bother her a bit. Not a bit," John Ames said. "Come on, let's go see her. Latrelle is not there, but she told us to take you there."

So we drove to Highway Dog's home. She was resting in a flowerbed. At first she was afraid of me. She hid behind Martha and then ran under a picnic table on the patio.

"Highway Dog, this is Jon. He interviewed you once. Remember? He's your friend," Martha said.

She looked at me. I leaned over and began talking to her.

"Highway Dog, I know you are famous. But I like famous dogs. Won't you let me pet you?" I asked.

She eyed me with those brown eyes boring into mine. Then I swear she grinned. I moved closer and petted her. I rubbed behind her ears and her back with its crazy splashes of brown and black that are typical of a blue heeler.

I continued petting her until my palm had oil from her coat. Then she let my friend John Tushim pet her.

When we prepared to leave, I looked at the oil on my hand. She looked at me. I told her goodbye. She gave me that crazy smile again.

It is nice knowing a famous dog.

## Jason—Fort Worth

I sat there in a rather dispirited state. Doc Keen sensed it and said:

"You know, dogs are funny. You become attached to them and then they leave and their spirit is still here. You turn around and you swear that you have seen them; and you have. You have seen their spirit."

He was talking about the absence of Jason and the reason for my depressed state.

I'd promised myself many times to never become attached to an animal after several painful emotional experiences brought on by unplanned departures of other dogs.

But the fact remained, I have always been a sucker for dogs. Always will be.

That became rather obvious when I met Jason some six or seven years ago. He's a giant mass of black Labrador and something else that we spent many hours pondering.

"Maybe he's part buffalo," Jane said one night while we were camping and watching Jason chasing sparks from the campfire and knocking over pots with those happy wags from his thick, strong tail.

He belonged to my stepdaughter and son-in-law, Terry and Brian Billeaudeaux. They sometimes asked us to baby-sit him.

It only took one of those episodes to realize that I wasn't strong at all. Jason had hooked me.

He loved to ride in my pickup and go fishing. He would sit and eye my casting for hours.

Jason loved people, and he did not like to be by himself. Consequently, when we left him in the backyard, you could bet he would be sitting on the front porch when we got back.

He accomplished this in several ways. He would leap over the gate, or he would simply rip some of the wooden planks from the gate and crawl outside. He reminded me of an old saying I once heard when somebody asked a man who raised buffalo how he drove them.

"You drive a buffalo just anywhere he wants to go," he had said.

That's the way it was with Jason. You kept him wherever he wanted to be kept.

Jason soon had anchored himself into a very special spot in my emotions. So special that I started calling him my granddog.

Then Brian and Terry announced they were moving to California. We kept Jason during the preparations for and after the move. That lasted two months. And with each day, I knew that I was facing one heckuva emotional separation.

That finally came when I was to meet Brian at DFW with Jason for his trip to California.

So I loaded him and his huge kennel into my truck. As I drove, Jason lapped at my arm with his tongue. He seemed to know that I was not feeling exactly happy.

Brian was there. He had a box under his arm. "This is for you. But don't open it until you get back home."

Then we marched into the airport. Brian purchased the tickets. An attendant led us toward an elevator.

"You will have to put him into the kennel and then put it on the elevator," she said.

Jason wagged his tail.

We reached the elevator. Suddenly, I knew I had to go. I reached over and hugged Brian. Then I leaned down and hugged Jason and did something I have never done. I kissed a dog.

I turned and walked away. I looked back once. Jason was looking at me. His tail was wagging. He seemed to be saying, "It's okay, Jon."

I drove home and went inside and made myself a drink. Then I remembered the box that Brian had given me. I cut through the heavy tape. A heavy object was wrapped in paper.

The present was a bronze of a black Lab puppy holding its head up. It looked like Jason.

I took it to my closet and put it into a far corner.

It would be awhile before I could look at it.

But Jason's spirit was strong in our house.

## Sassy—Granbury

This is not a sad story. It's about Sassy, a blond cocker spaniel.

Sassy would not have wanted the story to be sad. She spent her life trying to make people happy.

Her antics in our house for thirteen years were renowned.

Consider her insatiable appetite.

She never seemed to be full. She ate her regular feedings. Then she perfected the art of clandestine eating.

Her favorite pickings were in Jeff and Sue Cummer's garage. The Cummers, who are next-door neighbors, fed their cats there. Sassy loved to cut herself in for snacks.

As a result, she put on weight. That showed one day when the grandchildren had gone outside with her. She treasured these times because she loved children so much that she allowed them untold freedoms, including pulling her ears without growling.

But on that day, the children came screaming into the house. I wondered if Sassy had finally lost her temper. Kyle dispelled those fears, saying, "Sassy is stuck in the garage door."

I checked. She was indeed stuck halfway in the pet door leading into the garage. She looked at me as if saying, "Well, Jon, get me out."

Aw, what a dog.

She loved our family celebrations. She knew these meant food. And that meant we had to watch her closely. Woe be unto us if we did not.

One Thanksgiving, Jane and her daughters, Sue and Terry, had prepared a tremendous feast that covered the table.

But in a moment when we were all out of the room, Sassy struck. When we returned, half the turkey was gone.

But we quickly forgave her. I think she knew we would because she sensed our emotions and often tried to cheer us up.

There was the time when I came home from heart surgery. Sassy and Cinder, our cat, waited in the front yard. I sat down. Cinder rubbed against me.

Sassy sat at my feet and rubbed my legs with her ears. She looked at me with her dark eyes as if to say, "Jon, you are going to be okay. You're home with us."

I learned something from her. She slept on her bed in the garage, but every morning she was at the door early. I would let her in. She would quickly make her rounds and return to me. I would pet and rub her.

For years, I thought, "Gosh, this dog does have a need to be petted."

Then one morning, when I was a bit depressed, I realized that the petting went far beyond her need. She loved me and she was giving herself to me, thinking my touching her would cheer me up.

Then she developed heart problems. Despite a $40 monthly prescription, her heart kept slowing down. And finally, it simply quit.

Late that afternoon I watched the sunset. Brilliant red fingers from the fading sun split the clouds. I said, "God, thanks for my time with Sassy."

The next morning Sassy didn't meet me at the door. She was gone.

I began crying. I went inside. Jane and I both cried.

I made a small wooden cross in her memory. I placed it on the banks of the lake where she loved to sit.

I hand-carved this inscription on it. It reads, "Sassy, our girl."

She was.

# Chapter 12
# Veterans

$M$y strong feelings about what our veterans have done for this country surface in the darndest places and times.

Like once I was standing on the courthouse square in Stephenville watching a demonstration staged by the KKK. I don't remember what this group was protesting. But I do remember when they started blasting this country for everything wrong with their society, I felt anger surging into my emotions.

I thought of Uncle Ben McConal, who had fought in the trenches during World War I, had been wounded, and brought home a limp that he endured the rest of his life. I thought of a cousin, Marvin Murphy, who had lost his life fighting in Korea.

When I heard these tirades against our country continue, I thought, these people are soiling the memories of my relatives and the thousands of other veterans who have fought for this country to preserve its freedom. I had to fight to keep from screaming profanities back at them.

But, instead of focusing on these people, I focused on Uncle Ben and the veterans like him. I am damn proud of them and wrote many columns about their experiences.

I feel like every one of these people is a national hero.

## Decatur

R.N. Gregg of Decatur spent nearly three years working as a prisoner of war on the famed Burma-Siam Death Railway.

"I lost nothing there," he said. "I have no desire to go back."

Frank W. Ficklin of Granbury also worked on the railway and endured abysmal conditions. He has returned several times to visit. So why?

"I don't know. It's like an old boy getting bucked off a horse, and they say the first thing you do is get back up and get back on," he said. "If you go back and look at it that way, it doesn't well up inside you."

Ficklin, a tall slender man with freckles splashed across his arms and hands, smoked a pipe as he talked.

He told about his experiences on the railway. He was a member of the 2nd Battalion, 131st Field Artillery, a part of the 36th Division, Texas National Guard. The battalion was mobilized in November 1940 and eventually sent to Java. After fierce fighting with the Japanese, the unit surrendered in March 1942.

Ficklin remembers being transported in freighters from Singapore to work on the Thailand side of the railway.

"Hot? My gosh, it was 115 to 120 degrees in there," he said. "And all we had was standing room."

The conditions at the work camp were equally bad.

"Very little food. We lived on rice and a thing that looked like a radish," he said. "We'd cut it up and make soup."

Their clothes rotted off within a year.

"So we wore G-strings," said Ficklin.

He talked about their working conditions.

"We had absolutely no mechanical equipment. When we drilled holes for the dynamite used in cutting the right-of-way, we used hammers and chisels," he said. "Our biggest piece of equipment... elephants."

The Japanese officers gave orders in Japanese.

"If you didn't understand it, they'd whack the hell out of you," said Ficklin. "They also made you stand looking into the sun for hours. Sometimes they'd make you hold a piece of timber."

But he survived.

"If you worked or stayed busy, it wasn't on your mind," he said. "If you didn't get to the point of thinking that you were going to be there forever, you could handle it."

He stopped and tapped tobacco into his pipe.

"But I think if we had known from the first how long we would have been there, a lot more of us would have died."

He recalled the liberation. His weight had gone from 176 to 112. They placed him and others on a C-47 transport.

"The officer in charge assured us that they had plenty of food on the plane," said Ficklin. "Five hours after we took off, the food was gone. He said he had never seen anyone eat like that."

An item of food also made an emotional page in Gregg's memories. That item was a can of milk.

Gregg was also a member of the 2nd Battalion that became known as the Lost Battalion because it was years before people in this country learned what had happened to the group.

Gregg remembered working on the Burma-Siam Death Railway. The movie *The Bridge Over the River Kwai* is based on the experiences of British prisoners working on the same railroad.

"Right before we were captured, a lot of us figured they would kill us all," said Gregg. "I had this big cigar and lit it with a $100 bill because I figured I would never need that money again."

The Japanese did not kill them. But they worked them in conditions that later were compared to a living death.

"They'd whip you for anything," said Gregg, a tall man. "I got the worst whipping while trying to remove some rails from the railroad. I was not doing too good a job, and this guard began whipping me with a telephone line. Every time he hit me, it brought blood."

Death was a constant threat. His weight went from 200 pounds to 140. He credited his survival to having been reared on a farm.

"I knew what hard work was. Plus, during the Depression, we didn't have a whole lot of food," he said. "I lived three months at a time. Once I got through three months, I'd work on the next three."

He told about the work.

"We'd carry dirt and rocks in these baskets on our shoulders," he said. "All of us got these huge knots on them. Us country boys had worked horses before with sore shoulders. All of us swore we'd never work a horse with sore shoulders again."

Then he told the story of the canned milk. He had found it in a sack of other items just before the POWs were shipped to Burma.

"I put it with my stuff and carried it for two years," he said. "I was carrying it for me. I figured somewhere along the line I would need it."

A Dutch doctor who cared for the sick and injured with little medical supplies knew Gregg had the milk.

"One day I came in and he told me that this guy I knew was dying," said Gregg. "He said he couldn't keep anything down. And if he didn't get something down and hold it, he was going to die."

Gregg shook his head.

"He asked me for the milk. He said he could mix it with water and spoon-feed it to the guy and maybe he would keep it down," said Gregg. "So I gave it to him."

Eventually Gregg and other survivors were liberated August 15, 1945. Gregg remembers little about that day.

"I don't know. I kind of cut loose from all of that...discarded it," he said. "I've tried to forget it."

But there are things he does remember. One was the stacks of Coca-Colas that the liberators had.

He also remembered the can of milk. The man the doctor fed it to survived and lived in North Texas. Every time he saw Gregg, he hugged him. Then he started crying.

# Hamilton

Excuse Nora Sparks if emotion seeps into her voice as she talks of her little brother.

"See, when he was little, I took care of him. I took care of him until he got old enough to where I could lean on him," she said.

Her eyes flashed strong with those memories of her little brother, Charles Roy Sneed. The years tumbled backward. Back to those days when Hamilton had a tiny airport with a landing field full of rocks and chug holes.

"I can't imagine anybody landing out there," said Sparks. She laughed. "But, Charles did. He loved flying so much."

He took his first flight from that field. He told her, but he never told their parents.

Aw, the memories of those days. She recalled them from her office and beautiful home here in this county seat of Hamilton County. She is a pretty woman and speaks in a voice that lingers with soft echoes.

She was often feisty as she talked of her childhood days.

"We didn't have abortions in those days," she said. "So a woman stayed pregnant all of the time and had eight or ten children."

There were eight in her family. Charles Roy and she became very close.

"He could repair anything. We had two old Model Ts and one of them quit. He took one apart and rebuilt the other one," she said.

He loved flying and in 1935 joined the Army Air Corps.

"He was so glad," she said. "That was the Depression. You were lucky to get bread and gravy."

During his training he landed here a couple of times.

"Oh, he loved flying. He would tell me, 'It's wonderful to get up there and float through the air,'" she said.

During his last visit here, he told his sister that war was coming.

"He told me, 'Sis, no matter what happens, I want you to do your best to look after Mama and Dad. If something happens to me, don't take it too hard. Really, I'm worth more to the family dead than alive.'"

He was shipped to the Pacific and stationed at Pearl Harbor when it was bombed. He survived.

Then she repeated more stories of his service. Of being at Corregidor. Flying many times off that island in a tiny, beat-up trainer. Of receiving the Distinguished Flying Cross for extraordinary achievement, which included flying an old two-seater from Corregidor to Panay Island.

"I still dream of those times he went through over there. They must have been nightmares," she said.

She recalled the time when her brother and other pilots were supposed to be airlifted from an island. But an artillery colonel ordered Sneed to join a detail so he could get Sneed's seat.

"That still haunts me," she said. "When he got back, the plane was gone. I would have killed that man."

Sneed was captured after that. He survived the sinking of one POW ship. He was placed on another ship. It too was bombarded. Sneed was killed this time.

Sparks stumbled with words. She picked up a phone book.

"I could live a thousand years and I could never, never get over this," she said. "Look in this phone book. There is not a Sneed in there."

We drove to the cemetery and walked to Sneed's marker. There in a soft wind, we stood with Bill Snell, commander of the local American Legion post.

"Miss him? Oh, yes, I miss him," said Sparks.

The wind spun into her gray hair, stirring it so gently.

# Eastland

Ah, the stories that will be told over this Memorial Day.

Roy Blair, who lives on Lake Leon near this town, has one that ranks high in World War II adventures.

He was listed as killed in action after the bombing of Pearl Harbor. Certainly that's unusual. But Blair's theory behind this happening to him and others is really unusual.

"I think the government did it to cause people to buy U.S. Savings Bonds," he said. "Like in my case. They ran my name with a bunch of others in a full-page ad in the *Star-Telegram*, saying that these men had given their lives for their country, so buy U.S. Savings Bonds. I'll bet there were people from my hometown who read that ad and did just that."

Blair, a thick, balding man with blue eyes, had a voice with a growling edge. He told his story in short, no-nonsense sentences.

He was reared in Lipan in Hood County and joined the Navy after high school graduation. He was assigned to the *California* and was aboard it when the Japanese bombed Pearl. He fished through some photos and pointed at the *California* after a torpedo bomb had hit it.

Smoke engulfed the ship. Blair was lucky. He had been a turret electrician on one of those huge guns for just a week. The man who had replaced him in his former position in the lower part of the ship was killed.

Blair made it to safety. For days he worked on ships that had been hit.

Then he was assigned to the USS *Lexington*, an aircraft carrier. Shortly after he came aboard, an officer warned Blair and others, "You are not going to sink the Lady Lex."

The remark angered Blair. So did the fact that he was not given any new clothing.

"It was like they didn't want us on that ship," he said.

The carrier was attacked twice. The first time was unsuccessful when enemy planes dropped bombs that missed.

"I stood on deck and watched. Those bombs were falling like eggs. But all hit our wake," he said.

They were not so lucky during a May 8, 1942 attack. Torpedo bombs hit the ship. Blair was in the engine room.

"I remember hearing ammunition and paint exploding," he said. "I was among the last off. I climbed up through an air vent."

Not until years after the war did Blair learn about being listed as killed in action at Pearl Harbor. He heard the story from a woman who had been working as a telephone operator when the telegram came in about Blair's death. She had called his father and told him he had a telegram.

"She saw my father read it, and he fainted," Blair said.

His parents never mentioned any of that to him.

"I talked to them after Pearl and they didn't say anything," he said. "I think they were just happy that I was alive."

After the war Blair talked to several men who had the same thing happen to them.

"Yes, I think the government did it on purpose," he said. "I've got two buddies in this area that it happened to. Hostile? Yeah. Wouldn't you be, especially by the way they did it?"

Probably.

# Weatherford

Russell A. Gill's story of his three and a half years as a prisoner of war of the Japanese at first comes in short snatches.

He tells a story and tries to laugh. But you realize that his surviving the Bataan Death March then being taken to Japan in the hold of a ship filled with the stench of vomit and corpses is not funny.

I had come to the Gill ranch six miles west of this county seat of Parker County to see furniture he builds by hand and sells. It is indeed stunning work, as evidenced by a beautiful mahogany executive desk with symmetrical designs.

"I learned about this wood while I was in the Philippines," he said.

He's a strong man with washed blue eyes. He was reared in Big Spring during the Dust Bowl days, days when people were dying of dust pneumonia.

"Now here's a sideboard I made," he said.

As I looked, he explained that he started building furniture seven years after he retired from building houses.

"You can't just sit down, can you? You need something to do," he said.

We walked to the house and met his wife, Joy. The ranch has been in her family for more than 100 years.

She showed a beautiful round table with chairs with thick leather backs and seats that he had made.

"Our eating table," he said. "Enjoy doing this? Yeah, I like to back off and look at them. I might be caught looking at them anytime."

We sat down. White Dog, a miniature poodle, leaped into his lap. His huge hands petted the dog.

"Being on that ship was worse than the march. Men were puking, had diarrhea, dying...stiffs in there for days. Hotter than the hinges of hell," he said. He stopped. "Right then is when I realized I was a long ways from home."

He worked in a Japanese steel mill. He was always hungry and once got caught stealing some long, leather-like radishes and was whipped with them.

"I thought that guard would never get tired," he said.

One day they heard B-29s bombing the city near the POW camp. They looked out the windows through the smoke and flames and began hooting and hollering. His rasping laugh came.

"That was strong medicine, even though the next day they cut our rations in half," he said.

"Then one day a guard told us about the big bomb the Americans had dropped. And soon planes came with supplies. The first was a small single-engine craft whose pilot circled, came back, and tossed out a half-carton of cigarettes.

"We cut them into lengths about this long," he said, holding his fingers a quarter of an inch apart. "That way, everybody got at least one drag."

Then came planes with candy bars, gum, canned soup, and fruit cocktail.

"We poured the juice from the fruit cocktail, mixed it with sake, and got drunker than all get-out," he said.

We talked some more and then I had to leave. He followed me to the car, talking about friends he lost, ticking off their names. His voice cracked. He blew his nose into a handkerchief.

"I'm sorry, Jon. Sometimes my emotions kinda get away from me," he said.

We shook hands strongly. I said, "Thanks, Gill, for what you did. Very much."

I headed home.

# Glen Rose

John Wilson hesitated to share his memories of World War II because of fears that people would think he was lying.

He endured some almost unbelievable things during more than a year as a driver of an ammunition truck in the 6th Armored Division of Patton's 3rd Army.

There were months he went without sleep except for brief naps captured while collapsed over his truck's steering wheel.

There were the months he went without changing clothes.

And there were the months he went without a hot meal, eating rations with questionable contents like the mouse leg he found in one can.

He and his wife, Novella, relived those days in their home in this town in Somervell County. She has written a book about his experiences, much of that based on the 312 letters he wrote to her during the war.

"Because of censors on his letters, I actually kept up with him through stories in the *Star-Telegram*," she said.

He's a slender man. His voice was often soft as he told about his job hauling ammunition in a truck and trailer to the front lines.

"Yeah, you would think about the danger of getting hit," he said. "But still, you got to where it was just what you did."

He told about seeing Gen. George Patton in action, including one time when they were moving across France and were trying to get through a narrow gate in a sandy field.

Patton stood in his jeep cursing because a huge gatepost was hindering progress.

"He was hollering for somebody to knock that post over," Wilson said. "When I got to it, I straightened up my truck and hit it dead center with my front bumper. My truck hesitated, but I put the gas to the floor and it knocked the post over. Patton yelled, 'That's the way to do it, soldier. Now maybe the rest of those S&%#es will get their tanks through here.'"

Wilson seldom stopped his driving. But one night as he and his helper were on a mountain road, he got a feeling.

"Something just told me to stop...I don't know what. But we did and got out of the truck and slept with our backs to each other," he said. The next day they found the road had been heavily mined.

He paused.

"I don't know why I stopped. Still don't," he said.

"Maybe it was the good Lord sending him a message," his wife said.

Maybe. But there was one thing he did wish the good Lord had sent him...food.

"We hadn't had a hot meal since that November and did not have another until spring. One day I got the idea of putting a can of rations on my truck's engine to heat them," he said. "It heated them all right ...blew them up. And talk about a smell...gosh."

Then there was the day he opened a can of rations and found that mouse's foot.

"I never opened a can that I didn't think the people who prepared those ought to be out there eating them with us," he said.

But somehow he survived that and the mined road. And he really doesn't care if people think he is lying when he tells those stories or when he tells of what he saw when he helped liberate Buchenwald, the concentration camp where thousands were executed.

From these he learned the meaning of the words "War is hell."

## San Antonio

Every time the Vietnam War is mentioned, I think back to a week I spent at Brooke Army Medical Center in San Antonio.

Hundreds of casualties from Vietnam were brought there for treatment. I did a series of articles about them. There is one youngster who stands out in my mind like a windmill silhouetted in the West Texas blood sunsets.

The wards were full, particularly the burn ward. Brooke's burn unit, which has developed many innovative treatments for third-degree burns, is among the best in the country.

What I was doing there was no secret. Many of the young servicemen who lived in an area where the *Star-Telegram* was sold came to me and asked that I talk with them. So did a man and woman on the first day I was there.

"We've heard what you are doing...talking to the GIs," said the woman. She was nice looking, but you could tell something had been eating at her beauty. There were lines near her eyes that would take more than time to wipe away.

"Well, anyway, you've got to promise us before you leave that you will come and talk with our son. Will you promise me that?"

I promised. But I told her that I couldn't do it that morning as I already had a series of other interviews arranged. Then I left.

I talked to a man who had been a gunner on a helicopter. He was from South Texas. He had black hair and dark eyes. He was built like a bantam-weight fighter. His helicopter had been knocked out of the air by a rocket. When it crashed, he was pinned by his legs inside.

"I watched the flames come toward me. I always thought I was strong, but I could not move. I thought about getting my knife and cutting my legs off. But both my hands were broke. So I just watched the flames come and soon I was smelling myself burn," he said.

His legs were burned off. He was nineteen. He said he had no idea what he was going to do.

Late that afternoon I was back in the building where the man and woman were. I had finished an interview and was leaving. The man stopped me.

"My wife said she talked to you about talking to our son? Well, I sure hope you can do that," he said. He was dressed in a white shirt and dark slacks. "Our son was outstanding in his high school. I think you would really enjoy talking to him. We are from Arkansas."

Again, I promised I would talk to the young man. The week continued. I talked to this huge man of twenty. He had biceps the size of grapefruits. He was cheerful despite the fact that his legs had been blown off. He said he was going to be a disc jockey.

After I left that interview, the woman stopped me again.

"Our son was voted most likely to succeed and most handsome of his class. He was also captain of his football team. He played quarterback...was named All State. He also had an 'A' average and had been accepted as a pre-med student...you've got to meet him," she said.

I told her I would be there the next day.

"Oh, I appreciate this so much. I will tell Gary just as soon as I leave here. I know he will be so excited," she said.

I didn't sleep well that night. I kept dreaming about this man whose legs were on fire. He kept running and jumping into rivers and lakes. The fire kept burning...finally morning came. I went back to Brooke.

"We are so glad you came to talk to Gary. You will never know how much this means to us," the woman said. "And promise that you will send us a copy of your article."

Then we were in Gary's ward. We were standing beside his bed. His father was there. He held Gary's hand. He said, "This is Gary."

Gary had huge muscled arms. His legs were also nicely built. His eyes were blue. But just beyond that, Gary ended. It was as if somebody had taken a shovel and scooped away Gary's head just above the eyebrows. Gary had been lobotomized by a Viet Cong mine. Gary would never talk again.

I stood there for a few minutes. Nobody said anything. Finally, I said I had to go. The father followed me into the hall. We stopped. He shook my hand.

"We certainly do appreciate this," he said. "We are going to take Gary home soon. He was such...he is such a nice kid."

Our eyes caught and held. I felt mine stinging. I knew his were too. I left. But Gary has never left my mind. His was a story I wish I could have heard from his own mouth. I would have made it good. Maybe that would have helped take those premature lines away from his mother's eyes.

# Chapter 13
# **Personal**

W hen I first started writing my column, I made a pledge to myself that I would strive to write about people other than myself.

One reason I did that came from Phil Record and Horace "Chief" Craig, two editors who taught me so much about writing early in my career.

Both of these men, for whom I have a deep fondness and respect, hammered into me their belief that anyone can write stories about themselves.

"But, Bunky, you need to get the real people into your stories. They are the ones we should be writing about and not ourselves or relatives," Record, former night city editor at the *Star-Telegram*, told me many times.

So that is what I strived to do and did do the majority of the time. But when you write a column for twenty years, there are times when, well, it seems okay to write about yourself or put yourself into the column. I didn't do it a lot. But I did on occasion use myself to make a point.

The following are some of those times.

## Dub Manus—Pampa

Somewhere in this town in the Texas Panhandle and the territory north toward Arizona, Dub Manus will celebrate July Fourth.

And having known Manus for most of my fifty-seven years, I won't be surprised at what he fashions for the celebration. It will come near the end of a 2,600-mile bike ride that he and twelve high school students are making. That trip may sound unusual to some. But it is typical of stunts that Manus has staged throughout his life.

I met Manus in junior high school after we had moved from Midland to Midlothian. We became good friends and have maintained contact in the passing years.

Generally, any call from Manus brings a surprise about his latest adventure. They always tax his strength and sound like they have come from the latest script for an Indiana Jones movie.

One of Manus' long-time loves has been boxing. He fought as a heavyweight in the Texas Golden Gloves and once went to the national tournament.

So I should not have been surprised that night when he called after we both had reached our late thirties to tell me about his latest hobby. He said, "Hey, guess what I am doing?"

I knew better than to guess at anything that Manus might be attempting.

"I'm fighting professionally. As a hobby," he roared.

"Like in professional prize fighting? A hobby?" I asked.

"Yeah, that's right. Everyone has to have a hobby. And I thought, 'Why shouldn't mine be professional fighting?' I've always loved boxing. So why not do it as a hobby?"

So he fought professionally for a couple of years.

But he topped this feat the year he turned fifty. At the time I was really into distance running. I had run seven marathons. Manus knew about this, so he called.

"Hey, have I got a deal for you," he said. "This is the year we both turn fifty. Right?"

I knew something really big was about to be offered to me.

"So why don't you come along with me and help me celebrate my birthday," Manus said.

"How?" I asked.

"I'm going to ride a ten-speed bicycle from here [he then lived near Fort Worth], and in 50 days I'm going to ride a route that will carry me through forty-eight states."

I said that sounded delightful.

"Well, I want you to come along, and you can write stories. You also could run ten miles in each of the states as you accompany me," he said.

I thought it sounded like a great idea. Unfortunately, none of my bosses did. They could not imagine anyone fifty being able to do this nor could they imagine anyone fifty being able to write interesting stories about such an adventure. They didn't know Manus. He did it. I wish I could have made the trip. I think the editors would have learned I could have made it interesting.

But enough crying. When Manus called me last week, I was not surprised when he told me about his latest summer adventure.

He was calling from Pampa.

"You still running?" he asked.

"No, but I walk every day," I said.

"Great. Great," he said. "Guess what I'm doing this summer?"

I had no idea.

"Well, I am teaching at an Indian reservation in Arizona. So I decided why waste the summer. Why not go on a 2,600-mile bicycle ride with some of my students?" he said in his usual burst of enthusiasm. "They liked the idea. But they had no money to buy bicycles. So I just went to a Sears store and charged twelve of the cheapest mountain bikes they had to my charge card. And so here we are. We are making seventy-five miles a day. We should be finished sometime in mid-July. Now isn't that something?"

Well, it is. And it also means that they will be spending today plowing through the heat somewhere on those mountain bikes.

So I'm lighting a huge firecracker for G.W. "Dub" Manus.

To me, he's the kind from which our country was made. Kind of crazy, gutsy, adventuresome, and the kind to whom you don't ever say, "Hey, you can't do that."

Plus, I think he's darned interesting.

# Cow Talk—Granbury

I've started talking to cows again. I've found out that I haven't lost my touch.

That discovery came after Jane and I purchased bicycles a year ago. We began making rides in the countryside around here.

There are plenty of cows still grazing in the pastures in this area. Jane and I began talking to them.

It was this intellectual feat in her that made me know that I had found true love during our dating. We camped out frequently. On one of those trips, I was awakened by Jane. She was going, "Woooooooit. Wooooooit. Wooooit, cows. Wooooooooit."

Now for some men, that would have meant an immediate call for help, bellowing, "Hey, come here. My girlfriend has gone crazy. She is yelling this far-out stuff at me."

I knew better. I knew Jane was talking to some cattle that stood across the fence from our campground. I was impressed. I also knew that I was in love.

I mean, I had spent years before I found a woman who could talk to cattle. I did find plenty who used a part of a cow in describing my actions when I exhibited this ability.

Actually, this trait goes back to my childhood spent on ranches. Those years required ways of finding cattle so they could be fed. Some people used their pickup horns. Others, like me, used their voices. I got darned good at it.

I learned that not everybody talks to cattle the same way. For example, some people will arch their backs and bellow, "Soooooooock. Soooooooooock. Soooooooooock, cow. Come on."

Others prefer a medley of sounds. A kind of cross between cow language if you please. Something like this.

"Wooooooooooit, soooooooock, woooooooooit, sooooooooch, cows. Where are you? Soooooooit. Soooooit. Whooooooooooooock. Darn, honey, I think we are going to have to go get the horses to find them this morning. They just aren't listening."

Some people don't understand the importance of talking to cattle. Doc Keen and I learned that when we went on what was called a Texas Trek. We walked 350 miles around the area west of Fort Worth.

After several days of walking, you will do anything for entertainment. Like talk to cattle. We did this one day. Rick Moon, our photographer, asked us what we were doing. We told him. Then we tried to teach him to talk to cattle.

I told about his efforts in my story. He was embarrassed.

"You guys are crazy," he said.

Regardless, I find it fun to continue to talk to cattle. So on our bike rides around the ranching country, Jane and I frequently talk to them.

Reaction varies.

Generally, Herefords or those with a cross of Hereford blood listen better. Or maybe that is because they understand us better.

That could be traced to my childhood. Most of the cattle I talked to then had some Hereford blood in them, so I might have picked up their accent.

Or maybe there is another reason for their reactions as explained by a friend, John Tushim.

"When a cow is standing there minding her own business and somebody on a bicycle stops and starts babbling at her, well, they think you are crazy," he said.

Maybe so. Or maybe I'd better work on my accent.

## Flood Party—Del Rio

Nature has a funny way of bringing people together during its worst moments.

That fact has been repeated many times this week as a result of the gorging rains that hit this area, causing massive flooding.

So it was with me and about fifty other people in this country some twenty-five years ago. I had come to this town to cover a convention. This is normally a dry and arid country. But on this weekend, huge black clouds emptied excessive amounts of rain on the area.

By Saturday the rains swelled the Rio Grande and washed out the bridge leading to Ciudad Acuna. That's when I decided to head north for home.

So did bunches of other people.

The rains started again. Suddenly the dry riverbeds between here and Sonora were swollen with water.

When this happens, many crossings are covered. If you have any common sense, you know never to risk trying to go across one of these in a car. Find high ground and stay there.

That's what about twenty cars did after becoming trapped between two of the dry rivers, which now were bellering like stampeding cattle as a result of the flooding waters.

We parked in a long line on the edge of a hill. People got out and began looking at the swirling waters, which carried huge logs that sounded like shotguns being fired when they rammed into the rock river banks.

"We're going to be here awhile," said one man. "So we might as well sit back and enjoy it."

Others agreed. Then somebody opened their car trunk. They began pulling out goodies bought in Mexico. That included some tequila and food.

"Let's celebrate," said someone.

Somebody produced cans of juice. We made some cocktails.

"Hey, honey, why don't you get that guitar you bought?" a woman asked her husband.

He looked around.

"Anybody play?" he asked.

"Well, I've been known to pick a tune or two," said one man.

I echoed his comments.

"I also bought a gui159tar," I said. "I might be able to follow you if you don't get too fancy."

We began playing and singing.

The rain started again. We put on raincoats and kept singing. Somebody began "Your Cheating Heart." Everyone joined in on the chorus.

"Know 'Fraulein'?" asked someone.

We did. People took turns singing verses with all of us singing the chorus. A kind of skinny man smoking unfiltered cigarettes had been standing in the back. He walked to the center and cleared his throat.

After the chorus, we nodded at him. He began singing. His voice was high and mournful, bouncing off the hillsides like a dog barking in a hollow. When he finished, people clapped.

Then someone built a small fire. Heated up some tamales and tortillas they pulled from an ice chest. Passed them around.

We sang some more songs. One older couple began dancing as I sang "Release Me."

"He hasn't danced with me in years," she said. "But he still cuts a mean two-step. No wonder I married him."

During a break, someone checked the crossing in front of us. He hollered:

"It's down. I think we can make it across."

We looked at the river. Only a trickle passed over the road. We loaded our things into our cars, got in, and hollered at each other about how we would keep in touch. Then we drove on.

I've never seen or heard from any of them since. But I still remember the party that nature created for us.

## Bull Nettle—Gorman

There's more to get hot about than summer temperatures when a person gets off the trail in country like this.

I've had encounters with many of these products from nature that cause me to howl in pain.

Of course, there's a variety of insects that can cause pain. These include yellow jackets, ants, spiders, and scorpions. I've been bitten or stung by all of them, including the black widow, the tarantula, and the brown recluse.

But one of the most painful encounters I've suffered has come from a plant called the bull nettle. It grows abundantly in sandy soils like those in this country where peanuts generally thrive. The plant is quite pretty. But it can make a grown person cry.

I learned early in my life to respect the bull nettle. That respect came in my crazier days when we did such things as have grass bur fights.

Grass burs come from a green plant that grows heads with needlelike stickers. We'd cut these stickers and throw them at each other.

Their puncture marks often triggered explosions of anger and profanity.

Oh, the Sundays I've spent kneeling in church and asking the Lord's forgiveness for those eruptions of profanity that ripped from my mouth after encounters with grass burs.

The preacher always had blistering words of condemnation for those who used such language.

I did feel some guilt. But on further contemplation, I thought that the good Lord was not going to close the gates of heaven for those who had such encounters. I often wondered what that preacher would say if he suddenly felt a head of grass burs tearing through his socks and into his skin with their sharp prongs.

Would he really just say, "Aw, gee whiz, guys, that hurts"?

I doubt it.

I also doubt that a preacher or anyone could keep from using a little raw language after the sudden pain rocketing into one's flesh from an encounter with a bull nettle.

The plant is a vibrant green and has, if you can just back off and look at it objectively, beautiful yellow flowers.

Though the plant loves sandy land, it will grow in any kind of soil.

I had a cousin who said that bull nettle kernels were delicious. But I never figured out how she could pick them without getting the fire stung out of her fingers.

One trouble with bull nettles is that they often thrive in places known to have rattlesnakes. That's where the trouble comes in. You can't see them. So you brush up against them, and you swear you have been bitten by a rattlesnake.

When that happens, the bull nettle sting can bring the toughest of individuals to their knees.

Such was the case with a man to whom we once sold cattle. He was known for his ability to take pain and not flinch.

One day we were taking him to a pasture to look at some cattle. We had a gate leading into the pasture. Both sides were choked with grass and other plants. A sure place for rattlers. And bull nettles.

The man opened the gate. In so doing, he suddenly screamed a line of profanity.

"G-------, a snake bit me," he yelled.

My dad and I quickly got out of the pickup to offer assistance. That's when the man screamed again.

"The s-------- bit me again," he yelled.

My dad ran to him. As he neared him, he realized that the bite had not come from a rattler. It had come from a bull nettle.

I probably would have laughed had not the man been known for his tough character. I thought what a time for one of the old good news, bad news jokes. It could have gone:

"The good news is that it wasn't a rattler that bit you."

To which he would have probably asked, "Well, what's the bad news?"

"The bad news is that it was a bull nettle," I would have answered.

# Baker's Crossing

Some go to elaborate church chapels for their praying.

I go to Baker's Crossing.

This is a low-water bridge over the mercurial and enduring Paluxy River. I watch the river surge across flat rocks and spill under the bridge.

I listen to it charge south, its symphony often accompanied by crows making their harsh "caw caw" calls along with lonely bawls of cattle.

This for me is a natural place to get my batteries recharged or to ask for help for someone facing death.

I've been here twice recently. Brought my companion, Sassy, a cocker, who is growing older and hard of hearing like I am.

She loves it here as much as I do. Her nose goes into overtime, and as I talk she answers me with a whine like she is agreeing with me that there is something of strength here.

Maybe it's nothing. But I can smell the rawness and sense something a lot more powerful than I am.

We stood where the river makes its head-on crash into the tiny spillover. Water splashed into our faces. Sassy strained at her leash.

I thought of the years flying by like leaves falling from trees after the first hard frost. They mean nothing to some as they are registered in faces. The lines and wrinkles gather, and only friends really care.

So it was with me for these two friends…one lean and built like an old cowboy. Gosh, how I have admired his writing and the absolute power he has with words.

I've seen more of that power recently with his way of facing cancer. He's tight-lipped. Makes those tart, sarcastic remarks. But he has that look in his eyes like an old cowboy saying, "Well, I'll come to the house in a little while. I've got to work a couple more head of cattle."

I thought about our talk on the telephone last week. About the loss we both had felt over the death of a friend.

"He was a good person, Bunky, a good person," he said.

Yeah. Then I blurted: "So are you, man. So are you. And I don't pray like most people, but I want you to know that me and Sassy went out to Baker's Crossing this week to say a few words for you."

We talked some more. I asked if there was anything I could do. There was nothing. Except:

"Bunky, would you and your dog go back to that crossing again and say a few words for me."

So we did. And again I thought of this person's power with words. And how on down this river lives John Graves, another writer whom I absolutely worship.

Then we started home. Winding our way through the back roads of this rugged and beautiful country. Sassy sat in the passenger seat.

I saw a mother cow. Standing beside her was a calf that I knew hadn't been here long. I stopped and looked.

I had seen many calves being born. Coming out like a huge loaf of meat and their mothers licking that away and then the calves nursing like this one was. Out-of-place thoughts spilled into my mind. God, I miss you, Tony. God, I admire you, Jerry.

Sassy whined as she watched and smelled the young calf and its mother.

Life goes on.

# Blackland Farm—Midlothian

Even the whiskey's fire didn't cool the memories.

They were abundant as Tom Dodge and I drove down the old Fort Worth highway north of this town in Ellis County to the section of black land where my family spent two hard years.

We passed fields covered with tiny white flowers and the remains of an old dairy where I used to go and help with the milking. They gave me all of the ice cold milk I could drink from one of the cans pulled from a freezer kept cold by a compressor panting like a runner out of breath.

Finally, there's the old home place. Nothing left but the windmill. It looks like it has had brain surgery, with only a twisted blade left.

We walked to where the old barns stood. Through some hay and cow manure, strong, pleasant smells for somebody reared in the country.

I look down a hill where a creek always ran when rains came. Where one time, while clearing trash away from the fence, I stuck a pitchfork through my shoe and foot. I remembered letting go and closing my eyes and thinking if I open them, this will not have happened.

But the pitchfork is kinda weaving back and forth in the ground when I open my eyes. Then comes the smell of my father, chewing tobacco and sweat. He puts his foot on my foot and yanks the pitchfork out. I began screaming. I thought he was going to slap me. Instead he glares at me and says, "G........., why aren't you more careful. Now we are going to have to take you to the doctor."

I looked at the back portion of land where my brother and I plowed on that old F20 and little Ford tractor. Still the Johnson grass grew. Hot black dust blew into our lungs already on fire with heat.

I looked down the road and remembered Bill and Marvin Redmond, my best buddies. We prowled the countryside on old bikes. God, the problems we solved sitting on the banks of Mountain Creek, watching turtles, playing marbles and tops. Old games. Simple games.

I looked down into a draw with ragged edges eaten into it by erosion. A draw where I walked for hours looking for cattle and treasure left by I didn't know whom. Maybe a pirate had come through here and buried a treasure. A kid's dream. Anything to get him through the hard times.

We looked at the old foundation where our bedroom was. Where I discovered Twain's and Stevenson's characters and dreamed with them.

In the yard is a huge nest of cactus with neon-yellow blossoms like the hair of a painted prostitute. Nearby are two pieces of an old wrench, maybe one of the many we lost fifty years ago and my dad said, "You boys lost enough wrenches out here that some day somebody will think they've found an iron mine."

The humidity caught my shirt. Under my arms I smelled like those summer nights when we lay there with our windows wide open and sweating and smelling worse when we got up than when we went to bed. Listening to the old man in the next room, lying close to Momma and bemoaning the fact we ever came to this country from West Texas.

Dodge handed me a drink. I killed it.

"Here's to life," he said. "Or whatever."

Yeah.

Two years after I made that visit to the old farm, my old man died. I always figured he would outlive me.

I figured he'd probably call me on my deathbed and recite in his rusty voice that old poem that began, "The lark is up to meet the sun, the bee is on the wing."

Gosh, how long have my brother, Mack, and I heard those words? Ever since we were a family in that raw part of the state called West Texas.

My dad was as tough as the country. His philosophy was spare the work and spoil the child. So my brother and I were riding horses and working cattle by age six. We were driving tractors by the time we were eight.

But then, it took that philosophy to survive in that tough land. At least, that's what the old man said.

He and my momma both worked hard. He learned auctioning and drove hundreds of miles in a pickup to sell and trade cattle.

He awakened us shortly after he got up by thundering out the next line of that poem, "The ants, their labor have begun, the woods with music ring."

He seldom complimented us. His physical touch was limited to a crushing handshake.

But he instilled in us early in our lives that because we were brothers, if somebody picked a fight with one of us, they were going to fight both of us.

Fights were frequent in those days when we rode a school bus for sixty miles coming home from school. Halfway through the route, we could get off, walk a mile, and get back on the bus after it had made a loop. One day when we got off the bus, an older student jumped on my brother.

I grabbed a tree limb and broke it over this guy's head. The fight continued. I got an even larger limb and began pounding the guy. But the other students pulled me off, and the larger guy proceeded to beat the hell out of Mack.

When Daddy saw his black eye that night, he immediately began cursing me for not helping Mack.

"He tried, Daddy," Mack said. "But the other kids wouldn't let him."

The next day when the bus reached the spot where we got off, there sat my father in his pickup. He stepped into the bus and said, "I want to tell you people something. If you jump on one of my boys and the other one tries to help him, then you'd better leave him alone. If you don't, then you are going to have to deal with me."

That was it. He got back in his pickup and left.

That was my dad, a man who hammered us physically but who never hesitated to hammer anyone threatening us.

But he never softened his criticism when we did things he did not agree with, like my growing a beard. He called me Brush Face until he died.

He was there in his own way, however. Like the day he yanked the pitchfork from my foot. Or the day that my brother, riding a green bronc, got bucked off coming down a hill. He somehow escaped injury and I know expected some sympathy from the old man. He didn't get any.

"Get back on that horse. We got cattle to work," Daddy thundered.

That was M.G. Mac McConal. He was ninety-seven when he died. I thought of the last lines of that old poem when we buried him.

"Shall ants and birds and bees be wise, while I my moments waste. Oh, let me to the morning rise, and to my duties haste."

## Dale McPherson—Glen Rose

Death can come as quickly as a flash flood on the Brazos River.

Both are shocking in their finality. So it was with the death of my close friend Dale McPherson, a former long-time Somervell County judge.

He was fifty-seven. Way too young to die. Way too young to have the voice of this natural storyteller and the fine tunes from his fiddle silenced.

Our friendship went way back to the wild days of our teen years. We both were products of fathers who made their living from this raw old country, raising cattle, peanuts—anything that would make a dollar.

McPherson and I sometimes worked together. Once we were at the Armstrongs' farm combining maize in weather hot as the inside of a furnace.

I always hated combining. That chaff from the grain drove me nuts. I had escaped it this day until lunch. As was the custom, we went to the Armstrongs' house to eat.

Dale, his brother Wendell, and I went in with grease and sweat dripping from our clothes and smelling like we were first cousins to the hogs.

Mrs. Armstrong had a table set that would have fed twenty hungry city people. There were only three of us.

Dale, who always had an appetite, did put that food away. He used his obliging manner when he wanted seconds, saying, "Excuse me, ma'am, but these beans are some of the best I've eaten. Would you care if I took another helping?"

He made several approaches to those beans, and Wendell and I winked at each other because we knew that furnace out there had not gotten cooler.

Dale found that out after he made two rounds on that old combine. He jumped off and began losing his lunch. I thought it was funny until I realized whose job it became to drive that cyclone of chaff...mine.

For years after that he always greeted me, "Bunky, you been driving any combines lately?"

Then would come that rasping laugh. He sounded a lot like his father, Wallace, a man who captivated me with his fiddle playing. He, too, was a great storyteller. On those Saturday nights when I played my guitar with him and Dale as they fiddled, he told stories of this country when it was rough and a person could find a jug of home-made whiskey by following the smoke easing up from a still in the cedar brakes.

Those sessions stretched past midnight. I was always amazed looking at the fingers of these men, so hard and strong and thick from hard work yet how they made them look like tiny ballerinas dancing across the fiddle strings.

Dale could equal his father in storytelling as I learned on our camping experiences. We would stand around a campfire. I would listen to him and that old Brazos echoing in the background like the chorus behind a fine singer.

I thought of these stories during his funeral service. Flowers surrounded his casket. One arrangement was appropriately in the shape of a fiddle.

I remembered our good times and how I tried to keep up with him while I played the guitar. Back then we both chewed tobacco. For years, every time I saw him, he would hand me a plug and say, "You still like this stuff?"

I never told him I had quit. So on my sixtieth birthday, when he brought his band and played in honor of the occasion, he eased over to me and said, "Bunk, I brought you a present."

He gave me a plug of tobacco with two chews gone.

Today, when I go walking and wear my old red vest, I reach deep in my inside pocket and feel that plug, dry as parched peanut hulls. I probably should get rid of it. But I won't.

It reminds me of fiddle music and the Brazos River and a good friend who died too young.

# Andrew Cummer—Granbury

If Andrew Cummer's appetite whims include any exotic Thanksgiving dish, he'll get it.

Tables of friends, relatives, and his parents, Jeff and Susan Cummer, are weighted with love for this youngster. And because Andrew—Andy to all of us in his neighborhood—is only three months old, he will probably want nothing heavier than milk.

Andy is the Cummers' first child. What a long road that has been for this couple.

We personally know about the hardships they've faced in getting an infant because they are our next-door neighbors.

They're the kind who, when you say, "Hey, we've got a problem," respond quickly by saying, "How can we help?"

Their response knows no limits. They have even given us access to their house when ours becomes overloaded with family. We've tried to do the same for them.

Susan and Jeff were ecstatic when they learned she was pregnant.

Jeff was out of town when that pregnancy ended with a miscarriage. Susan spent the night with us. We all cried.

Then came the day they decided to try to adopt a baby through the Gladney Center in Fort Worth. A social worker called us for a reference. We were overjoyed.

The good news came. They had been selected. Everything seemed final.

But the birth mother changed her mind. Jane and I and other neighbors wondered how much more the Cummers could endure.

Susan said, in her no-nonsense way, "If God wants us to get a baby, then we will get a baby."

They were selected again when Andrew's mother chose to give him up for adoption.

When they brought Andy home, he was an instant hero. Art and Pat George, Becky and Leo Orlowski, Marsha Moore, and the McConals...we all gushed about Andrew like he was a member of our families.

The Cummers' emotional reaction is hard for a writer to capture without being trite. So just say that Jeff and Susan dearly love Andrew.

He does indeed look like part of the family. Many think he more closely resembles his father, with his kind of long face and that quick grin.

His birth mother feels good about the adoption.

"I'll bet Andrew is getting to be a big boy," she said in a recent letter.

Then she asked if they had heard about the young mother in Irving who left her baby for dead. She said that was so sad. She closed by saying:

"Well, give Andrew big hugs and kisses for me. I miss him. But I know he has a great mom and dad that love and nurture him."

Does he ever.

The whole community nurtures him. And he responds. One day this week he was wearing sports shoes that had "Dallas Cowboys" written on them.

"Hey, Andy, are you going to be a Dallas Cowboy?" I asked. I patted his foot.

He flashed that grin that would stop a defensive line.

Aw, Andrew, I am so glad you are here. For the Cummers. For us. For this November, which is National Adoption Month.

For this Thanksgiving with its palette of colorful leaves that makes people think that somebody a lot more powerful than us made this beauty and this youngster.

Andy, you've made this a special Thanksgiving.

Author's Note: Since I wrote this two years ago, Susan became pregnant and in July gave birth to Alex, a nine-pound-three-ounce boy. When Andrew first saw him, he retrieved a toy beside his brother's crib and handed it to him. When I later asked him how his brother was doing, that Cummer smile flashed quickly across his face.

# Sarah—Granbury

We knew before the announcement came over the radio that the news would be bad.

For hours, helicopters had chopped through the air like giant ceiling fans. Seemingly everyone was looking for Sarah Patterson, eleven. Then suddenly the sound stopped.

During the two-day search, I had winced several times at TV and radio reporters, their voices shellacked with doom as they said, "People in Granbury are shocked because things like this don't happen here."

On Thursday I had driven north. I looked at the small town of Thorp Spring, packed by officers and members of search parties. Here Sarah's brother, Cody, nine, was found beaten.

I thought of the irony that here once sat Thorp Spring Christian College, a campus of old-time beliefs so stern that young lovers sneaked to the shadows just to hold hands.

Yet here had become the scene of a crime so nauseating, so unthinkable.

I drove farther north, up toward Tin Top. I watched the people on the side of the road, searching for clues in grass thick with chiggers and ticks.

Sometimes I get a feeling. Don't know what it's called, but I feel like I can sense something.

My ears began ringing. I drove to a small, public boat launch.

I walked around. The ringing got louder. I stopped at a huge trash container. I shuddered as I opened it. Nothing.

But I felt that Sarah had been there.

I went back to Granbury. Listened to stories in the Pirate's Den barbershop, owned by Darrel Grober, a man who spends hours answering calls as a volunteer fireman. A man who does it all just for the good feeling of helping people. He shakes his head about Sarah. More harsh language comes from other customers.

"By gosh, they should just take a b-------like that one out and kill him," said a man, referring to the suspect in the case.

As a kid, I once came searching for the Granbury girls because they supposedly were so much "purtier" than those in Glen Rose. Then a kid's wildest crime was stealing watermelons.

The helicopter charged across our side of the lake, heading west down a slough where I've watched vivid sunsets slash across the sky.

Jane's face was white. She listened. She talked of our grandkids charging up the hill outside. Playing freely over in a park by McKelvey's Marina.

"I wish we could do something," she said.

So did I.

"I feel so sorry for her. She is a hard worker. A good mother. A loving mother," said Pam Graham, a close friend of the children's mother.

Words. Thoughts. Not in Granbury. Not where the Lady Pirates girls basketball team is always top-ranked.

The search had shifted to Rock Harbor. Just across from us. Rock Harbor where I walk every day and the grandkids play in another park.

More helicopters chopping the air. Sounding like a rolling drum beat for a funeral dirge. Not in Granbury.

Then suddenly the quiet. Nothing but the wind sifting the leaves. Tiny ripples in the water. Bass jumping.

And less than a mile away, they announced they had found Sarah's body. Less than a mile away.

The bluebonnets wept on this day. Their blueness matches the tears.

In Granbury, Texas.

# Homemade Malts—Santo

I don't drink malts anymore. But if I did, I'm certain I would like the old-time malts made at Jackson's Grocery in this town west of Fort Worth and off I-20.

I got plenty of testimony about their goodness from people who pay $1.99 for malts and milkshakes made by Monteen Jackson.

"Those things in those fancy places don't compare to Mrs. Jackson's," said Kyle Rucker, twelve. "Besides, I like to talk to Mrs. Jackson."

Well, who doesn't? She is a gray-haired grandmother type. She knows practically everyone in this area and chats about their welfare as she makes malts and milkshakes the old-fashioned way, with old-time mixers.

She has three mixers in a line. One is new and was bought when one of the old-timers sounded like it was coming apart.

"So Stoney [her husband] ordered this new one," she said. "So, what I do is use it to kinda break the ice cream up and then let the old one finish the job."

To start the job, she puts two large scoops of ice cream into a steel container from the old days and pours in some milk and a large helping of sugar from a plastic jug. None is measured.

After mixing, she gives the customer the container and says, "Be sure and pour out the leavings."

The Jacksons, who have owned the business for forty-three years, thought of closing until a daughter, Diana Kidwiler, joined them in October and added videos for rent.

"That did help our business," Monteen said.

She attended a customer. I sat at the counter and spun around on one of the old-time seats. I looked at an old RCA radio behind the counter.

"My daddy bought that when I was a kid," she said. "We didn't have electricity, so we had a wind charger and some batteries that they charged. This radio ran off that. We thought we were really up to snuff."

Raymond Martin, a long-time customer arrived.

"I can't live without having at least one of her malts each week," Martin said.

The Jacksons sell other things. Like Martin buys some of his groceries here. The store also sells fresh meat.

"We put out ground meat, roasts, and steaks on Friday," Monteen said. "If we don't sell it all by Saturday, we take it home and eat it."

A customer arrived. He plucked a paper-shell pecan from a large open sack. He removed the shell and ate the meat.

"Those are purty good," he said and left without buying any.

I looked under the counter and saw rows of old-time charge accounts, the kind in which tabs are kept in small paper books with the customer's name on top.

"Oh, yeah, we still use these," Monteen said. "I'm glad you brought that up. I forgot to write down that bar of candy and soft drink that girl bought."

Monteen knows that youngster and practically everybody else in town by their first names.

Let's see, that would be how many people in this town, I asked.

"I tell people that the population is 302, if you count the dogs and cats," she said.

And everyone, including those dogs and cats, loves her milkshakes.

# Backyard Wedding—Granbury

The holy clouds of matrimony will be raining in our backyard today.

I'm making fun. I do hope the rain stops. But right now I feel like Steve Martin in that movie *Father of the Bride*. Only I'm the stepfather. I'll get to that as soon as I wring out my clothes from the latest drenching.

Why, oh, why does anyone plan to have a backyard wedding in Texas? Many people are glaring at me with that question. Because I'm the one who said, "Let's have it in our backyard. It's not going to rain."

Well, it has rained and rained and presented me with a problem. Where can I find a vast supply of mud boots?

That is one of my duties, being stepfather of the bride, Susan, a delightful woman who came into my life when I fell madly in love with her mother.

Susan is marrying this charming man Barry Sandacz, who has the fastest quip in the West. He could earn his living as a stand-up comedian. Only right now, he is not saying many funny things when looking at the ocean in our backyard.

That's where we've been planning for six months to have the wedding. It's been raining for the past six days. We sort of changed our schedule.

Umbrellas will be issued at 5:30. Mud shoes at 5:45. Bring your own slickers. Game time is 6:30 P.M., God willing and the creeks don't rise.

Hey, Barry, I've been waiting all of my writing life to use that phrase. But it brought no laughter as our latest efforts were curtailed by another shower.

Helpers at our house have included Carrie, a long-time friend; Terry, Jane's other daughter, and her two children; Jane, mother of the bride; John Tushim, family friend; and Sassy.

Sassy is the family dog. We've tied sponges to her feet to try to absorb some of the water.

So while I'm trying to figure this all out, I thought of the other step, as in stepfather.

I've never liked it. Step is something that is walked on. Put that in front of father, mother, son, or daughter, and it is sort of like belching in church.

Since Jane and I married, I have considered her three children like blood kin, though I do admit they all are taller than me. But I've loved them, shouted at them, and cursed them. As my son Patrick said after he and Kevin heard one of my outbursts, "Hey, Daddy, you really do like them. You curse them just like you do Kevin and me."

I don't know who invented this term step. Like, now, am I supposed to call Barry my stepson-in-law?

So it's proper. But I think in our scramble to make things proper, we forget that emotions can forge a strong love regardless of whose blood runs in the veins. To me, if I feel kin to somebody, then by gosh, they are a part of my family. And they aren't step.

So back to the wedding. I'm sure everything will go as planned. I welcome Barry to our family.

I'm sure that welcome will be recorded in several toasts tonight. So many times that when I wake up tomorrow, I'll probably feel like I have been treated like somebody's stepson.

# Old Stone Church—Cranfills Gap

My Christmas gift to readers is to take them to the old stone church near this community.

Many times in the past forty years, I have driven to this spot in Bosque County just to recharge my emotions with the smell and feel of the raw power of the outdoors.

Jane and I recently came here by way of Glen Rose on Texas 144, passing over Squaw Creek. Its banks were full and ate at the sides of dark soil like a hungry kid gobbling chocolate.

We drove along the Paluxy River, which twists through Glen Rose, passing the old white frame Community Center, a building with kind of a bulging look like a young man wearing jeans a size too small for him. It was here that I learned to two-step and that, yeah, dancing could quickly ignite a young man's emotions.

We drove toward Walnut Springs, passing the road to Eulogy, a tiny community that was once as wild as the poison oak growing in the brush. But that is another story. We continued south.

We passed three hills sitting like three ice cream cones in a ranching pasture. I had always wanted to climb them. When I was a youngster, the word was that there were huge rattlesnake dens at the top of each one.

We reached Walnut Springs, with its lovely city park and sprinkling of antique shops. We passed a house painted lemon yellow that sits near the road leading to Iredell. This hamlet was once known informally as Snuff City because of the tremendous quantities of snuff its residents used.

We passed tiny creeks, with shrinking water levels holding clots of moss on top.

We went through Meridian, with its many beautiful old homes. We looked at one called Rose Hill Terrance, once a bed and breakfast where we celebrated an anniversary and is now closed for renovation.

We headed west on Texas 22 past fields of winter grass being grazed by sheep so far away they looked like tiny white dots on a green blanket. Nearby is Meridian State Park, one of my favorites, where Jane and I once camped on a New Year's Eve. I knew I had found my mate when she agreed to camp out for a New Year's celebration.

Finally we reached the Gap with its wide streets and places like Gap Hardware, the Viking Theater, St. Olaf Lutheran Church, and the Nothing Fancy Café. A sign on the front of the café read, "We'll be back at 5:30."

We looked for our friend Mark Johnson, long-time resident here and fierce defender of this city. Don't ever offer any criticism of it being small or you will risk the wrath of Mark in his weekly column for the nearby newspaper in Clifton.

We followed a sign that said, "Stone Church three miles."

We drove down a narrow paved road. Suddenly the old church spiraled through a break in the cedars. It stared at us like a piece of white majesty that had been planted there in 1886.

Built from native stone, it was originally called St. Olafs Kirk, and it was entered in the National Register of Historic Places in 1983.

I walked inside. In the silence, I knelt on the wood floor, made bowl-shaped by thousands of resting knees.

I looked at the arched wooden ceiling and heard a norther wailing outside.

I felt warmth in my eyes as I thought of my forty years of writing and of what a great job I have that allows me to visit such places.

I tried to pray. I couldn't. My voice cracked like somebody walking on thin ice. But finally I gained control. I said:

"Thanks, Big Fellow, for allowing me this privilege of being a writer. And Merry Christmas to everyone."

I've always considered writing as a profession heavy with responsibility.

As a result of that feeling, I have tried to be extremely sensitive toward the feelings of those about whom I was writing. I have never deliberately tried to hurt or insult any person.

Sometimes that did require an extra effort on my part since I always liked to give the reader some idea of what the person to whom I was talking looked like.

I hope the reader can sense that in the columns I chose for this book. That in itself caused some apprehension on my part in choosing which ones out of the nearly 3,000 columns I wrote to use. In selecting those, I truly felt that any of my columns could have been used.

It was not a matter of picking the best. It was really more like flipping a coin to see which ones I chose. So if a person I have written about is not in this book, please do not interpret this as a put-down from me. It's not. I just did not have enough room to list everyone.

My feeling of a writer's responsibility came to me when I was in Houston covering a hurricane. I had been out all day, interviewing people, and had finally found a room in a cheap motel that had not been blown away.

While sitting on the patio, trying to relax, I thought of my job and the obligation of writers. I wrote a free verse poem about this. It goes:

Soft footsteps of humanity
Dig into the night.
The houses' doors are shut, locked tight
to everyone but the burglar and
the writer.

The burglar can
rip, pry, and batter his way inside and dash
off with things bought by hundreds
of yesterday's sacrifices.
And the wronged call the police
And fill out reports.
But the writer has even more
to take.
He can hammer, unlock
and smash secrets of the heart and mind
and nobody reports him.

For the night swallows his existence
as he tromps the
dim meadowlands
and smells the bodies' emotions and
the sour grease of
hamburger joints
belching their nakedness
to humanity.

And with that, I say, "Adios y vaya con Dios."

# Index

# About Jon McConal

*Jon is a master storyteller, one who can capture a moment and place in time and then write the experience in such a way that the reader finds himself there—living it and feeling it. He has a magnificent talent for using words to sculpt people with such care that we are able to not only see them, but to touch their inner spirits.*

*His words speak with a delicate power, engaging his readers without manipulating them, guiding them without forcing them. His columns sing and dance and laugh and cry. They breathe fresh air and often tug at the heart while soothing the soul.*

> Bob Ray Sanders
> Vice president/associate editor & columnist
> *Fort Worth Star-Telegram*

*Jon McConal's columns celebrate people. His words paint a real-life picture of life in his native West Texas. His readers are drawn to a writing style that projects warmth and earthiness. No wonder the author developed such a devoted following.*

> Jack B. Tinsley
> Former executive editor
> *Fort Worth Star-Telegram*

From a letter to the editor of *Fort Worth Star-Telegram* January 5, 2001, at McConal's retirement:

> For 20 years Bunky waltzed across West Texas, painting in prose everyday scenes that Frederic Remington and Charles Marion Russell would have painted in oils. With only a few words from the palette of his imagination, he portrayed well-defined West Texas character. He painted beautiful word pictures. For instance: "Night came on quickly. The sky was clear and dark and the stars looked like somebody had spilled table salt onto a black tablecloth."
>
> No matter if the headlines heralded tornado, hurricane, flood, drought, pestilence, war, or rumors of war, Bunky—painting in the glorious colors of the English language the sights and people he saw—never failed to brighten the day.
>
> Hasta la vista, amigo mio! We will miss your smiles and similes.

> Don Woodard